DRAW

:

)

95

5

93.933

APPLIED QUALITATIVE RESEARCH

CRPYK

APPLIED QUALITATIVE RESEARCH

Edited by
Robert Walker

Gower

Published by
Gower Publishing Company Limited,
Gower House
Croft Road,
Aldershot,
Hants GU11 3HR,
England

Gower Publishing Company,
Old Post Road, Brookfield,
Vermont 05036,
USA

Reprinted 1988

British Library Cataloguing in Publication Data

Applied qualitative research.
 1. Sociology——Methodology
 I. Walker, Robert L. (Robert Lloyd)
 301'.072   HM24

Library of Congress Cataloging in Publication Data

Applied qualitative research
Includes index.
 1. Social sciences — research. I. Walker, Robert,
1949–.
H62.A626 1985 300'.72 85-5409

ISBN 0 566 00897 1 (cased)
          00898 X (paper)

Printed and bound in Great Britain by
Biddles Limited, Guildford and King's Lynn

Contents

Acknowledgements

Chapter 8 is taken from pages 41–54 of Ritchie, J. and Matthews, A., 1982, *Take-up of rent allowances: an in depth study*, London, Social and Community Planning Research and is reproduced with the permission of the Controller of Her Majesty's Stationery Office.

The editor is most grateful to Dr Bastin who wrote Chapter 6 at great speed to fill a gap left by a prospective contributor whose work had taken him unexpectedly to the Antipodes. Welcome assistance was also received from Peter Abell, Lesley Andrews, Su Bellingham, Helen Charnley, Rob Flynn, Pamela Park and Jennifer Park, to mention but a few.

Contributors

Dr Ron Bastin, Freelance Consultant with Social Analysis Anthropology Associates.

Dr Alan Branthwaite, Lecturer in Psychology, University of Keele and Consultant Director of Cooper Research and Marketing.

Caroline Cantley, Research Assistant, Department of Social Administration, University of Glasgow.

Jeremy Gray, Research Fellow, Policy Studies Institute.

Alan Hedges, Freelance Consultant, social and business planning.

Dr Sue Jones, Lecturer, School of Management, University of Bath.

Tony Lunn, Chairman, Psychological and Social Investigations Limited and Deputy Chairman, Cooper Research and Marketing Limited.

Alison Matthews, Senior Research Officer, Department of Health and Social Security.

Jean Morton-Williams, Field Director, Social and Community Planning Research.

Jane Ritchie, Research Director, Social and Community Planning Research.

David J. Smith, Senior Research Fellow, Policy Studies Institute.

Dr Gilbert Smith, Professor of Social Administration, University of Hull.

Dr Robert Walker, Research Fellow, Social Policy Research Unit, University of York.

PART I

The Basics

Drawn and scripted by a university researcher based in a government-sponsored research unit.

1 An Introduction to Applied Qualitative Research

Robert Walker

There are many occasions when the traditional methods of social research – notably the social survey – are inappropriate. Perhaps there is insufficient information or inadequate theory on which to ground and order a logical interview schedule. Perhaps a survey has already been conducted but has produced confusing results. Maybe the subject of the enquiry is inherently complex and understanding of this complexity is part of the research brief. Perhaps the subject is sensitive so that an interview schedule would elicit only superficial responses. Then again, maybe the objective is to study an institution with a focus on understanding the relationships within it.

This volume describes a series of techniques which are ideally suited for use in such circumstances. The techniques are traditionally termed 'qualitative' for they are generally intended more to determine 'what things "exist" than to determine how many such things there are' (Hedges, 1981; also van Maanen, 1983; Smith and Manning, 1982; Bogdan and Taylor, 1975). Because qualitative techniques are not concerned with measurement they tend to be less structured than quantitative ones and can therefore be made more responsive to the needs of respondents and to the nature of the subject matter. Typically qualitative methods yield large volumes of exceedingly rich data obtained from a limited number of individuals and whereas the quantitative approach necessitates standardised data collection, qualitative researchers exploit the context of data gathering to enhance the value of the data. Analysis of qualitative material is more explicitly interpretive, creative and personal than in quantitative analysis, which is not to say that it should not be equally systematic and careful.

Whether qualitative techniques are considered a sufficient basis for scientific description or explanation or whether they offer merely a prelude to scientific enquiry ultimately depends on the philosophical stance taken with respect to the nature of social science. Indeed, as we shall see, some have argued that qualitative data provide the only empirical foundation on which social science can be built. What is indisputable, however, is that on occasions when the more established research techniques are impotent, qualitative methods can yield information of considerable value to decision takers and social scientists. Moreover, as we shall again see, there are numerous other occasions when qualitative methods are preferable to quantitative ones.

Methods of qualitative research

Before furthering our discussion of the nature of qualitative research it is appropriate to introduce the four methods which come under special scrutiny in this volume: depth interviews; group interviews; participant observation; and projective techniques. These methods, which are among the most important in a large and growing repertoire of qualitative techniques, differ rather in kind. While observation is commonly considered to be the archetypal qualitative method, it contrasts with the other three approaches in that the research subjects are studied in their own 'social' or 'natural' environments. In group discussions artificial situations are created by bringing together individuals who would not in normal circumstances interact. Similarly projective techniques present research subjects with an artificial and seemingly absurd task, in part to release them from the constraints of their social environment. With individual interviews, the interaction is essentially artificial since it consists of a long detailed conversation between total strangers.

The four methods differ in another respect. Observation is usually employed in conjunction with other methods such as social surveys and interviews, but this is not necessarily the case with group and depth interviews. Extended creativity groups are a development of the group interviews or discussion approach making extensive use of projective techniques. Projective techniques can be administered in many contexts including relatively structured interviews, although they are probably used most frequently in group settings.

Depth interviews

The depth interview is a conversation in which the researcher encourages the informant to relate, in their own terms, experiences and attitudes that are relevant to the research problem. It provides:

> the opportunity for the researcher to probe deeply, to uncover new clues, to open up new dimensions of a problem and to secure vivid, accurate, inclusive accounts that are based on personal experience (Burgess, 1982a, p. 107).

The interviewer is not bound by a rigid questionnaire designed to ensure that the same questions are asked of all respondents in exactly the same way. At most the depth interviewer will carry an aide memoire. He is therefore free to follow up interesting ideas introduced by the informant. But a depth interview is not completely unstructured since the skilled interviewer constantly:

> appraises the meaning of emerging data for his problem and uses the resulting insights to phrase questions that will further develop the implications of these data (Dean, Eichhorn and Dean, 1967, p. 302).

The degree of structure necessary to provide a framework in which the informant feels free to elaborate his/her ideas depends on the topic, the informant and the personal style of the interviewer.

Depth interviews are usually recorded and transcriptions of the tapes are generally analysed individually, although in the context of concepts and categories developed in the analysis of earlier interviews.

Group interviews

Group interviews bring together small numbers of people to discuss topics on the research agenda (Burgess, 1982b; Hedges, 1981; Banks, 1957; Chandler, 1954). The task of the group interviewer – frequently called a 'moderator' or 'facilitator' – is not to conduct individual interviews simultaneously but to facilitate a comprehensive exchange of views in which all participants are able to 'speak their minds' and respond to the ideas of others.

The views expressed in a group may well be influenced by the group's dynamics and so differ from those elicited in individual interviews. This is not necessarily a disadvantage although it does emphasise the limitations of substituting group for depth interviews which is sometimes done on grounds of cost (Hedges, 1981). Rather, the group format aims to capitalise on group dynamics in order to throw light on the research topic. Ideas may be generated which would not have occurred to any one individual. Participants may find it necessary to justify their position so that ideas and weaknesses in argument may be thrown into greater relief. In certain contexts the interactions between group members may themselves constitute evidence relevant to the substantive research problem (in addition to being crucial to the interpretation of the data generated by the group). The group may also prove to be a heuristic experience for participants and this may be utilised in the context of an action research project.

The composition of groups usually depends on the research topic but the sample is usually a purposive one. Ideally groups should contain six to eight people and the number of groups in any one project is likely to vary depending on the heterogeneity of the research population and other data generated by the groups. Invariably, discussions are recorded and transcriptions used as the raw material for analysis. The units of analysis generally consist of ideas, experiences and viewpoints and the reported and logical relationships between them.

Participant observation

However long a group session and however 'at home' respondents feel, the situation remains artificial. Not so, the field of the observer who seeks to study people in their 'natural' environments and, more often than not, to participate in their day-to-day activities. The observer's task is to immerse himself in the host society: 'learning, as far as possible, to think, see, feel and sometimes act as a member of its culture and at the same time as a trained [researcher] from another culture' (Powdermaker, 1966, p. 9). Central to the participant observation method, as Powdermaker continues, is both involvement and detachment.

The settings need not be the isolated primitive community traditionally studied by anthropologists and, in applied research, rarely is. Nor need the 'immersion' be total or long-lasting. Moreover, the role adopted by the observer can vary along a continuum from complete participation through participant-as-observer and observer-as-participant to complete observer (Gold, 1958). Each approach will suit different occasions and problems and will necessarily result in varying degrees and types of insight.

Almost invariably observation alone is insufficient to satisfy the researcher. Other techniques including surveys, informal interviews, photographs and documents may be used alongside observation to cross-check the hypotheses generated by observation and perhaps to provide a better understanding of the context. The art of the researcher lies in his ability to integrate these different methods and their various data. How frequently integration is successfully achieved is another matter (Burgess, 1982c).

Projective techniques

Most of us are acquainted, through fiction, films or television, with the administration of the Rorschach test: an analyst asks his patient what objects he 'sees' in a series of inkblots (Wiseman and Aron, 1972). The Rorschach test is an example of a projective technique.

More generally, such techniques are based on the assumption that the way an individual organises a relatively unstructured stimulus reflects his perception of the world and response to it. In social science the most frequent use of projective techniques is as a means of:

> encouraging in respondents a state of freedom and spontaneity of expression where there is reason to believe that respondents cannot easily evaluate or describe their motivations or feelings . . . or where there are

topics on which respondents may hesitate to express their opinions directly for fear of disapproval by the investigator or when respondents are likely to consider direct questions as an unwarranted invasion of privacy or to find them threatening for some other reason (Kidder, 1981, p. 233).

This is achieved by asking respondents not to talk about themselves or their own feelings but about other people and their presumed feelings or about imaginary situations, pictures, objects or inkblots. The underlying conceptualisation is that, in so doing, respondents 'project' their own beliefs and hence make accessible attitudes and feelings which would otherwise have remained hidden. Moreover once such views are 'out in the open' respondents can often be encouraged to expand upon them. Frequently they spontaneously acknowledge them to be their own.

These techniques are available to the skilled depth interviewer but they may equally be used in groups. Once the initial postures are removed, groups can express shared feelings so that in the 'safety of the group', a respondent 'advances a feeling and this is a catalyst for others. Subgroups confront one another, and draw out real feelings' (Cooper and Pawle, 1982).

Groups in which projective techniques are used extensively are frequently termed 'extended creativity groups' and may generally be distinguished from ordinary group discussions by their length, their informality and the range of techniques and stimuli employed. In market research they usually have one of two orientations. Either they are probing, emotional and expressive when used to explore brand personalities and motivations. Or they are creative, inventive and incisive when applied to product development research (Cooper, Lunn and Murphy, 1982).

Table 1.1 summarises the characteristics of the four methods which are discussed more fully in later chapters. What the methods share is flexibility in execution, deliberate interaction between researcher and researched and a richness of data which stems from their largely textual nature and from their grounding in the language and experiences of the informants.

Value of qualitative research

No mention has yet been made of the methodological and philosophical traditions which have informed the development of qualitative methods. At first sight, this omission may seem strange or even inexcusable since much that has been written about qualitative methods stems either from a radical critique of the dominant philosophy or from proselytising accounts of alternatives. However,

Table 1.1
A choice of method

	Depth interviews	Appropriateness of Group interviews	Participant observation	Projective techniques
Where research objectives are:				
Descriptive	M		H	
Explanatory (in the sense of providing understanding)	M	H	H	H
Hypothesis testing (in the sense of subjecting ideas to common sense)		H		
Action orientated	M	H	H	H
To tap respondents' creativity		H		H
Where research topic is:				
Sensitive	H	L		H
Complex	H	H	H	H
Concerned with process	M	M	H	M
Concerned with institution		M	H	
Where research subjects are:				
Suspicious	M	M	L	L
Inhibited	H			H
Inarticulate			H	H
High status	H	M		M
Low status	H	H	H	H
Characteristics of method:				
Interactive	M	H	H	
Interpretative (i.e. by researcher)	M	M	H	H
Dependence on verbal communication	H	H	L	L
Artificial context	M	H	L	H
Responses constrained by social norms	L	H	H	L
Cost per respondent	H	L		

H=high(ly), M=moderate(ly), L=less so.

A blank indicates that the author is here unwilling to generalise.

It is assumed that projective techniques are administered in extended creativity groups.

qualitative research has contributed, and continues to contribute to knowledge generated under a host of traditions. Moreover, the characteristics of qualitative research outlined above remain largely undisturbed by the philosophical context in which they are employed. What differs is the significance attached to those characteristics and the status given to the findings (Halfpenny, 1979).

Risking the distortion which is frequently borne of simplification, it is possible to identify two main traditions within many of the social sciences. They have variously been labelled positivistic versus humanistic (Hughes, 1976), positivistic versus interpretive (Giddens, 1976), scientific versus humanistic (Martindale, 1974) and naturalistic versus humanistic (Poloma, 1979).

Positivistic tradition

A central tenet of the positivist position is the view that the study of society and human behaviour should be scientific in the mode of the natural sciences. Sociologists and others should therefore work 'as natural scientists are believed to' (Bell and Newby, 1977, p. 21) and look to them for a model of theory construction and precision. This is considered both desirable and possible because the distinction between 'the social and natural merely reflects a matter of convenience; there is no dualism in the world, but simply different aspects of the same underlying natural phenomena' (Hughes, 1976, p. 19).

Another fundamental belief shared by positivists is the view that the social and natural worlds 'conform to certain fixed and unalterable laws in an endless chain of causation' (Hughes, 1976, p. 19). Therefore:

> the major goal of scientific research is to establish causal laws that enable us to predict and explain specific phenomena. At a minimum, to establish these laws a science must have reliable information or facts (Labowitz and Hagedorn, 1971, p. 1).

The requirement to establish causal laws necessitates the formulation and empirical testing of explanatory theories (Brenner, 1981) which in turn 'tends towards a theory which is a deductively, indeed axiomatically structured system of empirically verifiable statements' (Mayntz et al, 1976, p. 2). With similar inexorability the requirement for reliable 'facts' leads to an emphasis on rigour, objectivity and measurement which is encapsulated in the statement attributed to the nineteenth century physicist, Lord Kelvin:

> When you can measure what you are speaking about, and express it in numbers, you know something about it; but when you cannot measure it, when you cannot express it in numbers, your knowledge is of a meagre and unsatisfactory kind (quoted in Harvey, 1969, p. 307–8).

The logical concomitant is that qualitative methodology fits uneasily, if at all, within a positivist tradition (the conception of qualitative data in positivist sociology is discussed more fully by Halfpenny, 1979). In making no pretence at measurement, and in relying on inductive reasoning rather than deductive, qualitative research must count as 'unscientific' or, at very least, pre-scientific. The tendency has therefore been 'to adhere to Lazarsfeld-Stouffer's position that qualitative research is exploratory in function – is prefatory to quantitative research' (Filstead, 1970, p. 5). Consequently, traditional texts tend to restrict the use of qualitative methods to the stage of questionnaire development and piloting; some also recognise that qualitative methods may be of value when existing measurement techniques are insufficiently advanced to facilitate certain topics being studied in a truly rigorous fashion. Then qualitative methods may have to be used, perhaps pending the development of more sophisticated techniques (Gardner, 1978; Hoineville and Jowell, 1978; Babbie, 1973; Moser and Kalton, 1971). In practice, the development of techniques seems not to have kept pace with researchers' appetites for new topics – a point emphasised by Glaser and Strauss (1967) – so that few have returned to ground originally defined qualitatively. Indeed much theory central to positivist social science has empirical foundations grounded in qualitative research (Barton and Lazarsfeld, 1969).

Finally, before considering a methodological basis of qualitative methods it is worth noting that a case has sometimes been made that certain qualitative methods are in fact close analogues of the techniques of natural science. Smith notes that 'the scientific model is one of direct observation' but that 'unfortunately, the social survey is a poor approximation of direct observation. ... Field research and structured observation come much closer to approximating our ideal models of direct observation' (1981, p. 184). Similar arguments occur in Herbert Blumer's discussion of the methodological position of 'symbolic interactionism':

> ... what is needed is to gain empirical validation of the premises, the problems, the data, their lines of connection, the concepts and the interpretations involved in the act of scientific enquiry. The road to such empirical validation ... lies in the [direct] examination of the empirical social world ... [which] is exemplified among the grand figures of the natural sciences by Charles Darwin. It is not 'soft' study merely because it does not use quantitative procedure or follow a pre-mapped scientific protocol. That it is demanding in a genuinely rigorous sense can be seen in the analysis of it to fundamental parts ... 'exploration' and 'inspection' (Blumer, 1969, pp. 34–40).

Humanistic tradition

There is now a very substantial literature devoted to positivism and its critics (e.g. Halfpenny, 1982; Harré, 1981; Giddens, 1977; Lally, 1976). However, it is only necessary here to draw attention to two distinct but related themes: (a) that positivist social science in its concern with scientific procedures, hypothesis testing, measurement, statistical significance and the like has become sterile and introspective; and (b) that fundamental differences between the natural and social worlds rule out the possibility of using the techniques of natural science to study social phenomena. In respect of the first theme, Blumer argues that faithful adherence to the protocol of research procedure is no guarantee that one will secure valid knowledge:

> inside of the 'scientific protocol' one can operate unwittingly with false premises, erroneous problems, distorted data, spurious relations, inaccurate concepts, and unverified interpretations (1969, p. 29).

He concludes that in 'current' social and psychological research:

> the predominant procedure is to take for granted one's premises about the nature of the empirical world and not to examine those premises, to take one's problems as valid because they sound good or because they stem from some theoretical scheme; to cling to some model because it is elegant and logically tight; to regard as empirically valid the data one chooses because such data fits one's conception of the problem; to be satisfied with the empirical relevance of one's concepts because they have a nice connotative ring or because they are current intellectual coins of the realm (Ibid, p. 32–33).

Bad science is bad science in whatever field of enquiry. However, there are very real problems associated with applying the measurement theory of the causal law paradigm in the social sciences. First, the axioms of deductive theory in the social sciences are rarely isomorphic with each other, so that a mapping from the language of theory into data is necessary (Hughes, 1976). Frequently the mapping 'depends on *presumed* relationships between observations and the concepts of interest' (Torgerson, 1958, p. 21) which on inspection turn out to be inappropriate. Second, the theoretical concepts are frequently insufficiently precise to suggest an appropriate measurement (Cicourel, 1964). Third, the control and simplification necessary for measurement may lead one to ignore the fundamental complexity of certain social phenomena. This problem is endemic in policy evaluation studies (Patton, 1975). Fourth, the objectivity and consistency necessary for the development of classification systems is difficult to achieve because the decision procedures 'are buried in implicit common-sense assumptions about the actor, concrete persons, and the observer's own views about everyday life' (Cicourel, 1964, p. 21). Finally, the data collection process itself is necessarily socially reactive. 'Thus, the "causal laws" paradigm is under-identified, as far as methodology is concerned, as it does not consider, nor elaborate, except in terms of measurement error ..., the social processes that constitute the practices of method' (Brenner, 1981, p. 2).

Deutscher has argued that the typical response to these dilemmas has been to focus on problems concerned with reliability rather than to address the issue of validity:

> We concentrate on consistency without much concern with what it is we are being consistent about or whether we are consistently right or wrong. As a consequence we have been learning a great deal about how to pursue an incorrect cause with a maximum of precision (1966, p. 241).

The same theme is taken up by Filstead (1970):

> by defining reality and validity synonymously to refer to the consistency with which researchers could replicate other empirical investigations, sociologists operationally defined away the concern for validity (1970, p. 4).

Moreover, in Filstead's view the problem of validity is most readily tackled by employing qualitative methods which enable the researcher to get 'close to the data'. Thus, citing Louis Wirth (1949), Filstead argues that objects 'can be known purely from the outside, while mental and social processes can be known only from the inside', as well as through the shared meanings and interpretations we give to the objects. 'Hence, insight may be regarded as the core of social knowledge. It is arrived at by being on the inside of the phenomena to be observed' (1970, p. 4).

This brings us to the second, and more important, theme – namely that the subject matter of the social sciences is intrinsically different from that of the natural sciences and that it is therefore inappropriate to ape its methods. Men and women are not particles acted upon by exogenous forces; they are 'purposeful, goal-seeking, feeling, meaning-attributing and meaning-responding creatures' (Hughes, 1976, p. 24). The natural and social worlds are viewed as fundamentally different. In attempting to understand human behaviour, therefore, it is necessary to discover the actors' perceptions of events and to ask how these relate to their behaviour. To appreciate the meanings 'conferred upon social events by interacting individuals, you must first interpret what is going on from the social context in which these events occur' (Schwartz and Jacobs, 1979, p. 8). Adequate descriptions of the social world, unlike those of the natural world, necessitate the researcher 'getting inside' the objects of his study so that he understands and knows them as subjects. This is facilitated by the fact that the researcher is himself a social being and is likely to share some at least of the social meanings of those he is studying and will have directly experienced analogous motives, reactions, emotions and feelings of his own. There is the possibility therefore to acquire understanding through empathy and to achieve the degree of insight that Weber termed *'Verstehen'* (Weber, 1949). Such insight can only be obtained if the researcher is permitted fully to engage his subjects rather than to adopt a stance of uncommitted neutrality. In facilitating this, qualitative methods have come to occupy an honourable position at the heart of the humanistic tradition.

The insight which the researcher gains into the meaning of the events for the individual he is studying is not the end point of the exercise. These 'first order concepts', to use Schutz's (1967) terminology, provide raw material for the development of second order concepts at a higher level of abstraction which constitute the basis of explanation within the discipline's own scientific paradigm.

Insight into human behaviour is only possible because the researcher and subject share a common humanity. However, because such insight or knowledge is acquired subjectively, the objectivity demanded by a positivist model of social science is impossible to attain. What the researcher learns from his research depends on the quality of his interaction with his subjects, his ability to interpret what he observes and is told, and his own ethical and social values. The qualitative researcher considers these influences explicitly in his analysis in a way that the positivist rarely does:

> ... few have questioned the inherent subjectivity of quantification which requires 'selection' of parameters and baseline data, the interpretation of findings, and the selection of facts and evidence. There is much to be gained by destroying the myth of objectivity since subjectivity is always intricately involved – but disallowed (Siedman, 1977, p. 415).

The humanistic view that a researcher is engaged in a social process leads ultimately to a relativistic interpretation of the knowledge that he uncovers (Douglas, 1970). The researcher, like those he is studying, is engaged in making sense of the social world. Like them, the researcher 'constructs versions of the social world, marshalls evidence to support those versions and tests them out in an on-going process of social interaction' (Hughes, 1976, p. 26). Consequently there can be no absolute objectivity but only agreements on truth and validity shared by people who hold the same meaning system, most notably by researchers of the same methodological persuasion.

Reconciling two traditions

There have been repeated attempts to bridge the gulf between positivistic and humanistic traditions of which the most influential is perhaps that of Weber (1949). His goal was the creation of causal explanations of social action. However, he recognised both the significance of individual motives and subjective meanings and the possibilities offered for understanding them by the researcher's own subjectivity. Such subjectively acquired knowledge was used to generate hypotheses about motivation, subjective states and human action which were then incorporated into theoretical models of social action. Finally the model's predictions were compared with actual courses of action. The superficial similarity of Weber's approach to that of Lazersfeld-Stouffer's positivistic model is illusory for the significance attaching to the qualitative component is altogether different. For Weber it is of paramount importance since, as Filstead wrote recently, 'one cannot infer the meaning of an event from data that does not have this dimension of information' (1982, p. 708).

Unfortunately Weber's bridge-building was incomplete. Not only did his own approach to research differ from the model presented above but the problem of reconciling human consciousness with deterministic law-building remained unresolved. In discussing this failure Schwartz and Jacobs (1979) point to the implications of an ancient observation:

> The presence of consciousness seems to result in one part of creation being able to be aware of other parts. When we consider what it is the part that is aware has in common with the part that is the object of awareness, many fascinating logical problems present themselves: Can a characteristic of one's own seeing apparatus be seen with that same apparatus? Can a creature subject to certain natural laws discover those laws, or do the laws themselves prevent this discovery? How does the universe change itself when it becomes aware of itself? (p. 21).

The researcher, who follows Weber, is forced to engage in 'as-if' thinking (Harvey, 1969). He would recognise the dilemmas posed by Schwartz and Jacobs and the heuristic status of his causal laws but nevertheless he would argue that for some purposes, depending on the level of aggregation and resolution of the research question, it is valuable to proceed 'as if' a causal explanation of social action did apply. In doing so he would have much in common with natural scientists working under the shadow of the so-called stochastic revolution (Rescher, 1964; Kemeny, 1959). Moreover, he would argue that explanations grounded in *Verstehen* have a greater 'social validity' than those derived from the hypothetico-deductive natural science model.

Peter Abell has recently proposed an alternative approach to the Weberian problem of devising 'a methodology in which explanations are deemed adequate at the levels of both causality and meaning' (Abell, n.d.). The central tenet of Abell's approach is that a social event may be explained by describing the set of interrelated actions that brought it about. This is termed a 'narrative'. Thus, the occurrence of social event o is explained by reference to an 'intentional syllogism':

Actor A intends o (the intentional premise)
A believed that in the situation perceived as C, only if he did X would o result (or be likely to result) (the cognitive premise)

Therefore A intended X
And A intentionally did X
And A intentionally did o

It should be noted that this explanatory model (unlike positivistic ones) is not dependent for its explanatory power on generalisation; that the cognitive premise is not dependent on the truth of the premise 'X leads to o'; and that 'intentionality' is crucial to explanation.

Narratives when expressed in terms of graphs may then be compared. 'The chances of (two particular events, o1 and o2) having identical narrative structure is perhaps rather remote, but if we are prepared to translate each to a higher level of abstraction then it may well be that the abstract (simpler) narrative structures will be more similar or even identical' (Abell, n.d., p. 19). In this way it is possible to build higher order explanations which, for example, address such issues as 'is o, if it is a recurring type of social event, always generated by a similar/identical sort of outcome?' (Abell, 1983, p. 75).

While Abell's 'syntax' of social life is intrinsically satisfying, it has yet to be tested as a practical research tool. The same cannot be said of Denzin's very influential concept of 'triangulation' (Denzin, 1970). Following in part Mannheim (1936), Denzin argues that 'sociology's empirical reality is a reality of competing definitions, attitudes and personal values' (1970, p. 300) and concludes that multiple methods and theoretical approaches must be used.

Four basic triangulations are proposed:

1 data with respect to time, place, person and level;
2 between multiple observers of the same phenomenon;
3 between multiple theoretical perspectives with respect to the same set of objects; and
4 methodological triangulation.

Methodological triangulation embraces between-method triangulation using dissimilar methods to measure the same unit and within-method triangulation which would employ variations within the same basic methodology. Denzin differs from Mannheim in his tendency to define phenomena according to the congruence between different triangulations. Mannheim, on the other hand, views different perspectives as complementary and additive, rather than competing, leading the researcher to 'constantly seek to understand and interpret particular insights from an ever more inclusive context' (Mannheim, 1936, p. 105).

However, Denzin's approach, like Weber's before it, is not wholly convincing. The differences between positivism and humanism go much deeper than merely theories and methods. The two traditions reflect fundamentally different epistemologies concerning the sort of knowledge about the social world which it is possible to achieve and different philosophies as to the nature of man. Moreover, even if triangulated studies are undertaken, questions remain as to how one should decide which results to accept and who should take the decision (Hughes, 1976). Certainly, Ackroyd and Hughes (1981) remain unconvinced by triangulation and conclude that 'data ... only have meaning within the method that produces them' and that 'outside of the appropriate theoretical context, theory specific methods can be more of a liability than an asset' (p. 136, p. 18).

But this conclusion may be altogether too negative in the everyday world of practical policy making. Certain questions simply cannot be answered by quantitative methods, while others cannot be answered by qualitative ones. (Frequently the reason is one of cost.) More importantly triangulation can add qualification to research that would otherwise be accepted uncritically. Different methods can also complement each other as when a survey provides a context for qualitative work which in turn permits commentary on the findings of the survey (Bebbington et al, 1983). Even the thorny problem of which results to accept may be less important than it seems, for research findings are constantly being evaluated and interpreted by the writers, readers and users of research in the light of their individual information needs. This is equally the case in the natural sciences (Knorr, 1981; Kuhn, 1970). An understanding of the methodological heritage of a particular technique is a necessary element in the interpretive process but in the end each person makes his own evaluation.

Finally, mention should be made of Runciman's attempt to 'close forever this long-running debate'. His view is that there is no fundamental logical gulf between the natural and social sciences. The meaningfulness of behaviour creates an additional problem for the social scientist but it 'does not render it inexplicable. On the contrary, the additional difficulty which it raises is not to do with explanation at all' (Runciman, 1983, p. 15). Instead it concerns 'description' in Runciman's fourfold distinction between the reportage, explanation, description and evaluation of human behaviour.

Description is concerned with conveying 'what it is/was like' and has no analogue in natural science. Description yields what Runciman terms 'tertiary understanding'. Good description is judged in terms of its representativeness and its authenticity, that is its ability to 'bring home' the experience to those who have not experienced it and although Runciman draws many of his examples from poetry and literature, he could equally have cited examples of qualitative research.

Reportage, explanation and evaluation do have parallels in natural science and the special problems encountered in the social sciences are not considered fundamental. Reportage concerns answering the question 'what?'. There are difficulties but, in Runciman's view, agreement about what is and what is not correct reportage is generally possible: one has only to ask the actors involved and, though they may sometimes be mistaken, this can usually be spotted. Once 'what is' is known ('primary understanding'), the logic of explanation, answering the question 'why?' which results in 'secondary understanding', is common to both the natural and social sciences.

Runciman is firm that tertiary understanding is not synonymous with *Verstehen* which he would argue confuses the very distinctions that he is at pains to draw. But whether primary and tertiary understanding are really distinctive and not simply aspects of the same process of characterising human action is, at the very least, questionable (Giddens, 1983). If they are not, and the difficulties attaching to tertiary understanding apply equally to primary, then the gulf between the social and natural sciences widens once more. Runciman's awaited application of his own methodology may be the critical test.

The market research tradition

An altogether different perspective on the role of qualitative methods is provided by the market research community whose contribution to the development of qualitative techniques has been substantial. It may come as a surprise to realise that 78 per cent of the firms listed in the British Market Research Society's 1985 Guide specialise in, or at least offer, qualitative research. Certainly the contribution of market research has frequently been overlooked by academic researchers perhaps because market researchers are too readily dismissed as 'technicians' or simply as 'trade'.

In 1979 a sub-committee of the Research and Development Committee of the Market Research Society reported on qualitative research. It argued that quantitative information, while indispensable to decision makers, was insufficient for their needs. Sometimes decision makers sought information that was:

> qualitative in its very essence – basic information about the nature and elements of a new or familiar or changing consumer market, for example, information which can only be provided by means of exploration and discovery (1979, p. 110).

At other times the information required was too subtle and too complex to be tailored to structured, standardised techniques or too detailed to be elicited by quantitative means.

The committee responded to fears about 'subjectivity' by suggesting, in a way reminiscent of Weber: 'That understanding – in terms of explanation and illumination of experience – does not derive solely from the realms of "scientific" thought and activity' (pp. 110–111).

Indeed, it stressed that: 'an input to some extent coloured by subjectivity from a properly informed and qualified source is a perfectly valid form of information (for decision-makers) (p. 111).

The committee concluded that in marketing, qualitative research provides 'the constant conceptual link between consumer and decision-maker in marketing and advertising development'. This it has achieved through its proven utility:

> Despite the difficulty of placing qualitative research, theoretically, its findings are normally found, materially, to enhance understanding of the consumer, and so facilitate marketing decisions and the marketing function generally. Thus, we are forced to conclude that qualitative research is justified by its indubitable usefulness, rather than by theoretical *bona fides* derived from any existing philosophy of science (Ibid, p. 15).

Applied qualitative research

There are, then, widely divergent views with respect to the legitimacy of qualitative methods. This book is concerned with the use of qualitative research in policy making and perhaps not surprisingly is much influenced by the pragmatism of the market research tradition. Hence the view that the value of qualitative research lies in its utility assumes central importance. Qualitative research has value when and because it is applied and can be validated with reference to the value placed upon it by policy makers and by the success or otherwise of policy decisions based on its findings.

Research is only one influence on the shape of decisions and generally a minor one (Bulmer, 1982; Filstead, 1982; Weiss, 1977). Even as a source of information, research may take second place to intuition, experience, the corporate memory etc. Nevertheless, the quality of decisions must in a very real sense be constrained by the research available. Most research used by decision takers – particularly those in the public sector – has increasingly been quantitative in form. As such it is based on the positivistic premise that social phenomena – rapes, muggings, fraud, poverty, performance, competitiveness, brand identity and the like – can be meaningfully measured, and consequently is subject to many of the same criticisms as have been levelled against positivism itself (Patton, 1979; Rist, 1977). Moreover, much of the quantitative material reaching policy makers is also suspect because theories underlying its collection are not made explicit. At the very least, therefore, there are grounds for increasing triangulation in policy-related research by adding to the qualitative component.

But there is an important place for qualitative research in its own right. As already noted, much of what needs to be known cannot be learnt from quantitative research and in such circumstances 'knowledge' has all too frequently been invented (Rosenhan, 1972). Qualitative research reaches parts that other techniques don't.

What qualitative research can offer the policy maker is a theory of social action grounded on the experiences – the world view – of those likely to be affected by a policy decision or thought to be part of the problem. The theory may, or may not, include specific references to the subjects' definitions of the policy problem, to their wishes or their likely reaction to policy initiatives. But it should be derived systematically and methodologically from the researcher's understanding of his subjects in a way that 'restores the legitimacy of subjectivity, and – even more important – gives it visibility and weight so that decisions and actions can be more accurately assessed' (Siedman, 1977, p. 415). Moreover, in their influential book *The Discovery of Grounded Theory* Glaser and Strauss argue that grounded theory should be developed in such a way as to 'facilitate its application in daily situations by sociologists and laymen' (1967, p. 237). First, it should:

> ... closely *fit* the substantive area in which it would be used. Second, it must be readily *understandable* by laymen concerned with this area. Third, it must be sufficiently *general* to be applicable to the multitude of diverse daily situations within the substantive area, not to just a specific type of situation. Fourth, it must allow the user partial *control* over the structure and process of daily situations as they change through time (p. 237).

Grounded theory – a principal output of qualitative research – should therefore be assessable and intended for use. If it is found meaningful by policy makers and employed successfully by them, this may constitute further evidence of the theory's validity. If it is employed and found lacking, questions will have to be asked of the theory, about its comprehensibility and comprehensiveness and about its interpretation in policy terms. If it is not used, the theory may be pregnant with validity, but have little value.

The fact that grounded theory is derived directly from the world experiences of people in the policy domain does not mean that it will be used in their interests. Indeed, policy making is usually concerned with deciding between conflicting interests. Information, whether quantitative or qualitative, confers power and if qualitative information is indeed more socially meaningful, then the power which it confers is all the greater. Moreover the qualitative researcher cannot avoid the uncomfortable dilemma that his research may be used against the interests of the people he has studied. Unlike the quantitative researcher he cannot distance himself from his data by retreating into the elegant world of mathematics. Instead he is continually confronted in his analysis by the social worlds of his research subjects. To the extent that the humanistic perspective reduces reality to an infinite set of competing definitions, the researcher will at very least wish to confirm that he has understood the viewpoint of the researched and to explore with them the implications of any policy recommendations he is making. Having understood their viewpoint he may quite naturally feel an advocate, if not of its truth, then at least of its social validity. In some small way the researched are thereby given a place in the decision taking although in large measure the moral dilemma remains, visible and challenging.

Uses of qualitative research

In discussing the uses of qualitative research it is helpful to distinguish three phases in research which may be more or less developed in any given project. They are the preliminary, principal and validation phases. Few projects lack a preliminary phase during which concepts are formulated, objectives defined, and ideally, piloting undertaken; but many progress no further, some through design, others because preliminary results are discouraging and yet others because resources are insufficient. Most published research has both preliminary and principal phases with a 'final report' that draws conclusions, frequently suggests further research and sometimes makes policy recommendations. However, projects rarely include a validation stage which would involve checking the conclusions against further data sets, testing the feasibility of policy recommendations or, perhaps, lobbying to get them implemented. More often than not this stage is left to other researchers, policy makers or lobbyists.

While qualitative and quantitative techniques may be employed during any phase of research (and, as has already been noted, there is much to be gained from triangulation) their different characteristics make them uniquely appropriate in certain circumstances (see Table 1.2). Thus the inherent flexibility and interactive nature of qualitative methods have guaranteed their primacy during the preliminary phase of research. (Indeed this is their only legitimate role under the positivistic orthodoxy.) However, this is not to deny quantification a place in exploratory research and descriptive surveys often precede ethnographic studies.

Findings from exploratory qualitative studies may assume 'taken for granted' status; indeed Glaser and Strauss view the *generation* of grounded theory as an end point in itself. Alternatively they may provide a starting point for further quantitative or qualitative work. In multi-method projects, group discussions and depth interviews are frequently used in piloting to clarify concepts and to devise and calibrate instrumentation for inclusion in structured questionnaires.

The choice of qualitative techniques as the main approach during the principal phase of a project frequently depends on the research topic. Maybe the topic is complicated or sensitive; concerned with

Table 1.2
A role for qualitative research

Phases of Research	Qualitative research	
	As the prime (or sole) approach	To complement quantitative research
Preliminary	Concept of formulation Generation of hypothesis/theory	Concept clarification Instrument design Piloting

Principal	Topic is:
	e.g. sensitive
	    complicated
	    unmeasurable
	    concerned with
	      interaction
	    concerned with process
	Research subjects are:
	e.g. inarticulate
	    'precious'
	    few in number
	Research objective is:
	e.g. brainstorming
	    action-orientated
		Interpretation
		Illumination
		Illustration
		Qualification
		
		Process evaluation

Validation	Between technique triangulation Testing 'consumer' response to policy recommendations	Between method

relationships or interaction; or with processes of change. Perhaps the phenomenon is not measurable (or, at least not yet). The choice may also be conditioned by the research subjects who may have limited communication skills or, alternatively, require 'VIP-status treatment' which prohibits the use of standard measurement techniques that 'require the "subject" to perform operations or give responses which may seem at best mystifying or at worst humiliating' (Young and Mills, 1980, p. 5). The research population might be extremely small, difficult to locate or discrete. This can sometimes lessen the concern about representativeness and inference, and thus tip the balance away from an interest in measurement. To summarise, the choice of qualitative methods may reflect limitations in the state of the quantitative art or a philosophical stance that quantification is inappropriate.

The research objective is also relevant. The researcher may want the research subjects 'to do his thinking for him' because they are directly involved with the issue or can bring a wide range of knowledge and experience to bear on it. Alternatively, the researcher may wish to gain first-hand experience of the situation or the problem. The research could be orientated towards action and reflect a concern to bring about change, in which case considerable emphasis is likely to be placed on dialogue and feedback. This would be particularly important if the subjects of the research were also the commissioners of the research or its main audience. Finally, returning again to philosophical positions, it may be that quantification results in the wrong questions being asked.

Qualitative research is increasingly being used to complement quantification during the principal phase of research (e.g. Bebbington et al, 1983). Often the two methods are used with different objectives. In evaluation research, for example, a distinction is made between impact and process analysis, the former using predominantly quantitative techniques, the latter qualitative ones (Hollister, Kemper and Wooldridge, 1979). Impact analysis is concerned to measure, or predict, the outcomes of policy programmes. Process analysis is then used most frequently to determine why a particular programme was unsuccessful although it should also facilitate elucidation of the reasons for success.

More generally qualitative research can help interpret, illuminate, illustrate and qualify empirically determined statistical relationships. The first two processes involve the application of grounded theories, the former to establish the substantive significance of relationships and to determine priorities; the latter to describe the processes involved. Illustration, typically seen as simply a means of enlivening a dull statistical text with case studies, is often crucial both to successful communication of the research findings and, more fundamentally, to the process of mapping theories or mathematical constructs on to the social world. The fourth process is similar to within-method triangulation except that instead of qualitative material being employed as a check on quantitative findings (see below) they are used, in the Mannheim tradition, to add another perspective on the phenomena of interest. Figuratively speaking, qualitative analysis is designed in this context to be read alongside the quantitative one.

Within-project validation to check the conclusions of research is rarely undertaken in a quantitative project since this would normally entail replication (although in some cases comparative designs may achieve the same objective, see Glaser and Strauss, 1967). Qualitative research may make such validation viable as a final stage of either a predominantly quantitative or qualitative study. Two aspects of validity may be involved, one relating to the findings and the other, where relevant, to the appropriateness of policy recommendations. The former corresponds with Denzin's use of between method triangulation. Vidich and Shapiro, 1970, argue that the degree of correspondence between quantitative and qualitative findings provides one measure of the former's 'external validity' and reveal the amount of 'bias' or 'selectivity' introduced by both methods. Such a view may introduce unwelcome assumptions about the nature of social reality. Nevertheless inconsistencies should cause the researcher to check for errors of reasoning, perhaps to devise refinements in theory or, at very least, to add qualification to the findings.

Testing the policy relevance of conclusions is often an integral part of qualitative research. In marketing research the final report may not be written until the research customers have had a chance to discuss the researchers' conclusions with them and perhaps to participate in the interpretation of some of the research findings. This procedure may be extended to include people responsible for implementing policy and, indeed, groups of individuals likely to be most affected by it. The results of these discussions may then be systematically incorporated into the final recommendations. Employing qualitative research in this way to integrate the key processes of devising, presenting and disseminating policy recommendations is equally appropriate whether the recommendations stem from qualitative or quantitative analyses. However, interpreted from a humanistic perspective, the procedure provides a unique opportunity for social actors to negotiate their competing definitions of reality.

References

Abell, P. 1983, *Comparative narratives: some rules of a sociological method*, University of Surrey, mimeo.

Abell, P. n.d., *Comparative narratives: the logical foundations of a scientific sociology?* University of Surrey, mimeo.

Ackroyd, S., Hughes, J.A., 1981, *Data collection in context*, London, Longman.

Babbie, E.R. 1973, *Survey research methods*, Belmont, Wadsworth.

Banks, J.A. 1957, 'The group discussion as an interview technique', *Sociological Review*, vol. 5, no. 1, pp. 75–84.

Barton, A.H., Lazarsfeld, P.F. 1959, 'Qualitative support in theory'. In G.J. McCall and J.L. Simmons (eds), *Issues in participant observation*, Reading, Massachusetts, Addison-Wesley, pp. 239–245.

Bebbington, A. et al, 1983, *Domiciliary Care for the Elderly, Research Design* (revised). PSSRU Discussion Paper 282/2, University of Kent.

Bell, C., Newby, H. 1977, *Doing Sociological Research*, London, George Allen and Unwin.

Blumer, H. 1969, *Symbolic interactionism: perspective and method*, Englewood Cliffs, Prentice-Hall.

Bogdan, R., Taylor, S. 1975, *Introduction to qualitative research methods*, New York, Wiley.

Brenner, M. 1981, 'Social method and social life: introduction'. In M. Brenner (ed.), *Social method and social life*, London, Academic Press.

Bulmer, M. 1982, *The uses of social research*, London, George Allen and Unwin.

Burgess, R.G. 1982a, 'The unstructured interview as a conversation'. In R.E. Burgess (ed.), *Field research: a sourcebook and field manual*, London, George Allen and Unwin.

Burgess, R.G. 1982b, 'Multiple strategies in field research'. In Burgess. R.G. (ed.), *Field research: a sourcebook and field manual*, London, George Allen and Unwin.

Burgess, R.G. (ed.) 1982c, *Field research: a sourcebook and field manual*, London, George Allen and Unwin.

Chandler, M. 1954, 'An evaluation of the group interview', *Human Organization*, vol. 13, no. 2, pp. 26–8.

Cicourel, A.V. 1964, *Method and measurement in sociology*, New York, The Free Press.

Cooper, P., Lunn, T., Murphy, O. 1982, *The social democratic party: A new political party or a new way of life*, Mimeo.

Cooper, P., Pawle, J. 1982, *Brand Personality – its place in the strategy planning process*, paper given at the BPMRG symposium, Bristol.

Dean, J.P., Eichhorn, R.L., Dean, L.R. 1967, 'Observation and interviewing'. In J.T. Dolby (ed.), *An introduction to social research* (2nd ed.), Des Moines, Meredith.

Denzin, N.K. 1970, *The research act*, Chicago, Aldine.

Deutscher, I. 1966, 'Words and deeds: social science and social policy', *Social Problems*, vol. 13, pp. 233–254.

Douglas, J.D. 1970 (ed.), *Understanding everyday life*, Chicago, Aldine.

Filstead, W.S. 1970, *Qualitative methodology*, Chicago, Markham.

Filstead, W.J., 1982, 'Qualitative and quantitative information in health policy making'. In E.R. House, et al (eds), *Evaluation studies, Review Annual*, p. 7.

Gardner, G. 1978, *Social surveys for social planners*, Milton Keynes, Open University Press.

Giddens, A. 1976, *New rules of sociological method*, New York, Basic Books.

Giddens, A. 1983, 'Understanding human and social activity', *New Society*, 3 March, pp. 348–9.

Glaser, B.G., Strauss, A.L. 1967, *The discovery of grounded theory: Strategies for qualitative research*, Chicago, Aldine.

Gold, R. 1958, 'Roles in sociological field observation', *Social Forces*, vol. 36, no. 3, pp. 217–23.

Halfpenny, P. 1979, 'The analysis of qualitative data', *Sociological Review*, vol. 27, no. 4, pp. 799–825.

Halfpenny, P. 1982, *Positivism and sociology: explaining social life*, London, George Allen and Unwin.

Harré, R. 1981, 'The positivist–empiricist approach and its alternative'. In P. Reason and J. Rowan (eds), *Human inquiry*, Chichester, Wiley.

Harvey, D. 1969, *Explanation in geography*, London, Edward Arnold.

Hedges, A. 1981, *An introduction to qualitative research*. A paper presented to the Market Research Society Winter School, January.

Hoineville, G., Jowell, R. 1978, *Survey research practice*, London, Heinemann.

Hollister, R.G., Kemper, P. Wooldridge, J. 1979, 'Linking process and impact analysis'. In T.D. Cook and C.S. Reichardt (eds), *Qualitative and quantitative methods in evaluation research*, Beverley Hills, Sage, pp. 140–158.

Hughes, J.A. 1976, *Sociological analysis: methods of discovery*, London, Nelson.

Kemeny, M. 1959, *A philosopher looks at science*, Princeton.

Kidder, L.H. 1981, *Selltiz, Wrightsman and Cook's research methods in social relations*, New York, Holt Rinehart and Winston, 4th ed.

Knorr, K. 1981, 'Social and scientific method or "What do we make of the distinction between the natural and the social sciences?"'. In M. Brenner (ed.), *Social method and social life*, London, Academic Press.

Kuhn, T. 1970, *The structure of scientific revolutions*, 2nd ed. Chicago, University of Chicago.

Labowitz, S., Hagedorn, R. 1971, *Introduction to social research*, New York, McGraw-Hill.

Lally, A.J. 1976, 'Positivism and its critics'. In D.C. Thorns (ed.), *New directions in sociology*, Newton Abbot, David & Charles.

Maanen, van, J. (ed.) 1983, *Qualitative methodology*, Beverley Hills, Sage.

Mannheim, K. 1936, *Ideology and Utopia*, New York, Harcourt, Brace and World.

MRS 1985, *Organisations book*, London, Market Research Society.

Martindale, D. 1974, *Sociological theory and the problem of values*, Columbus, Charles E Merrill.

Mayntz, R., Holm, K., Hueber, R. 1976, *Introduction to empirical sociology*, Harmondsworth, Penguin.

Moser, C.A., Kalton, G. 1971, *Survey methods in social investigation*, London, Heinemann.

Patton, M. 1975, *Alternative evaluation research paradigm*, Grand Forks, University of North Dakota.

Poloma, M. 1979, *Contemporary sociological theory*, New York, Macmillan.

Powdermaker, H. 1966, *Stranger and friend: The way of an anthropologist*, New York, Norton.

R & D Sub-committee, 1979, 'Qualitative research – a summary of the concepts involved', *Journal of the Market Research Society*, vol. 21, no. 2, pp. 107–124.

Rescher, N. 1964, 'The stochastic revolution and the nature of scientific explanation', *Synthèse*, vol. 14, pp. 200–215.

Rist, R. 1977, 'On the relations among educational research paradigms: from disdain to detente', *Anthropology and Educational Quarterly*, vol. 8, pp. 42–49.

Rosenhan, D. 1972, 'On being sane in insane places', *Science*, vol. 179, pp. 250–258.

Runciman, W.E. 1983, *A treatise on social theory: Vol 1; the methodology of social theory*, Cambridge, Cambridge University Press.

Schutz, A. 1967, *The phenomenology of the social world*, Evanston, Northwestern University Press.

Schwartz, H., Jacobs, J. 1979, *Qualitative sociology: A method to the madness*, New York, The Free Press.

Siedman, E. 1977, 'Why not qualitative analysis', *Public Management Forum*, July/August, pp. 415–417.

Smith, H.W. 1981, *Strategies of social research: the methodological imagination*, Englewood Cliffs, Prentice-Hall, revised edition.

Smith, H.W. 1975 *Strategies of social research: the methodological imagination*, England Cliffs, Prentice-Hall.

Smith, R., Manning, P. (eds) 1982, *A handbook of social science methods: Vol II: Qualitative methods*, Cambridge, MA, Ballinger.

Torgerson, W. 1958, *Theory and methods of scaling*, New York, Wiley.

Vidich, A.J., Shapiro, G. 1970. 'A comparison of participant observation and survey data'. In N.K. Denzin (ed.), *Sociological methods: a sourcebook*, London, Butterworths, pp. 512–522.

Weber, M. 1949, *The methodology of the social sciences*, Glencoe, Free Press.

Weiss, L.H. 1977, *Using social research in public policy making*, Farnborough, Saxon House.

Wirth, L. 1949, *Preface to Karl Mannheim's Ideology and Utopia*, New York, Harcourt, Brace and World.

Wiseman, J.P., Aron, M.S. 1972, *Field projects in sociology*, London, Transworld.

Young, K., Mills, L. 1980, *Public policy research: a review of qualitative methods*, London, Social Science Research Council.

2 Making Qualitative Research Work: Aspects of Administration
Jean Morton-Williams

Qualitative research uses an essentially unstructured approach to data collection; nonetheless, qualitative studies require careful planning and involve a considerable amount of administrative detail. This chapter reviews the issues that a researcher needs to consider in planning a qualitative research project, the decisions that have to be made before work can be started and the procedures that are usually followed in undertaking it.

Each study is, of course, unique; it is therefore impossible to draw up a blueprint that will apply to all. Observational studies in particular closely reflect the environment in which they are conducted and for this reason are not discussed in this chapter. All then that can be done is to provide an aide memoire that covers most of the points that a qualitative researcher should bear in mind.

Planning the study
The starting point for the researcher's thinking and planning is the research context in which the qualitative study is to take place. The most common use of qualitative research is as a preliminary to a quantitative study to help plan the content of the questionnaire and the design of the questions; sometimes it is used in a complementary role to quantitative research, perhaps to put flesh on the otherwise rather bare bones of information obtained with a structured questionnaire by following up and interviewing in depth certain particularly interesting sub-groups. Occasionally, despite its limitations, a qualitative research project will be undertaken in its own right because the need for depth of understanding outweighs the need for quantification (perhaps on a particularly sensitive topic that would be difficult to investigate with a structured interview). These three different types of context for qualitative research will all have a bearing on the method, scope and sample that are appropriate.

It is also necessary for the researcher to define precisely the objectives of the qualitative study. This may seem obvious but a common fault, when qualitative research is used as part of a larger programme involving quantitative studies, is for the researcher to assume that the objectives of the qualitative research are identical to those for the programme as a whole. The qualitative research will have a particular role to play in the programme and its objectives should be defined in terms of this role. For example, the specific objectives of a preliminary qualitative study might be to establish the *range* of attitudes to the topic area and to identify attitude *dimensions* that could form the basis of attitude scale questions in the structured questionnaire. The major planning decisions (choice of method, the scope of the project, the sample design and the development of the topic guide) all flow out of the precise definition of the objective of the qualitative study.

Choice of method

The subject matter and the sort of people to be studied all have bearing on the choice of method as is discussed more fully elsewhere (Chapters 1, 5 and 11). Often there is a case for using more than one method in a qualitative study. For example, group discussions might be used to explore the range of attitudes, taking advantage of the stimulus that group participation provides; individual depth interviews might serve the purpose of covering particular sub-groups of the population that are difficult to persuade to attend group discussions and to explore in detail the interrelationship between attitudes, characteristics and behaviour. Sometimes a small number of group discussions might be used as a first stage in helping to develop the topic guide for more extensive individual interviewing.

Methods may also be adapted according to the research topic or objectives. 'Depth' interviews can vary considerably in the degree of real depth; some subjects require a great deal of skill and insight on the part of the interviewer; others are less demanding and one can employ an interviewing approach that is more structured than is the case in a true 'depth' interview. The latter is often referred to as 'semi-structured'; the interviewer may be supplied with a rather detailed topic guide or with a skeleton questionnaire in which the key questions are specified but a great deal of space is provided for writing down detailed and lengthy answers. A semi-structured questionnaire may be used when some of the flexibility and detail of qualitative research is required in conjunction with the opportunity to aggregate answers (the hallmark of quantitative research), for example when interviewing minority groups who are expensive to contact. It was the method chosen for a study of nurses from overseas working in British hospitals (Thomas and Morton-Williams, 1972) in which the sample was around 250. While such studies combine some of the advantages of both qualitative and quantitative research, they also combine their disadvantages; the analysis in particular can be extremely difficult and time-consuming.

The scope of the project

All research is subject to time and cost constraints which must be weighed against the ideal requirements of the project. It must also be remembered that the analysis of qualitative material is very time-consuming and demanding; precious little of it can be delegated even to another researcher. Furthermore, there comes a point with un-structured information beyond which further interviews or discussions add very little in the way of insight or understanding and the researcher is advised to take a broadly based approach to the design of the project and to avoid the danger of being swamped by too much data that cannot usefully be synthesised. In particular, it is necessary to get away from the quantitative researcher's way of thinking about sampling: a qualitative study can never cover the whole population in such a way that different sub-groups that may be important can all be looked at in detail. The art of designing qualitative research lies in dipping into the population rather as a marine biologist may take samples of water from a lake by dipping in a bucket at judicious intervals.

Qualitative studies being undertaken as a preliminary to a quan-tified survey will usually comprise between 20 and 40 depth interviews or from four to twelve group discussions, depending on the com-plexity of the subject and the need to cover various sub-groups and different parts of the country. A qualitative study that has to stand as a piece of research in its own right may be larger: for example, a study of male attitudes to contraception (Morton-Williams, 1976) consisted of 70 depth interviews in order to cover adequately men in different age and socio-economic groups and married and single men; also to incorporate some joint interviews with men and their partners. A study of attitudes to life in a London borough (Hedges and Stowell, 1978) involved 16 groups, each of which met four times to discuss their views on different aspects of the topic and to consider what improvements might be made in the borough.

When larger studies are undertaken, it is often appropriate to divide them into a number of phases – an approach recommended in par-ticular for research that involves the development of a theoretical model (Glaser and Strauss, 1967). The large qualitative study of male attitudes to contraception was undertaken in three phases: six inter-views were undertaken by a highly skilled depth interviewer; these led to some modification of the theoretical concepts in the researcher's mind and the structure of the interview was more clearly defined. A further 20 interviews were then carried out and used to develop preliminary hypotheses about some of the main attitude areas and as a basis for developing interviewing strategies to explore sensitive topic areas more effectively. The remaining 54 interviews were used to confirm, modify and extend the preliminary ideas gleaned from the first two phases.

Sample composition

Decisions regarding the composition of the sample for a qualitative study emerge from the objectives and are modified by considerations governing choice of method and the scope of the study. It is essential that respondents should be objectively selected and not be friends or acquaintances of the interviewer but the rigorous sampling procedures used in quantitative research are inappropriate to the nature and scale of qualitative work.

Sample design in qualitative research is usually *purposive*; that is, rather than taking a random cross section of the population to be studied, small numbers of people with specific characteristics, behaviour or experience are selected to facilitate broad comparisons between certain groups that the researcher thinks likely to be important. For example, in the study of male attitudes to contraception, the preliminary interviews indicated that age was likely to be a very strong indicator of attitude although socio-economic group had always been considered the more important. It was therefore decided to take equal numbers within six groups defined by three age categories within two socio-economic categories. In addition, there was a specification for a minimum number of interviews with single men and with men and their partners together. Areas were selected in different sized towns in various parts of the country and respondents were then found simply by knocking on doors.

A further consideration, when sampling for group discussions, is that each group should be relatively homogenous with respect to those characteristics that might influence participation in the discussion or the views expressed: working-class people may feel inhibited by people with very 'posh' accents or by obviously very wealthy people; the very young or the very old may feel out of place in a group consisting largely of people in a different age group; people from ethnic minorities are likely to be unforthcoming about their experiences of prejudice in a mixed group, and so on. On some topics, the researcher may gain something by deliberately bringing together people whose views are likely to diverge markedly, but usually the discussion is more productive if they are kept separate.

Since the scope of the study is likely to be limited, it is necessary for the researcher to exercise judgement in deciding how to divide the resources available among different sections of the population. The phased approach described earlier can be very helpful as it allows the sampling for the later stages of the project to be guided by the initial findings.

Developing the guide

A group discussion guide should ideally be no more than two pages so that the group facilitator can see at a glance which topics have been covered and which remain; a depth interview guide can be longer but is unlikely to be more than four or five pages. The guide consists of a list of topics to be covered which may be set out with headings with a number of sub-topics that might be posed as questions grouped under each heading. The questions, however, are addressed to the interviewer, indicating the sort of information he or she should find out; it is the interviewer's function to devise his or her own questions to introduce topics and then to draw out the respondent by appropriate probes. The skilled depth interviewer will use the guide only as a guide, and not as a prop; he or she will have been thoroughly briefed on the detailed objectives of the study and will have worked over the topic guide, relating it to the objectives before starting interviewing, so that he or she will be using the guide simply as an aide memoire.

A few preliminary depth interviews or one preliminary group discussion can be very useful in helping to develop the subject matter and the strategy for tackling the topics to be covered: particular ways of approaching certain topics might be suggested (for example, the use of a projective technique or presenting pictures) and the most appropriate topic for starting with might be determined. The specific tactics for eliciting the expression of views will, however, be developed by the interviewer or the group discussion facilitator in response to the requirements of the situation, but also through building on the experience gained in the early stages of the project.

A depth interview may follow the guide in terms of the order of broad topic headings though it will not necessarily do so; the detail under each heading is not only likely to vary in order but also in content from one interviewer to another. A group discussion is unlikely to deal with topics in the order set out in the guide as the group will itself develop the theme, following its own path, only lightly guided by the facilitator.

Who should do what?

Enough has been said to indicate that qualitative research is very different from quantitative research, with its own expertise and demands. The researcher who decides to undertake a qualitative survey may consider sub-contracting the whole of that phase to a qualitative research specialist. In making such a decision, the researcher must take into account not only his or her own level of expertise in qualitative research, but also his or her other commitments (qualitative research is very time-consuming) and the amount of background knowledge of the research subject that is required.

An alternative is to sub-contract part of the project, such as conducting the group discussions or the depth interviews. If this is done, then extremely close liaison needs to be maintained with the specialist researcher on a day-to-day basis in order to ensure that the objectives of the research are fully understood and are being borne in mind. Specialist depth interviewers are often used for some of the interviews but again they must be fully briefed and close liaison is essential with the researcher especially in the early stages of the interviewing.

There can be advantages (as well as disadvantages) in sharing data gathering, and even analysis; another view on how to tackle the difficult subjects and how to interpret what is emerging can often be a helpful stimulus. Sometimes depth interviewers or group discussion facilitators are asked to write a brief interpretative summary on each interview or discussion; occasionally researchers may share the data collection and detailed analysis, the latter typically divided in terms of topic areas. The dangers of fragmentation are obvious but can usually be overcome if there is adequate liaison and if one researcher is responsible for the final synthesis.

Choosing an agency or consultant. If the qualitative work is to be sub-contracted, how does one choose an agency to undertake it? There are three main possibilities: to go to a general research agency with experience in both quantitative and qualitative research; to use an agency specialising in qualitative research; or to retain the services of an independent consultant. Which of these should be given preference will depend on the type of qualitative research being undertaken and on the degree of expertise and involvement of the sponsor. For example, the combination of quantitative and qualitative skills required when a qualitative study serves as a preliminary to quantification is most likely to be found in an agency that undertakes both qualitative and quantitative research.

A specialist qualitative research agency or a consultant might be more appropriate for a study that has to stand in its own right without quantification. The advantages of a specialist agency over a general agency are (usually) the wider range of researchers available with qualitative expertise and the fact that the organisation is specifically geared to the setting up of group discussions, depth interviews and other kinds of qualitative fieldwork which it should thus be able to do very efficiently.

An independent consultant is often cheaper than an agency which has more overheads to cover – and the sponsor knows precisely whose expertise he is buying. On the other hand, an agency takes responsibility for ensuring that its contractual obligations are met. If a consultant falls ill or turns out to be incompetent, the sponsor may have little chance of getting the project completed to his or her satisfaction.

In choosing an agency or consultant, it is necessary to bear in mind the level of expertise and intellectual input required. If the sponsor simply needs some specialist help with a project in which he will be closely involved or if the project is small-scale and not complex, then a competent but not necessarily senior researcher may be adequate. Qualitative studies that are tackling complex and sophisticated issues require researchers with a high degree of expertise founded on experience, intelligence and preferably some grounding in one of the social sciences. When an agency is being chosen, it is important to establish who will actually conduct the group discussions and/or depth interviews; who will analyse the information and who will report on it. As explained earlier, too much fragmentation should be avoided. It is also necessary to keep in close touch with the agency researchers to ensure that those who were assigned to the project are actually working on it as agreed.

Evaluating the expertise of a researcher is always difficult, whether an agency researcher or a freelance consultant. Past experience is clearly important and, if possible, the sponsor should read some reports that the researcher has written. It is also advisable to obtain a detailed written proposal and to discuss it so that the quality of thinking in relation to the specific problem can be assessed.

Timing and cost

Good qualitative research cannot be rushed. At least four weeks should be allowed for developing the guides, planning the sample, designing and printing the recruitment questionnaire and any other documents, organising venues and briefing the recruiting interviewers. The amount of time required for taking the discussions and depth interviews will depend on the number of each and the availability of group facilitators and depth interviewers. It must be remembered that the work is very intensive. Although an experienced researcher might take two group discussions in a day, or three depth interviews, this should be very much the exception rather than the rule unless they are below average in length.

The analysis is also very demanding and time-consuming; four to six hours should be allowed per transcript; reporting might then take anything from one to four weeks depending on the type of report and the complexity of the issues.

It is apparent from the above that the cost of data collection in qualitative research is likely to be quite a small proportion of overall costs; research time in planning, analysis and reporting is likely to represent at least 75 per cent of the costs and often more.

Organising fieldwork

Successful qualitative fieldwork requires much forethought, careful planning and attention to detail. This section covers some of the considerations which need to be taken into account when organising group discussions and depth interviews.

Group discussions

Ideally, a group discussion consists of up to about eight participants meeting in an informal atmosphere in comfortable surroundings: the discussion is tape recorded so that thorough analysis can be undertaken without having to rely on note taking or memory, both of which are likely to be extremely unreliable. Achieving this ideal, including the end product of a good quality tape recording, is often difficult. The following notes outline the pitfalls and suggest ways in which they can be avoided.

Day and time. In deciding which day of the week to hold group discussions, it is best to avoid Friday evenings or weekends when people often want to be with their families or to go out. It is also advisable to check whether there are any important events such as a local carnival or a cup final on television, and whether it is half-term or when the local firms are closed for holidays.

Discussions with non-working housewives or pensioners can be held in the afternoon; children's discussions can take place in the early evening or on Saturday. Discussions on topics legitimately connected with participants' work may be arranged during working hours, preferably after lunch so that participants have the morning to 'clear their desks'. Discussions with most other sections of the population need to be held in the evening. The time that is most appropriate varies in different parts of the country: in London and the surrounding commuter belt, discussions usually start at 8pm to allow people time to get home from work and to have their meal; in other areas, a 7.30pm start is usually feasible; sometimes, in areas where people start work early and finish early, 7pm is more appropriate. Local interviewers can often advise as to the most suitable time.

Finding a suitable venue. An essential ingredient in obtaining respondents' cooperation is that the venue chosen should be close to where they live and easily accessible. Sometimes the discussion is held in the home of a local interviewer who recruits participants from the surrounding neighbourhood. This kind of venue has the advantage of being close by and informal but some people are embarrassed at being asked into the home of a stranger and feel more comfortable going to a public place. There is also the danger that if the same interviewer is used frequently for recruiting, he or she might invite the same people to participate in different discussions, leading to a group of people who are over-sophisticated in the technique and who may become atypical.

Often, therefore, the recruiter is asked to find a venue in or near the area in which he or she is going to recruit and will look for a convenient hotel, community or church hall, or perhaps a room in the local library. The local authority, library or police can often suggest suitable accommodation. Public houses are usually avoided unless there is a room with an entrance that does not entail going through the bar.

If for any reason a suitable venue cannot be found near the recruitment area or if the area to be covered is very widespread provision may be made to transport participants to and from the venue. Transport may be necessary if the participants are elderly or disabled.

The venue must be acceptable to respondents – neither too grand nor too dilapidated – and preferably in the sort of district in which the participants will feel at home. The room itself should accommodate ten to twelve people comfortably but should not be too large as this can be intimidating. Preferably it should be furnished with easy chairs set around a low central table on which the microphone can be placed, but upright chairs around a table 'boardroom style' is acceptable. The ideal is to seat participants in a three-quarter circle with the group facilitator in the gap so that all participants are in front of the facilitator yet not obviously set apart from him or her; this layout allows the facilitator to see all participants, to notice if anyone is failing to have a say in the discussion and to control anyone who tends to dominate the discussion, without being too prominent; it also encourages discussion between group members. 'Theatre style', where chairs are placed in rows facing the front, should always be avoided as it will focus participants' attention on the group facilitator and discourage discussion between members (see also Chapter 5).

The room must be quiet so that the participants are not distracted or the tape recording rendered unintelligible. Even a background hum from machinery or traffic can make a tape recording difficult to hear. Rooms that are too large or are sparsely furnished can affect the quality of the recording by producing echoes. There should preferably be an electric point in the room for the tape recorder (rather than relying on batteries) and light refreshments must be available. Alcoholic beverages should usually be avoided as they tend to turn the occasion into a party and reduce the seriousness with which the research is regarded.

Recruiting respondents. This is usually undertaken by an experienced survey interviewer; it is often found, however, that not all good interviewers make successful group recruiters. The work is demanding in quite a different way from interviewing, requiring a high degree of persuasiveness and the temperament to persevere and remain cheerful in the face of refusals. One of the limitations of group discussions as a technique is that a high proportion of those approached usually refuse; the interviewer must realise that he or she may have to approach five or six times as many people as are required. It is necessary to brief the interviewers carefully about their task, to provide them with notes about the rules governing recruitment and with tips on how to ensure that recruited respondents turn up.

Sometimes specific individuals are 'head hunted' for group dicussions when, for example, the aim is to bring together key actors in the system under study. Such individuals may first be invited by telephone and followed up by a letter. Alternatively they may be approached through an intermediary, possibly the research sponsor.

Usually, however, the interviewer is provided with written instructions describing the quota of people to recruit, and is typically asked to recruit ten to twelve people in order to ensure that eight to ten turn up. Participants are usually found simply by knocking on doors and enquiring for people with the required characteristics; sometimes a stipulation will be imposed that houses approached must be at least five doors apart. Interviewers must not recruit their friends; nor as a rule are they allowed to 'snowball', i.e. to use people already recruited as a source of other people to approach, as this would lead to groups in which participants know each other and are likely to have similar views. A short recruitment questionnaire should be provided which the interviewer uses to establish eligibility and on which are recorded the name and address (and telephone number if available). A letter of explanation should also be provided giving some details about the study, thanking them for agreeing to take part and also stressing the importance of attending once they have agreed to come: 'Someone is coming especially from ... to run the discussion' is a useful way of conveying that the discussion is part of a serious research project. However, respondents also have to be reassured that no special knowledge is required and that the other participants will be local people just like themselves or they may feel too overawed to agree to take part. The interviewer thus has to convey that it will be an interesting, enjoyable, unembarrassing and unalarming experience but also that there is a worthwhile purpose behind it and that, having once committed themselves, it will be very inconvenient if they drop out. The interviewer should leave a card giving the time, date and venue of the discussion and his or her own telephone number and respondents should be asked to contact the interviewer if they are unable to attend so that the interviewer has a chance to recruit someone else.

Recruiting will normally take two to two-and-a-half days (longer for special sub-groups) and should be carried out three or four days before the discussion is due to be held. If it is done earlier, then those recruited are likely to forget about it; if it is done later, more people will have made other arrangements; also there may be insufficient time for the interviewer to complete the recruitment by the due date if it proves to be a difficult task.

The day before the discussion is due to take place, the interviewer should visit or phone the participants to remind them and to make sure that they still intend to come. This again encourages respondents to make a firm commitment and also conveys to them that the discussion is taken very seriously by the research organisation.

An important element in persuading people to take part in a discussion is the offer of a small incentive payment; this is currently usually £5.

Organising the session. Someone other than the group facilitator should act as 'host' or 'hostess' at the beginning of the session – preferably the recruiting interviewer since he or she will already be familiar to participants. This person should be stationed where he or she can greet people as soon as they arrive, mark them off in the list and show them into the room. Refreshments should be served as they arrive, partly as a useful mechanism for breaking the ice and partly to avoid having to have a break during the discussion itself. The facilitator will have been given the recruitment questionnaires and will be passed the list of attenders. It is useful to draw up a plan of who is sitting where so that the facilitator can address people by name during the discussion; this makes for good relations and also helps to identify who said what during the analysis (but see Chapter 5).

It is also advisable to pay participants their fee before the discussion starts – another useful ice-breaker and it also avoids problems if some people have to leave before the end.

Tape recording the discussion. It is essential to tape record the session as one's memory is likely to be highly distorted by such factors as the emotional intensity or the loudness of voice with which views are expressed, or even by one's own preconceptions. A good quality cassette tape recorder should be used, preferably with two omnidirectional microphones to register the voice of everyone in the group. Good quality cassettes should always be used. Those with 45 minutes' play per side (C90) are recommended since longer tapes tend to be so thin that quality suffers and tapes may break while shorter ones involve too many irritating interruptions to change the cassette.

The tape recorder should always be very carefully checked to ensure that it is in working order before setting out and again at the venue before the discussion starts. It is also advisable to carry an extension lead fitted with a multi-purpose adaptor plug in case the power point is inconveniently situated or is the wrong sort. The microphones should be placed on the table in the centre, nearer to the participants than to the facilitator whose voice will normally be the most audible in the room because he or she will be the most confident person present. Care should be taken that teacups, ashtrays or papers are not moved around close to the microphones.

The facilitator should explain that the tape recorder is being used to dispense with note taking and is to enable him or her to concentrate on what is being said. It should also be made clear that the recording will be used solely for analysis purposes.

Transcription. Carrying out the analysis directly from the recording is very cumbersome and limiting; unless only two or three discussions have been taken and the time schedule is very short, transcripts should always be made. Transcribing a recorded discussion that lasted perhaps one and a half hours is likely to take three to five hours but is well worth the expense. Using a transcript, the researcher can identify topic areas quickly, easily go back to verify points, find quotations to support hypotheses, and generally avoid biased reporting arising from too much reliance on first impressions.

Depth interviews

The organisation of depth interviews is considerably simpler than for group discussions and there are only a few points that need to be made. Usually they are carried out in the respondent's own home although if the subject is to do with business or employment and the respondent is recruited via his or her place of work, the interview may be held in his or her own office or a quiet room away from colleagues. Occasionally there may be grounds for asking respondents to come to an alternative central venue; for example, interviews with young people on certain topics (e.g. sexual experience or delinquent behaviour) have not been carried out in the home because it was felt that the presence of other family members would inhibit the respondent.

Recruitment of respondents. Occasionally the depth interviewer may be asked to find his or her own respondents but preferably recruitment should be undertaken by a different person, usually a survey interviewer. One reason is that it is uneconomic to use the time of a specialist for this purpose. More important, the two functions involve very different roles and types of relationship with the respondent: the recruiter has to ask a favour and be persuasive; the depth interviewer has to be able to take charge of the situation, establish a role as a professional researcher and convey what the respondent's role should be. It is much easier to do this if someone else has set up the appointment.

The recruiting interviewer should be provided with a brief recruitment questionnaire (as for group discussion recruitment) to establish eligibility and to record any background details that it would be useful for the depth interviewer to know before starting the interview. A letter explaining the purpose of the survey and a card giving the time of the appointment and the name and telephone number of the depth interviewer should be left with the respondent.

Respondents are often (but not always) offered a fee of £3 to £5 for giving their time as the interview is likely to take at least one hour and might take two.

Organising the interview and tape recording. As soon as the depth interviewer arrives, he or she should take charge in a calm and professional way, indicating that privacy and quiet are necessary so that both interviewer and respondent can concentrate. The need to tape record the session should be explained and seating politely re-arranged if necessary so that interviewer and respondent can sit near each other with a table or arm of a chair on which the tape recorder can be placed. Positions half facing each other are recommended as this allows eye contact and observation of each other's facial expressions without forcing constant confrontation.

A small unobtrusive cassette tape recorder with a built-in microphone is most convenient for depth interviewing. Those currently fashionable for carrying on the body with earphones for listening to music while travelling provide an adequate standard of recording and excellent play-back quality over the earphones (providing an opportunity for the interviewer to listen to the interview while travelling home!). The tape recorder should be placed very much closer to the respondent than to the interviewer as respondents often talk very quietly and it is always worth checking that the tape recorder is working before setting out and again in the respondent's house before starting the interview.

The depth interviewer will often be offered a cup of tea or coffee by the respondent; if this happens before the interview starts, the interviewer should accept or decline according to their need and judgement of the situation. Offers made in the middle of the interview should usually be declined unless the respondent expresses a strong desire for a drink, as stopping can sometimes seriously disrupt the flow of the interview. Offers are in fact sometimes made as a way of evading emotionally loaded topics.

Hospitality offered at the end of the interview should usually be declined (though the interviewer must use his/her own judgement); the interview may have covered sensitive and intimate topics and it may therefore be best to maintain a professional neutral manner right to the end of the interchange rather than to enter into a more conventional social relationship with the respondent.

Transcripts. It is even more essential to have transcripts made of depth interviews than it is of group discussions as the researcher will want to go back several times over the material and may want to carry out some detailed content analysis of some parts of the interview.

Preparing the report

Analysis of qualitative material

The analysis of a large amount of qualitative material is a daunting task; since the data are largely unstructured, it is the function of the researcher to impose order and structure upon them. Chapter 4 describes in more detail how the analysis of depth interviews can be undertaken; in this chapter we set out only the basic principles and some of the strategies that might be adopted.

The necessity for transcripts and for adequate research time has already been stressed. Although it is sometimes possible to share the analysis with another researcher (usually by dividing the topics covered between them), it is rarely possible to delegate any of the analysis to junior or clerical staff. It is particularly inappropriate to try to code qualitative material in the same way that open-ended questions in structured questionnaires are coded; apart from the impossibility of devising suitable coding frames, any such attempt would fragment the material and deprive it of its essential holistic nature.

Order and structure are imposed on the material by the researcher's approach; the primary underlying structure is imposed by the objectives of the research which provides a conceptual framework within which the analysis can be organised. If the qualitative study is a preliminary to quantification, this will affect the researcher's orientation towards the data; he or she will be looking for quantifiable hypotheses and trying to identify measurable dimensions of attitude in addition to interpreting the findings in the light of objectives of the research programme as a whole.

Much of the analysis process consists of listening to the tapes while reading the transcripts, noting the topic numbers from the guide on to the transcripts and perhaps marking particularly relevant passages. Listening to the tapes is important as it gives tone of voice, expression and emphasis that will be missing from the transcript. The researcher might then make notes of initial ideas under various topic headings and proceed to gather data relating to each topic systematically, developing hypotheses and assembling quotations from the transcripts to support them.

More detailed analysis might play a role in two ways: first, a summary of the most salient points from each respondent's interview (or from each group discussion) might be made; this might include a straightforward notation of facts and views and/or an overview that draws conclusions about underlying attitudes and motivations; it might also involve classifying the respondent in several ways in order to make comparisons between sub-groups. To some extent this summarising might be carried out by the depth interviewer or group discussion facilitator who can add his or her impressions formed at the time of the interview or discussion, but it will almost certainly be added to by the researcher.

The second form of more detailed analysis consists of taking certain key topics and summarising each respondent's view on them; if the summaries are done within broad groups, then any major differences between groups can readily be seen. However, it must be borne in mind that such comparisons can only provide indications of possible differences; the small numbers preclude drawing any firm conclusions.

Reporting
The report on a qualitative study will be completely different from that on a quantitative study. The structure for the report will have emerged from that used in the analysis; the findings will be presented in terms of impressions gained, as hypotheses rather than as firm conclusions. There will be no tables (apart from those describing the sample composition) and no references to numbers or percentages; at most the researcher will use such phrases as 'most respondents' or 'around half' or 'a minority view was ...'. The researcher will be mainly concerned to identify and describe the range of behaviour and opinions rather than to indicate whether people feel strongly or how many hold each view. In all cases the description of beliefs, attitudes and motivations should be supported by evidence in the form of verbatim quotations from the interviews or discussions. This is a very important part of the discipline of analysis and reporting on qualitative material. The collection of quotations (or the failure to find supporting quotations) is an essential corrective to false impressions that may be formed during the reading of the transcripts.

When the qualitative study is a preliminary to a quantified follow-up survey, a section of the report will be devoted to a discussion on the implications of the findings of the qualitative study for the conduct of the follow-up survey; these implications will be particularly relevant to questionnaire design but might also affect sampling procedures and other survey design aspects.

The report should of course contain a full description of how the research was carried out, the sample interviewed and attending discussions, how respondents were selected, where and when discussions were held, and so on. In addition, a copy of the recruitment questionnaire and of the depth and group discussion guides should be appended.

Sometimes researchers are asked to give a verbal presentation of the results of a qualitative study; this is not an easy thing to do without the danger of misrepresentation, particularly if it is asked for in order to glean first impressions before the full analysis has been completed. First impressions can often be misleading, and the researcher should be careful to point this out to his or her audience. Another problem is that the supporting evidence in the form of quotations cannot be given in a verbal presentation and it is easy to become more dogmatic than the results warrant. Verbal presentations should, like the written report, be anchored firmly to the study objectives and not become a series of anecdotes based on the most memorable, amusing and dramatic incidents or views given in the interviews.

From the foregoing, it will be apparent that the conduct, analysis and reporting of qualitative research requires a blend of imagination, flexibility, receptivity, discipline and hard work that enables the researcher to process the information as objectively as possible while making his or her own contribution to the analysis and synthesis of data.

References

Glaser, B.G., Strauss, A.L. 1967, *The discovery of grounded theory: Strategies for qualitative research*, Chicago, Aldine.

Thomas, M., Morton-Williams, J. 1972, *Overseas nurses in Britain*, PEP Broadsheet 539, PSI, 1/2 Castle Lane, London SW1.

Morton-Williams, J. 1976, *The role of male attitudes in contraception*, SCPR, 35 Northampton Square, London EC1V 0AX.

Hedges, A., Stowell, R. 1978, *Community panels in Southwark*, SCPR, 35 Northampton Square, London EC1V 0AX.

PART II
Some Methods

Bill 1 – Gas £ 10

Bill 2 – Coal £ 20

Bill 3 – Electricity £ 30

Total £ 60

Gap £ 27.50

Money in hand

1 week's pension

= £ 32.50

'Need' as portrayed by a senior policy-maker in the DHSS (handwriting changed to maintain anonymity).

3 Depth Interviewing
Sue Jones

No book concerned with the practice of qualitative research would be complete without some discussion of the personal interview as a research tool. Indeed the interview is so integral to social research, its prime currency, talk, so central in our social lives, that its complexity as a social interaction can sometimes be forgotten or obscured. The purpose of this chapter is to consider some dimensions of this complexity and in so doing to stress the crucial *practical* implications of theory about the social process of one person seeking to interview another, 'in depth'. In a single chapter consideration of even a few of the key theoretical questions precludes an accompanying 'blow-by-blow' account and prescription about how best to conduct a depth interview. Indeed I shall argue that such a prescription would be inappropriate. The following is thus a partial (both incomplete and 'biased') discussion of some of the issues that have engaged me, and, it should be pointed out, many others, when thinking about and undertaking depth interviewing. They include: the degree of structure in an interview, the concept of 'interviewer bias', the social skills of the interviewer, obtaining trust, and the relevance of the research to the interviewees.

Exploring meaning
In characterising what they do, I have heard different researchers use the label 'depth interview' to cover many different approaches. These have ranged from the supposedly totally 'non-directive' to that where the main difference from the formal questionnaire interview seems to be that the interviewer does not have a typed sheet of paper, varies the exact wording of the questions and perhaps asks more 'probe' questions than is usual in a formal questionnaire. Between these two extremes is an abyss of practice and therefore theory about the purpose and nature of the qualitative interview.

There is, of course, a considerable literature on the theoretical bases for qualitative methodology to which justice cannot be done here. To summarise my own theoretical starting point: it comes from a particular 'model of man' which sees human beings not as organisms responding, Pavlovian fashion, to some external stimulus, nor inexorably driven by internal needs and instincts, nor as 'cultural dopes', but as persons, who *construct* the meaning and significance of their realities (see e.g. Thomas and Thomas, 1928; Kelly, 1955; Berger and Luckmann, 1966; Ball, 1972; Bittner, 1973). They do so by bringing to bear upon events a complex personal framework of beliefs and values, which they have developed over their lives to categorise, characterise, explain and predict the events in their worlds. It is a framework which, in a social world, is shared in some parts with some others but one in which the points of commonality cannot be assumed as self-evidently, non-problematically, 'given'. In order to understand *why* persons act as they do we need to understand the meaning and significance they give to their actions. The depth interview is one way – not the only way and often used most appropriately in conjunction with other ways – of doing so. For to understand other persons' constructions of reality we would do well to ask them (rather than assume we can know merely by observing their overt behaviour) and to ask them in such a way that they can tell us in their terms (rather than those imposed rigidly and *a priori* by ourselves) and in a depth which addresses the rich context that is the substance of their meanings (rather than through isolated fragments squeezed onto a few lines of paper).

Structure and ambiguity

The above leads naturally to consideration of one central issue in the conduct of depth interviews, that of the degree of structure in the interview. It is an issue I have found to be of recurring concern among those just starting to do qualitative research, reflected in such questions as: How non-directive can I, ought I to be? Do I always ask open-ended questions? Can I never disagree with the respondents? Qualitative research methodologies seek to learn about the social world in ways which do not rigidly structure the direction of enquiry and learning within simplifying, acontextual, *a priori* definitions. Thus, interviews in which interviewers have prepared a long list of questions which they are determined to ask, come what may, over a period of say an hour and a half, are not depth interviews. This is so even if the researchers are contingent enough to alter the exact wording and order of their questions and even if the questions all centre around the same broad topic. For in this way the interviewers have already predicted, in detail, what is relevant and meaningful to their respondents about the research topic; and in doing this they have significantly prestructured the direction of enquiry within their own frame of reference in ways that give little time and space for their respondents to elaborate their own. They are additionally likely to be so anxious to cover all their questions that even if they hear something they know they ought to follow up, they do not. Often they will not hear such crucial clues anyway.

Yet the issue of structure is not straightforward. There is no such thing as a totally unstructured interview and the term is over-used and often carelessly used. The point is not simply that researchers have a 'right' to define the relevance of the data they collect from respondents, even if their respondents are not interested in the data themselves. For, if the topics of relevance and significance to the researchers have no relevance or significance to their respondents, then the researchers should think seriously about the quality of the data they are getting (except in so far as it is data about the irrelevance and insignificance of the topics to the respondents). Nor is it simply that the interview is a 'conversation with a purpose' initiated and guided by the researcher. For there are persons with the social skill, if not always the overt positional power, to manage and control an interview as effectively as their researchers, including being able to declare that the question they have just been asked is irrelevant and/or meaningless to them.

The crucial point is that there is no such thing as presuppositionless research. In preparing for interviews researchers will have, and should have, some broad questions in mind, and the more interviews they do and the more patterns they see in the data, the more they are likely to use this grounded understanding to want to explore in certain directions rather than others. The process of interviewing is one in which researchers are continually making choices, based on their research interests and prior theories, about which data they want to pick up and explore further with respondents and those which they do not. The making of these choices is the imposition of some structure.

Yet although we are tied to our own frameworks, we are not totally tied up by them. If we ask more questions arising from what we hear at the time than we have predetermined we will ask, if we hold on to, modify, elaborate and sometimes abandon our prior schemes in a contingent response to what our respondents are telling us is significant in the research topic, then we are some way to achieving the complex balance between restricting structure and restricting ambiguity.

The problems of ambiguity is illustrated by the 'non-directive' style of interviewing, where researchers encourage interviewees to ramble in any direction they choose and give no indication of what they themselves are interested in. 'Non-directive' interviews are anything but non-directive. What one person will say to another depends on what he or she assumes the other is 'up to' in the situation. If the respondents have no clear idea of what the researchers' interests and intentions are, they are less likely to feel unconstrained than constrained by the need to put energy into guessing what these are. Furthermore, the level of ambiguity means not only that the interviewees do not know 'what questions the researchers are asking' but also, and therefore, that the researchers do not know what questions the respondents are answering. In short, researchers are more likely to get good data, and know what data they are getting, if the interviewees are told at the outset what the research topic is, even if initially in relatively broad terms, and why the topic is of interest.

Interviewer bias?

The issue of structure is closely related to that of 'interviewer bias'. Many of those who come to qualitative methods in policy-related research come from a quantitative tradition in which the need to avoid interviewer bias is usually regarded as crucial. It is a concern bound to ideas, for example, of reliability and replication. In qualitative research the notion of some kind of impersonal, machine-like investigator is recognised as a chimera. An interview is a complicated, shifting, social *process* occurring between two individual human beings, which can never be exactly replicated. We cannot get at some 'objective truth' that would be there if only the effects of interpersonal interaction could be removed.

Yet again the matter is not straightforward. Are we not concerned in some ways with avoiding the bias of imposing our own definitions to the extent that we do not see those of our respondents? The answer has to do with the way in which we understand and use the concept of bias, not as something to be avoided at all costs but as something to be used, creatively, contingently and self-consciously. We use our 'bias' as human beings creatively and contingently to develop particular relationships with particular people so that they can tell us about their worlds and we can hear them. In doing this we use ourselves as research instruments to try and empathise with other human beings. No other research instrument can do this. (See Diesing, 1972, and Filstead, 1970, on the introspective method of understanding.)

To see bias in this way does of course make the activity of research a much more demanding and sometimes awesome activity than if there were neat prescriptions we could follow to preserve our objectivity and ensure that all our research encounters were pre-enactable and manageable by a set of rules. This does not mean that there are no guidelines as may be instanced by bringing the issues of structure and bias together. It has already been argued that a high level of ambiguity is not a good way for researchers to know what data they are getting nor for making interviewees feel comfortable. Open-ended questions are used extensively in depth interviews because they give greater freedom for respondents to answer in their own terms rather than within the tramlines of set alternatives in 'closed' questions. Yet there are typically some occasions in most interviews when researchers will want to focus on discovering responses to specific alternatives. The reason why researchers are extremely careful about the extent to which they show strong disagreement with some of their respondents' opinions is that, as in other social situations, this may prevent respondents feeling able to tell what they sincerely believe at the time. Alternatively, however, the same reasoning applies to not refusing to give some answer if respondents ask for the researchers' own opinions.

There cannot be definitive rules about the use of open-ended questions, leading and loaded questions, disagreement with respondents, and so on. Such choices must depend on the understanding researchers have of the person they are with and the kind of relationship they have developed in the encounter. Some relationships may allow, without destroying trust and comfort, much more of the to-and-fro of debate and discussion between two human beings than others. What is crucial is that researchers choose their actions with a self-conscious awareness of why they are making them, what the effects are likely to be upon that relationship – and indeed whether their own theories and values are getting in the way of understanding those of the respondents.

A social interaction

People develop over their lives a personal framework of beliefs and values with which they selectively and subjectively build meaning and significance in events. It is this framework, or schema and its 'real consequences' for action that the qualitative researcher is interested in learning about. But people also, therefore, attribute meaning and significance to the particular research situations they are in. The actions they take – what data for example, they will give a researcher – depend on this situational definition. A central part of the theoretical framework á researcher brings to preparing for, and indeed analysing, depth interviews must be awareness of the factors which affect the data their interviewees provide.

Respondents' interpretations of the researchers' interests, attitudes, values, reactions to them and so on, are clearly fundamental to their definition of the research situation. For example, we all have our stereotypes which we use to make assumptions about other people's attitudes, values and characteristic modes of behaviour on the basis of apparently minimal 'external' data – dress, voice, sex, age, social role and so on. These are elements in the 'first impressions' we all seek to manage in social interactions in order that others will form the impression of ourselves that we want them to have. In research situations, interviewees will seek to 'suss out' what the researchers are like; what they want, why, with what consequences for themselves; and what the researchers seem to think of them. They will also take into account any previous experiences they have had of being interviewed. The conclusions they draw will affect what they themselves want out of the interview and the persona they choose to present to achieve this end and how they manage the impressions that the researchers have of them. Human beings present different personae in different situations, to different audiences. In the giving of accounts to others, they are concerned not only with 'intelligibility' – making their actions comprehensible – but also 'warrantability' – the legitimation of action and the presentation of a credible and legitimate 'self'. (See Harré and Secord, 1972; Harré, 1979; also Goffman's writings on the presentation of self, e.g. 1959, and Mangham, 1978.)

To take a few obvious examples, if we as interviewees believe that an interviewer may use what we say to damage us in some way, we are unlikely to reveal data that could be so used. If we have had experiences to suggest that this could happen we are likely to be extremely wary of talking to other researchers. We may not refuse to talk to them if we feel that the costs of refusal are too high. We *may* be bothered to put energy into finding out whether this new researcher is different and can be trusted. We may just seek to get the interview over with as quickly as possible, with enough detail and enough feigned interest to satisfy the researcher that he or she is getting something of value but without saying anything that touches the core of what we actually believe and care about in the research topic. In doing this we may have a well rehearsed script that we produce, about what we do and why, and about what we think is important and worthwhile about what we do, and so on. Some of what we say we may sincerely believe, some of it we may not, but we are certainly not going to tell the researcher which is which, and we are certainly not going to say too much about the things that confuse us or move us or distress us.

We may, if we are powerful senior managers, wish to make it clear to any researchers that we are doing them a favour by talking to them at all and they certainly have no right to ask about sensitive and confidential data. We may wish to manipulate them in various ways – perhaps, for example, to reveal certain data to certain others we want to influence. On the other hand, if we have never been interviewed before, and we are somewhat unnerved by the researcher's neat appearance, middle-class voice and quietly confident manner, we may be defensive and antagonistic. Alternatively we may be very anxious to present the image of a dutiful, thoughtful citizen, to avoid looking stupid, to please the researcher by saying what we think that he or she wants to hear, and so on.

If we as researchers want to obtain good data it would be better that the persons we are interviewing trust us enough to believe that we will not use the data against them, or that we will not regard their opinions as foolish; that they are not trying very hard to please; or are not so untouched by us as individuals and the process of being interviewed that they produce a well-rehearsed script that tells very little about what actually concerns and moves them; or that they do not see an opportunity to manipulate us to suit certain personal ends of which we are unaware, and so on. Thus, the stress in much that is said about interviewing is on the need to assure respondents of confidentiality, on using and developing the social skills (verbal and non-verbal) which we have all used at some time or other to convince others that we want to hear what they have to say, take it seriously, and are indeed hearing them.

We do need to pay attention to the crucial non-verbal data – of posture, gesture, voice intonation, facial expression, eye contact, and so on – by which we can communicate, for example, interest, encouragement, warmth and caring, on the one hand; or boredom, disapproval, coldness and indifference on the other. We need not only to ask questions in such a way that the others are encouraged to answer and elaborate further, in their terms, but also to give them enough time and space to do so. We also of course do need to listen – to hear what seems to be significant to the respondents in the research topic and explore this further, to be aware of the data that tell us we have misread significance and should change the line of probing. We need to know how to judge when we are getting data that are off the track of what we are interested in, be very sure that we are not just making this judgement on the basis of our own preconceptions and missing data that are relevant to the research topic as construed by the respondents; and then how to bring them back gently. We need to check meaning when we are not sure that we have understood, and not assume too quickly that we have understood. (See also Ivey, 1971, on attending behaviour and Spradley, 1979; Somner and Somner, 1980; Simon, 1981.) And just as we need to think very carefully about the types of people we are going to interview, the likely range of their experiences and possible responses, and adapt our approach and self-presentation appropriately, so we need to adapt our style to the particular person we are with (that is, the individual, not the 'type') and to the shifts and developments during the interaction.

These are essential skills that have to be thought about and practised, and if researchers do not develop such skills the likelihood of overcoming some of the problems outlined earlier is significantly reduced. It is perhaps worth noting at this point that I regard them as much more important than the question of tape recording that concerns some researchers. It is my belief not only that most people quickly forget about a tape recorder but also that if they do not believe in the researcher and the research the presence or otherwise of a tape recorder is not the determining factor. However, if people seem very uncomfortable with the tape recorder, then it should not be used and full notes of the interview should be made immediately afterwards.

Yet such skills are of themselves not always enough. Certainly issues such as trust and power are more complex than implied by the sometimes bland exhortations to 'establish rapport'. We can consider here the central question of the relevance of the research to the respondents.

Relevance and commitment

This is an issue graphically addressed by Maruyama (1981). He describes the attitudes of prison inmates to being interviewed by people such as psychologists, sociologists, students, newspaper reporters, whose purposes in doing the research – proving a theory, writing a book, getting a degree, getting promotion and so on – are totally irrelevant to the inmates. The latter feel exploited by the researchers and develop sophisticated phoney answers to minimise the intrusion.

It is not necessary to presume that all research respondents will feel exploited by researchers and deliberately develop phoney answers to acknowledge that respondents, who can see no intrinsic relevance or purpose in the research, may equally see little reason to give good data to an outsider who can offer no benefit other than the remote possibility of some future policy change. The issue of relevance is particularly pertinent to those instances where researchers want data that interviewees would regard as too sensitive or difficult to reveal unless there were good reasons for doing so.

Of course, not all the data that researchers are interested in are of the kind their respondents find threatening and difficult to reveal. Some people may well value the possibility that what they have to say could have some impact on policies affecting them. Some people may feel rewarded by knowing that the interview is important to the researcher. Some people may find that the process of being given the opportunity to talk to someone who wants to listen is of itself worthwhile. These benefits, however, cannot be assumed to be universal.

Let us take, for example, the interviewing of 'elites', that is, persons with power. Such people have the considerable social and political skills with which they have acquired and retained their position.

Potentially they also have much to lose by revealing personal and political data to others. Getting access to, and being taken seriously by, such persons is clearly helped by being of equal status and/or by appropriate self-presentation by the researcher. (See, e.g. Cannell and Kahn, 1968.) Yet such persons are most likely to be engaged if they can see some benefit to themselves of articulating certain data. (See also Mangham, 1982.)

How can the issue of relevance be addressed? One approach involves being aware of, and accepting in analyses and interpretations, the limits on the kind of data that are likely to be obtained in the archetypal form of the 'one-off' interview of an hour or two; being attuned to the difference between those who seem to be engaged for reasons such as those above and those who are not; taking oneself seriously as a research instrument who can, with care and explicitness, make judgements about this and about whether some data 'ring true' or not. Depth interviewing can never involve a simplistic 'face-value' treatment of data. We have to think beforehand, during and after the interviews about what is likely to, is, and has affected the data obtained in the interview and the relationship we are involved in.

Another approach is to consider ways of carrying out the interviews, as components in a different kind of relationship. The 'simplest' way is to conduct more than one interview. This not only allows a deeper exploration of a complex topic but also provides some evidence of commitment by a researcher to the person and a topic. With this can be built some higher level of trust and the opportunity for negotiating relevance. This may be developed yet further with a definite commitment to feed back the findings to the persons concerned at a not too remote date in the future.

More direct and immediate benefits to research participants can, however, be negotiated in interviewing that becomes action research. Here processes of data collection become linked to those of feedback and dialogue whereby persons can work on specific problems within the research topic for themselves. For example, Fineman (1983) describes an intervention method for research into the meaning and significance of unemployment to white-collar workers. This involved a process of counselling, lasted between one-and-a-half and two hours with 100 people, of whom approximately 20 per cent asked for and received a second session. The research was a 'contract' in which Fineman offered counselling and advice in return for the research participants allowing this very process to be used for his understanding of their unemployment situation.

I and my colleagues have used the techniques of cognitive mapping, described in the next chapter, sometimes with repertory grids (Kelly, 1955), for research through consultancy (e.g. Eden, Jones and Sims,

1979). Cognitive mapping is a tool for explicitly representing people's complex qualitative beliefs in such a way that they can explore, reflect and work on their own thinking about a particular situation. Often the research involves a relatively intensive long-term involvement but this is not always the case. Thus, for example, mapping can be done 'on-the-spot' with a person in a single session. Or a first interview of a more traditional form can be followed by a second feedback interview which facilitates further elaboration, checking understanding and the fulfilment of a 'contract' with the research participant to work on an issue of concern to them in the research area. In this way the interviewees become involved in an activity that is meaningful and useful to themselves. The reason for participating, for articulating their thinking, in its complexity and perhaps sensitivity, therefore ceases to be primarily in order to please a researcher.

Not everyone wants to be 'helped'. There are different ways of offering help, some of which can be highly coercive and structuring (e.g. Clark, 1972; Eden and Sims, 1979). Thus the approach to action research requires as much care and thought as any other qualitative research method. The key point, however, that I wish to make is that there are different ways of depth interviewing and different sorts of relationships in which they take place.

All research involves choices. These choices will depend on the nature of the research topic, on the particular data that are sought about the topic, on the researchers' 'models of man' and theoretical perspectives about the kinds of issues discussed earlier. They will also depend on such practical constraints as the time, energy and money available to do the research, and the acceptability of particular approaches to research clients. It is pointless to pretend that these constraints do not exist, and these may be determining factors in, for example, a choice of single interviews with respondents rather than more in depth involvements. This does not mean that such a choice should be made without an awareness of its implications for the kind of data that are likely, or unlikely, to be obtained. Indeed, that we should approach the practice of depth interviewing with a self-conscious awareness of what we are doing, why and with what consequences has been the central theme of this chapter.

References

Ball, D. 1972, 'The Definition of the Situation: some theoretical and methodological consequences of taking W I Thomas seriously', *Journal for the Theory of Social Behaviour*, vol. 2, no. 1, pp. 61–81.

Berger, P.L. and Luckmann, T. 1966, *The social construction of reality*, New York, Doubleday.

Bittner, E. 1973, 'Objectivity and realism in sociology', in G. Psathas (ed),

Phenomenological sociology: Issues and Applications, New York, Wiley.

Cannell, C.F. and Kahn, R.C. 1968, 'Interviewing', in G. Lindzey and E. Aronson (eds), *The handbook of social psychology*, vol. 2, Reading, Mass, Addison-Wesley.

Clark, P.A. 1972, *Action research and organizational change*, London, Harper and Row.

Diesing, P. 1972, *Patterns of discovery in the social sciences*, London, Routledge and Kegan Paul.

Eden, C., Jones, S. and Sims, D. 1979, *Thinking in organizations*, London, Macmillan.

Eden, C. and Sims, D. 1979, 'On the nature of problems in consulting practice', *Omega*, vol. 7, no. 2, pp. 119–127.

Filstead, W.J., 1970, *Qualitative methodology: firsthand involvement with the social world*, Chicago, Markham.

Fineman, S. 1983, *White collar unemployment*, Chichester, Wiley.

Goffman, E. 1959, *The presentation of self in everyday life*, New York, Doubleday Anchor.

Harré, R. 1979, *Social being*, Oxford, Basil Blackwell.

Harré, R. and Secord, P.F. 1972, *The explanation of social behaviour*, Oxford, Basil Blackwell.

Ivey, A.E. 1971, *Micro-counselling: innovations in interviewing training*, Springfield, Ill, Charles C. Thomas.

Kelly, G.A. 1955, *The psychology of personal constructs*, New York, Norton.

Mangham, I.L. 1978, *Interactions and interventions in organizations*, Chichester, Wiley.

Mangham, I.L. 1982, 'The research enterprise' in N. Nicholson and T. Wall (eds), *The theory and practice of oganizational psychology*, London, Academic Press.

Maruyama, M. 1981, 'Endogenous research: rationale' in P. Reason and J. Rowan (eds), *Human inquiry: A source book of new paradigm research*, Chichester, Wiley.

Simon, H. 1981, 'Conversation piece: The practice of interviewing in case study research', in C. Adelman (ed), *Uttering, muttering: collecting, using and reporting talk for social and educational research*, London, Grant McIntyre.

Somner, R. and Somner, B.B. 1980, *A practical guide to behavioural research*, New York, Oxford University Press.

Spradley, J.P. 1979, *The ethnographic interview*, New York, Holt, Rinehart and Winston.

Thomas, W.I. and Thomas, D.S. 1928, *The child in America: behavioural problems and progress*, New York, Knopf.

4 The Analysis of Depth Interviews
Sue Jones

A great deal more has been written about methodologies of qualitative data collection than about those of data analysis. This is not particularly surprising. The analysis of qualitative data is a highly personal activity. It involves processes of interpretation and creativity that are difficult and perhaps somewhat threatening to make explicit. As with depth interviewing there are no definitive rules to be followed by rote and by which, for example, two researchers can ensure that they reach identical conclusions about a set of data.

The difficulty of explication should not, however, lead to the extreme of mystification. Indeed a great deal of qualitative data analysis is rather less mysterious than hard, sometimes, tedious, slog. In this chapter I shall attempt to describe and explain the kinds of processes I go through when I analyse qualitative interview data. There is no intention to be prescriptive, but rather to offer a personal account of a personal process, in sufficient detail to enable those who are interested to try something similar to do so.

Grounded theorising
The analysis of qualitative data is a process of making sense, of finding and making a structure in the data and giving this meaning and significance for ourselves, and for any relevant audiences. As with data collection methodologies, the way we do this and the kind of structures we look for in the data depend on the purpose of enquiry and what we see as the underlying purpose of qualitative research. As with depth interviewing, therefore, my starting point is a concern to understand the world of the research participants as they construct it. As Psathas (1973, p. 12) argues, the key issue for social research is 'whether the results of an enquiry fit, make sense and are true to the understanding of ordinary actors in the everyday world'. It is a concern which is intensely practical. Theory which is 'grounded' (Glaser and Strauss, 1967) in the concepts and theorising of the people it is about is likely to 'fit and work' as the basis for explanation and prediction.

I know I cannot empathise with the research participants completely. I also know that I am likely at some points to set my understanding of their 'concrete' concepts – those which they use to organise, interpret and construct their own world (Diesing, 1972) – within my own and/or audience's concepts and frameworks that are different from theirs. When I do this, however, I try to be clear that I am doing this and why, and to ensure that this 'second level' of meaning retains some link with the constructions of the research participants. This is because of my concern to avoid what Lofland (1976) calls 'undisciplined abstraction', leading to concepts which bear little relation to the social world that they are supposed to refer to, either because they are not apparently based in any empirical research, or are wondrously elaborate edifices of theory based on very little empirical research. As Lofland (1976, p. 11) argues, 'an empirical science is constructed . . . out of the interplay of data and perplexed perception that *gives rise* to concepts yet contains and *constrains* them by a context of concrete empirical materials'.

I am trying to do this whether I am doing 'academic' research without a direct research client, or research commissioned by clients. My audience is different. When it is an academic one I am likely to make more references to existing theory within that audience, and I use words like concepts, models, theory and so on, relatively freely whereas I might be more circumspect with certain clients to whom they might smack of 'ivory tower' academicism. With some commissioned research I may also be less concerned with moving beyond a relatively concrete or substantive analysis of the data than for an academic audience. I am still however, theorising and cannot but do so.

As Bulmer (1982) points out, there is a tendency among the commissioners of policy-related research, whether in government or other organisations, to see it as primarily concerned with the gathering of 'facts' – objective information on the basis of which informed policy decisions about specific policy problems can be made. Researchers undertake this information gathering activity against the specific brief of their clients, and in analysing and reporting their findings are required also to be objective, impartial and descriptive. But the analysis of data about the social world can never be 'merely' a matter of discovering and describing what is there. The very process of deciding 'what is', and what is relevant and significant in 'what is', involves selective interpretation and conceptualisation. As Bulmer (1982, p. 38) also points out, 'There is a constant interplay between the observation of realities and the formation of concepts, between research and theorising, between perception and explanation'.

Structuring through categories

I start off with tapes or, if for some reason the interview was not taped, the notes about the interview made immediately afterwards. I also have the notes that I make after each interview which are not detailed records ſ what went on but rather more general comments on the nature of the interaction. They cover such things as: whether the interview seemed to go well; if not why not; how distracted, comfortable, nervous, confident, relaxed, wary and so on, the interviewee (and I) had been; whether I felt I had, or had not, managed to get behind the person's legitimating scripts; whether there were any particular parts of the data that did not quite ring true and why. In short, I note any factors about the place, time and relationship with the interviewee that seem likely to be important to take account of when I come back to the data. I make these notes because otherwise it is all too easy to forget these additional contextual data which can so importantly affect the interpretation of the interview content.

I sometimes have transcripts. They are a help in managing the data and holding on to the detail which can be missed by selective jottings from the tape. However, it is important that reading the transcripts does *not* become a substitute for listening to the non-linguistic data on the tapes: emphasis, mood, intonation and so on that crucially elaborate meaning. Transcribing tapes does, of course, take a long time, and is expensive if someone else is paid to do it. Thus I usually code the data directly from the tapes. Since this is typically done in considerable detail I do not feel particularly concerned that I am going to miss key data by not having transcripts.

Like many qualitative researchers a great deal of my analysis is concerned with 'coding' the data into categories. The quickest and easiest way to do this is to decide upon your categories in advance and simply go through the data putting the appropriate sections of data into the particular categories they illustrate. However, while it is in principle possible to do this and still remain sensitive to the unanticipated categories which derive from the concepts of the research participants, in practice it is difficult to do so. The data all too easily become structured within the *a priori* definitions of the researcher in precisely the ways that data collection methodology was intended to avoid.

Thus, Glaser and Strauss (1967) argue, in *The Discovery of Grounded Theory*, that theory about the social world which 'fits and works' is that which is generated inductively from the data. Categories emerge out of the examination of the data by researchers who study it without firm preconceptions dictating relevances in concepts and hypotheses beforehand. The problem with this, if taken literally, is that categories do not just 'emerge' out of data as if they were objectively 'there' waiting to be discovered. As Kaplan (1964, p. 133) points out: 'We always know something already and this knowledge is intimately involved in what we come to know next, whether by observation or any other way. We see what we have reason of seeing.' Different persons, with different perspectives and different curiosities about the area of investigation will inevitably find different categories with which to structure and make sense of the data. Furthermore, in commissioned research, the clients of the research will also have their own theories, even if sometimes inchoate and relatively implicit. They will inevitably bring these to bear when confronted with the framework of the researchers' conclusions to respond to and evaluate. To ignore them is merely to increase the likelihood of the researchers' analyses and conclusions being ignored themselves.

Nevertheless, the enormous influence and attraction of Glaser and Strauss' ideas in the literature of social research lies within the perspective discussed earlier, that is, in their stress upon building understanding about the social world which is firmly grounded in the concepts and theories of the persons inhabiting and acting in it. Thus I try to develop my conceptual categories from the crucial base of the categories and concepts of the research participants. However, in comparing and contrasting and bringing them together I will inevitably formulate broader superordinate or 'sensitising concepts' which are not identical to the former, and also reflect my own and/or my audiences' research relevances. (See Diesing, 1972, on the nature and relationship of concrete and sensitising concepts in qualitative theory development; also Glaser, 1978, on a similar substantive/theoretical concepts distinction.)

In doing this I am also inevitably making connections, as carefully and as explicitly as I can, with the concepts and theories I already have about the area of investigation, in ways which can confirm, elaborate, modify or reject them. I also make connections with what I understand to be the concerns and preconceptions of any research clients. By this I do not mean just what is set down in a final brief, but what I believe (and have usually put some energy into finding out) to be the typically more complex, less neatly organised set of ideas and interests they have about the topic. I would expect to take these into account in any debriefing and report.

Although I do not start with a list of categories into which the data are to be slotted, thinking about these and the broad question taken into the research represents the 'focusing' I will do before starting the detailed analysis. I prefer to listen to the tapes of each interview at least twice: the first time to get a sense of the whole interview, its themes and dynamics; the second time to examine the data in more detail. Then I begin to 'map' the interview, using the technique of cognitive mapping.

Mapping the data

Cognitive mapping is a method of modelling persons' beliefs in diagrammatic form. It was developed in the context of action research and consultancy, as a tool to enable clients to make explicit, explore, and work through their thinking about a particular problem in order to devise ways of handling it (see Eden, Jones and Sims, 1979, 1983). However, I have also used mapping extensively in analysing interview data that was not part of an action research project.

In mapping we are listening for, and seeking to represent, persons' explanatory and predictive theories about those aspects of their world being described to us. A cognitive map comprises two main elements: persons' concepts of ideas in the form of descriptions of entities, abstract or concrete, in the situation being considered; and beliefs or theories about the relationships between them, shown in the map by an arrow or simple line. An arrow represents a relationship where one thing leads to, or is explained by, another; a simple line represents a connotative, or non-causal link. So the following statements taken from an interview may be coded as shown:

> Our ability to carry out additional desirable policies rests in part on our making best use of current resources on current policies. We cannot carry out additional desirable policies if there is fundamental waste of resources on current policies. This means being able to make rational and accurate decisions based on adequate information, not decisions just on a gut basis.

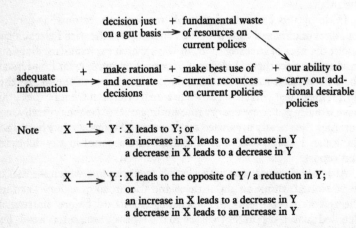

This is the simplest form of coding, one which those trying out the method often find helpful to begin with. However, more complete coding takes account of the way in which the particular meaning of an idea for a person is elaborated through its contrast, explicit or implicit, with some psychological alternative (Kelly, 1955). For example, the notion of 'being bored' only makes sense because there is some implied opposite notion, of say, 'being interested', although it is important to note that different persons may have very different opposite poles and thus different personal constructs; perhaps 'bored ... excited' or 'bored ... happy'. They may, furthermore, use either of these constructs at different times, depending on the situation they are in. Persons do not, of course, always express explicit discrete alternatives, but when they do these can be coded for, and furthermore the opposite poles can sometimes legitimately be inferred. The above quotation was chosen because it is a good example of expressed bipolar constructs. We could recode the statements, now, as follows:

adequate information... $\longrightarrow$	+	make rational and accurate decisions...' decisions just on a gut basis $\longrightarrow$	+	make best use of... fundamental waste of current resources on current policies $\longrightarrow$	+	our ability to carry out additional desirable policies

Note: Dots separate discrete alternative poles or indicate 'void' poles where the alternative has not been made explicit. Concepts without dots are monotonic concepts where the inferred poles are 'an increase in', 'a decrease in' respectively. A +ve sign between constructs indicates a relationship between similar-sided poles. Thus, for example, 'make rational and accurate decisions' leads to 'make best use of current resources on current policies' while 'decisions just on a gut basis' leads to 'fundamental waste of current resources on current policies'.

A −ve sign would indicate a relationship *across* poles so that the first pole of a construct 'A' would lead to the second pole of a construct 'B' and the second pole of construct 'A' would lead to the first pole of construct 'B'.

I code the interviews on large sheets of paper so that each interview, as far as possible, is coded on to one sheet. If there is not enough space I simply attach further sheets. At the end I therefore have a map of the whole interview in front of me. It is often untidy, bitty, but a map that I can make sense of, and it is worth noting that the skeleton rules for coding outlined above are often elaborated with additional personal conventions by others who use the technique. What is important is the use of mapping as a tool to help understand the way in which the interviewees make sense of their world – attributing meaning and significance through explaining and predicting the consequences of events, for themselves and/or others.

Whilst I am coding I also make a great many notes, some on the map itself, others on separate sheets which I then clip onto the map. For example, the use of lines to represent relationships between constructs clearly omits the verbal and non-verbal data which elaborate the particular strength, or tentativeness, or subtle qualification, of beliefs about these relationships. Where it seems important to do so, I therefore put these data in. I may put words along an arrow or draw heavy or dashed lines to indicate emphatic or tentative assertions, add question marks to represent questions and so on. I have no firm conventions for this activity because I do not wish to become bound up in an elaborate system of rules for coding. I underline or ring constructs or groups of constructs that seem to be particularly significant to the person, including those for example that seem to express strong preferences or values, and note why I am making the inference.

I comment on any apparent contradictions in the data, thinking about whether, for example, they reflect genuine inconsistency, or apparent consistency that is in fact reconciled by underlying beliefs, a change in thinking over the course of the interview, or indeed greater honesty later in the interview. I make notes about any data that feel more like legitimation than sincere belief, why they seem to be of this kind, and what inferences I can justifiably make about them. I note where I seem to have influenced the data by misreading significance and 'over-probing' in a certain direction or, on a second hearing, seem to have missed clues which I should have probed further. I continually jot down ideas that spring to mind about the significance and implications of the data for my research interests, including connections with existing theory. If there is a research client I record those things which are likely to be particularly pertinent to him and which I could expect to comment on in any report. I also note connections with and implications for previous interviews I have looked at and future ones I am going to analyse. I make a tentative list of possible categories.

At the end of this process I thus have a map and a series of notes that represent my inferences and interpretation of the data. At this point I look at the map as a whole, and draw out the clusters of constructs and relationships that seem to form the substantive categories in the data based on the 'concrete' concepts of the respondent. I also note other categorisations that reflect my own ways of organising the substantive categories in accordance with my own research relevances. These further categorisations may well change as I examine the rest of the data. Finally, I produce a summary diagram of the categories and their relationships which I use to help me relate interview to interview when I put the analyses together.

To give an example of this process, see figures 4.1, 4.2 and 4.3 which relate to part of an interview with a local politician concerned with exploring his perceptions of his role. It sets out part of the answer to a question asking him to elaborate further on the factors he saw as important in trying to effect 'change in a long established situation', a concept he had used previously in the interview.

> To get change in a long established situation an essential starting point it seems to me is that you yourself recognise that something is wrong and want to change it, you are not just prepared to patch and mend. I suppose I am the sort of person who if I see a problem I am not happy until I do something about it. Then, of course, you have to convince a lot of other people that something is radically wrong. You have to convince Committee, Council

and some of the officers that something is radically wrong. Obviously you have to be able to argue your case persuasively, logically and with adequate information. This is actually another question that we ought to look at at some point. We are in a way running a business, not with products but with services and we need the tools of any business, including information storage systems, to enable us to manage as efficiently and effectively and cost-consciously as we can. Anyway, in getting change, it is a fact of life that outside pressure is an important impetus to change. No politician wants a bad public image. No politician likes reading headlines in the papers saying that the Council is a failure in this field or that. Most Chairmen, for example, would feel that it reflected to some degree on them, on their department and certainly it reflects indirectly on the Council and on the ruling party. Ultimately of course, it affects the possibility of losing or keeping your seat. But it is also a personal concern as well as a political concern about how well you do the job you have chosen to do.

Comparison and integration

I go through this process with each interview and then I bring the resultant analyses together. With the help of the summary diagrams, I locate the categories that have similar labels and then compare the content of the categories, putting together the categories that seem to go together because they are about the same topic and/or illustrate a particular conceptual theme. I sometimes use computer software, specifically designed to assist with the analysis of cognitive maps (e.g. Jones, 1981; Eden, Smithin and Wiltshire, 1980), but it is important to point out that the process is not computer-dependent and this chapter concentrates on manual analysis. In the latter I literally cut up the maps, using photocopies but retaining the original, and put the categories next to one another. The process of comparison will usually result in further categorisation, such as finding superordinate concepts that bring together similar categories and perhaps further sub-categorisations beneath these.

The superordinate conceptual categorisations may be very closely related to the original concrete category labels and/or comprise those that particularly reflect the client's relevances and/or go further in conceptualisation to employ wider theoretical concepts. Thus to give one example, the notion of 'significant audiences for performance in a problem' is one that emerged for me as an important theme in interviews with local government members and officers. This was grounded in my understanding of what they construed as significant to pay attention to in performing their role but also reflected my own way of bringing together and conceptualising their constructs.

As Glaser and Strauss point out about their constant comparative method of analysis, this process of comparison (albeit somewhat different from their method) is one which very soon leads to ideas about the dimensions and properties of the category, including its relationship with other categories and including the differences as well as the

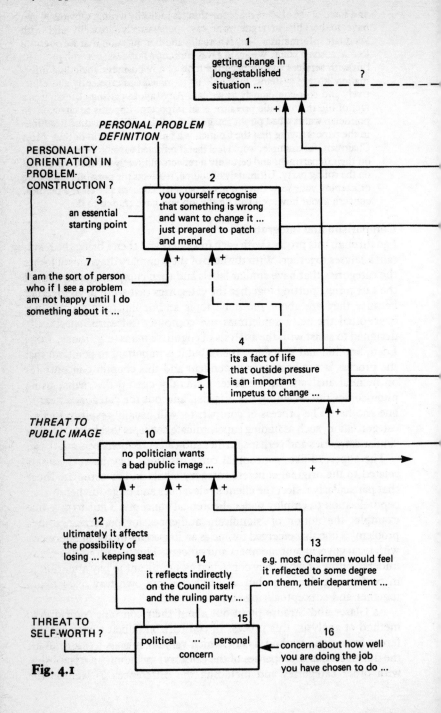

1
getting change in
long-established
situation ...

?

*PERSONAL PROBLEM
DEFINITION*

PERSONALITY
ORIENTATION IN
PROBLEM-
CONSTRUCTION ?

3
an essential
starting point

2
you yourself recognise
that something is wrong
and want to change it ...
just prepared to patch
and mend

7
I am the sort of person
who if I see a problem
am not happy until I do
something about it ...

4
its a fact of life
that outside pressure
is an important
impetus to change ...

*THREAT TO
PUBLIC IMAGE*

10
no politician wants
a bad public image ...

12
ultimately it affects
the possibility of
losing ... keeping seat

14
it reflects indirectly
on the Council itself
and the ruling party ...

13
e.g. most Chairmen would feel
it reflected to some degree
on them, their department ...

THREAT TO
SELF-WORTH ?

15
political ... personal
concern

16
concern about how well
you are doing the job
you have chosen to do ...

Fig. 4.1

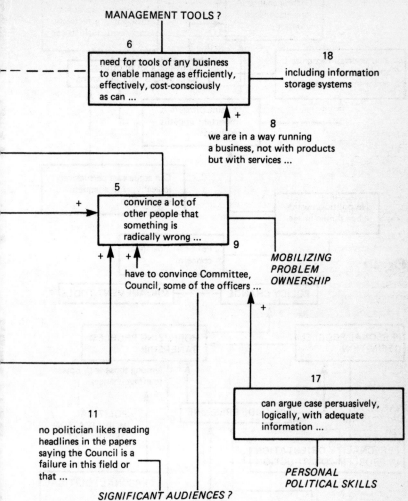

MANAGEMENT TOOLS ?

6

need for tools of any business to enable manage as efficiently, effectively, cost-consciously as can ...

18

including information storage systems

8

we are in a way running a business, not with products but with services ...

5

convince a lot of other people that something is radically wrong ...

9

have to convince Committee, Council, some of the officers ...

MOBILIZING PROBLEM OWNERSHIP

17

can argue case persuasively, logically, with adequate information ...

11

no politician likes reading headlines in the papers saying the Council is a failure in this field or that ...

SIGNIFICANT AUDIENCES ?

PERSONAL POLITICAL SKILLS

Fig. 4.1 A cognitive map of the transcript on pages 62 and 63, illustrating what an initial categorization might look like. Numbers are merely arbitrary identification codes used to identify constructs and often differentiate between interviewees. Blocked constructs represent potential category labels from the constructs of the interviewee, subsuming as the content of the relevant category those constructs traced back from these until another category label is reached, and the subordinate category related in the way. Thus, for example, the category indicated by construct 10 would contain constructs 10, 12, 13, 14, and the subordinate category indicated by construct 15, containing construct 16. Concepts in capitals indicate potential 'second order' categorizations, grounded in those of the interviewee but nevertheless reflecting my own perspectives and research interests (and no doubt other researchers with different perspectives and interests would find different categories). Dashed lines and question marks indicate tentativeness in inferences and interpretations that I would expect to come back to or require further evidence for and my maps typically have many of these as 1 code.

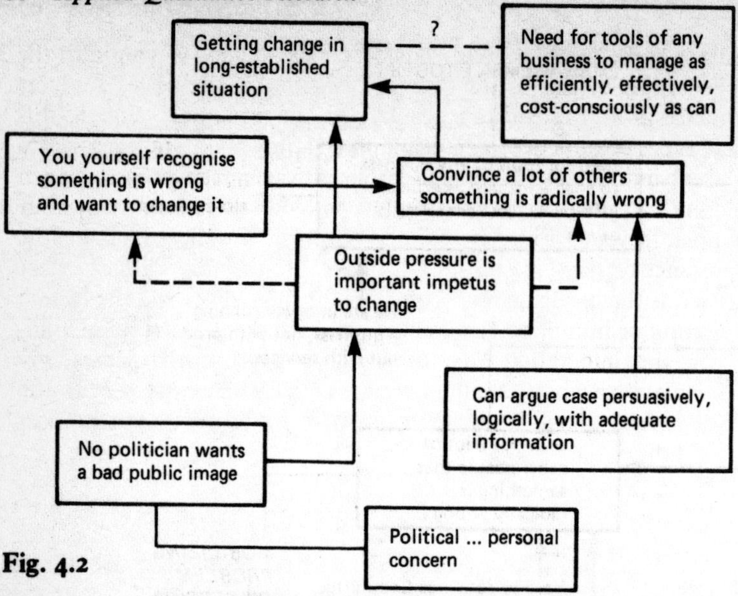

Fig. 4.2

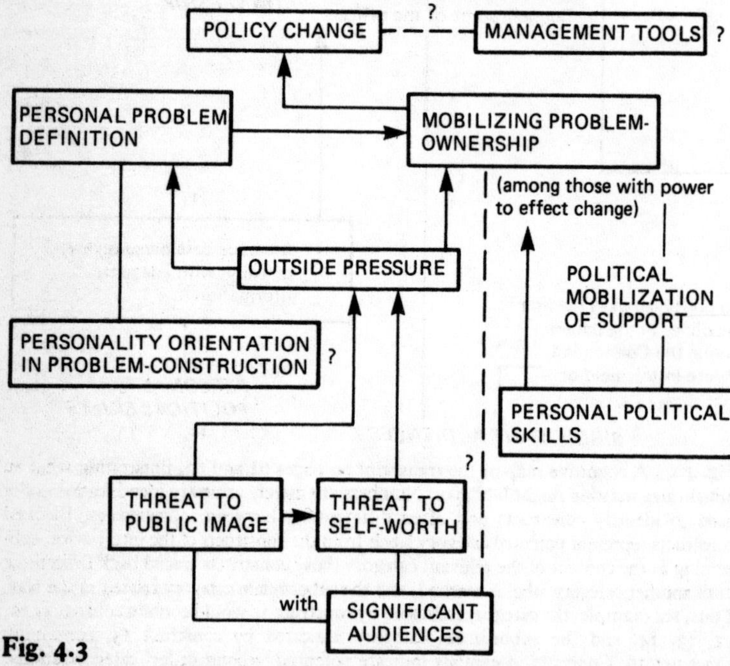

Fig. 4.3
Fig. 4.2 and 4.3 show examples of 'summary' diagrams that illustrate the category relationships that might be built from the map in Figure 4.1. One would of course expect both categories and their relationships to be elaborated and modified in the light of the related data in the rest of the interview.

similarities between people's constructions. Thus, to continue the above example, the broad category 'significant audiences for performance in a problem' can be mapped out through a range of different types of audience, significant for a variety of different reasons to different individuals. Here exploration of the relationships between concrete categories perceived by the individuals is important. For example, several interviewees may express a concern about the importance of 'good ... bad public image' but they may differ in what they see as the particular consequences for themselves and the factors facilitating or inhibiting this image. Throughout the process of comparison and integration I continue to make yet further notes, my commentary on what I am doing and why. It is these notes, with the data they refer to which, finally, form the basis of any research report and/or debrief. *

Involving clients

I usually write for any clients a traditional report, with quotations from the data, but I also refer to and include, in appendix form, maps of the categories and their contents on separate pages. I also provide summary diagrams of category labels and the relationships between them. I do not always put in all the data in each category. This is contingent upon the amount of data and the degree to which I feel justified in regarding some idea as so similar that it is not a distortion to remove the repetition and retain one chain of beliefs as representative of the beliefs of a number of the respondents.

The process of mapping I have described can be used by researchers for themselves alone. Maps can also, however, be used to involve the client in the data in a way that a few isolated quotes cannot. In most qualitative research the client is heavily reliant upon the summary interpretations of the researcher, with little direct access to the data. Yet clients will have their own interpretations of the particular significance of the findings to themselves. The good researcher will take account of what he or she understands to be the concerns and theories of the client about the research arena. Yet the process of building meaning and significance in the data is a dynamic activity of *direct* interaction with the data, and maps can offer more opportunity for this direct interaction than most typical research reports.

It is obviously the case that the maps produced by a researcher do not comprise 'raw data', but those which have been modelled and organised in a particular way. It is also the case that some clients are inclined to prefer brief summaries and recommendations from a researcher than become involved in the detail of the data underlying these. Nor do researchers always want clients to become involved in detailed examination of the data. Nevertheless maps do enable clients to explore considerably more of the language and theorising of respondents than can possibly be captured in selected quotations. Indeed the maps can be used as a strong tool of detailed evidence and backir for a researcher's interpretations and conclusions. More contingently clients can be invited to make their own interpretations of the data in a relationship where neither they nor the researcher have sole proprietary 'rights' to interpretation. They can become involved in 'negotiations' about particular meanings and significances.

Managing complexity

Cognitive mapping is not, of course, the only method for carefully and systematically analysing qualitative data. To take a very simple variation on the methods explored in this chapter, one may choose to categorise the data, not coded in maps, but in sentence form. Thus, for example, one may listen to the tapes and write down the content of categories collected as statements on different sheets of paper, or cards. As statements occur later on in an interview that seem to relate to an earlier category, these too are entered onto the relevant sheet. Alternatively, if working with transcripts, the categories in which one wishes to place sections of data can be marked by the side of them i the margin and the pieces cut out and aggregated later. While doin this, one can also simultaneously make notes about the relationship between categories as they are being constructed and additional note of the kind described earlier. Categories collected in this way will be compared and the process of comparison will lead to the development of further conceptualisation. This is a perfectly 'good' and thorough way to analyse qualitative data and one I have used.

It is perhaps worth noting at this point that, as Marshall (1981) points out, the debate within quantitative content analysis about the appropriate unit of analysis – whether it should be a word, phrase, sentence and so on – seems an unnecessary one. We find relatively easily 'chunks of meaning' and these may vary considerably in lengtl Not only is the debate unnecessary, it also seems inappropria Meaning is given by context. Words in isolation from their particu context of associated, elaborating beliefs are indeed meaningless. make them meaningful researchers have to 'put back' the cont from their own, and perhaps very different, framework of beliefs.

However, since this has been essentially a personal account should perhaps finish by explaining why I find myself repeate returning to cognitive mapping as a technique, despite the f. that it is somtimes a laborious and tedious process. First, rather tha distancing me from the data, I find that the discipline of mapping leads to an intense immersion in them. Second, I am helped by the confidence I have in the theoretical basis for the technique, provided by personal construct theory. Third, I find it easier to develop grounded concrete categories and their relationships in this way. Fourth, and perhaps most important, mapping helps me with the complex '*Gestalt*' of data. We need to 'fracture' the data in order to grasp and manipulate them; but the process of doing so by parcelling them into separate categories during coding makes it difficult to retain a sense of the relationships between the various elements in the data. I find that a map of a whole interview helps me to manage and also to retain the complexity of interrelated data better than if I follow a method which, for example, involves separating the data out as I proceed. In doing so I hope it also helps me retain and respect something of the unique 'wholeness' of unique persons' views of the world (e.g. Diesing, 1972, on holistic research).

Yet this has been a personal account and other people will inevitably find their own ways of managing and retaining complexity and *Gestalt* in data. There are many different methods that researchers can construct for themselves, all variations on the same themes of breaking down and building up analytic structure in the data. We can make some judgements about these as being more or less thorough, systematic, careful, non-pre-emptive, reflective, and so on, but some categorical determination of a 'best' method seems quite inappropriate. Finally, we all build and use the routines and tools with which we find, often through trial and error, we are most comfortable and which help us best make sense of the way other persons make sense of their realities.

References

Bulmer, M. 1982, *The uses of social research: Social investigation in public policy making*, London, George Allen and Unwin.

Diesing, P. 1972, *Patterns of discovery in the social sciences*, London, Routledge and Kegan Paul.

Eden, C., Jones, S., Sims, D. 1979, *Thinking in organizations*, London, Macmillan.

Eden, C., Jones, S., Sims, D. 1983, *Messing about in problems*, Oxford, Pergamon.

Eden, C., Smithin, T., Wiltshire, 1980, 'Cognition, simulation and learning', *Journal of Experimental Learning and Simulation*, vol. 2, pp. 131–143.

Glaser, B.G. 1978, *Theoretical sensitivity*, Mill Valley, California, The Sociology Press.

Glaser, B.G., Strauss, A.L. 1967, *The discovery of grounded theory*, Chicago, Aldine.

Jones, S. 1981, 'Listening to complexity – analysing qualitative marketing research data', *Journal of the Market Research Society*, vol. 23, no. 1, pp. 26–39.

Kaplan, A. 1964, *The conduct of enquiry*, San Francisco, Chandler.

Kelly, G.A. 1955, *The psychology of personal constructs*, New York, Norton.

Lofland, J. 1976, *Doing social life*, New York, Wiley.

Marshall, J. 1981, 'Making sense as a personal process'. In P. Reason, J. Rowan (eds), *Human inquiry*, Chichester, Wiley.

Psathas, G. 1973, *Phenomenological sociology: Issues and applications*, New York, Wiley.

5 Group Interviewing
Alan Hedges

Qualitative research is conventionally divided into two categories:

1 with single respondents (known as 'depth', 'focused' or 'individual' interviews);
2 with groups of respondents (known as 'group discussions', 'group interviews' or more simply as 'groups').

The line between the two forms is not as sharp as it sounds here. One might sometimes want to interview two people at a time – a married couple interviewed together, for example. This is not really a group, and in many ways has more in common with an individual interview.

The rationale for group interviews
Group and depth interviews both have advantages and disadvantages. Sometimes one is more appropriate, sometimes the other. Often the two techniques are best used together in the same project, because their respective strengths and weaknesses can complement each other.

The advantages of group interviews
Perhaps the most obvious reason for interviewing in groups is cost and speed. Although qualitative research does not set out to build a numerical sample like a quantitative survey would do, numbers are not irrelevant. If you talk only to a tiny handful of people your results may simply be untypical (although of course this depends on how you select the people as well as on the numbers involved).

But qualitative interviewing uses quite a lot of fairly expensive high-grade time, even though the numbers are comparatively small. You can obviously talk to a given number of people with less input of your own time if you take them in groups than if you take them one at a time. Similarly the analysis time is less per capita. This is not necessarily to say that a group project will be absolutely cheaper than an individual interview project, but it certainly will be if the number of respondents is constant, probably by a factor of two or three.

Cost is always a consideration, and this is certainly one ingredient in the recent popularity of group techniques. However, it is perhaps one of the worst reasons for choosing this method. If you do research using groups which is really better done within individual interviews you have only saved money in a very superficial sense, and may in real terms have spent it wastefully. Therefore one should concentrate first on the technical advantages and disadvantages, against which economic factors can be evaluated.

First, most human problems have a social dimension. People are to be understood partly through their relationships and interactions with others, as well as through their own internal workings as individuals. Interviewing people individually can minimise the impact of this because it encourages the participant to look in on himself rather than out at his relations with others. Groups provide an essentially social context. It is of course an artificial hothouse society created for the purposes of the research, but it still obliges participants to take account of other people's views in framing their own responses.

For example, suppose the research concerns the organisation of shopping facilities. Someone who does all their shopping by car will probably be absorbed by the need for good parking and access. However, in a group there may be others who depend on public transport or who cannot walk far, and the discussion will make both sides aware of the needs and perspectives of the others.

This kind of interaction can also have some disadvantages, as we shall see. In some projects the social context is particularly important, and it is valuable to explore the way in which people and ideas interact. In other cases it is more important to get an 'uncontaminated' snapshot of isolated individuals. Groups will best fit the former and individual interviews the latter need.

Second, social interactions can be particularly important in what are known as 'action research' projects – those where the research is designed to change as well as to study a situation. The experience of discussing in groups can often energise them to want to take things further.

For example, problems often flourish on inner-city estates precisely because the local community is socially ineffective, and lacks mechanisms for social cooperation. In this situation the very process of getting together to talk over problems in groups can lead to a realisation that neighbours have similar views, and a sense that collective action might be effective in tackling problems. This can create a more fertile soil for initiatives by community workers and others – or may even lead to spontaneous initiatives from those attending the groups. Individual interviews would have very little of this effect.

The 'action research' concept can be alarming to those researchers who traditionally want to see research as a purely passive measuring instrument and who find the idea of setting out to use it to *change* people somewhat heretical. It is certainly important to keep the two concepts separate in one's mind, but it is also important to realise that *any* interview-based research technique changes people in one way or another. Sometimes this is a useful, sometimes a harmful property, depending on the circumstances.

The idea of an interview as a totally inert measuring device has no possible foundation in reality. Groups are far from inert, which can militate for or against their use in a given context.

Third, talking together with other people is *stimulating*. There is more to react to, more food for thought, more diversity of opinion expressed than in a typical individual interview. This often helps people to analyse their own attitudes, ideas, beliefs and behaviour more penetratingly and more vividly than they could easily do if just alone with the interviewer.

This is most important, because it does not take much interviewing experience to recognise that most people (researchers no doubt as well as others) have remarkably limited capacity for self-observation and self-analysis, and equally limited ability to articulate the perceptions they do have. Often people in interviews are visibly (and with difficulty) addressing questions they have never really asked themselves before. So much of our normal behaviour is organised and motivated at sub-conscious or semi-conscious levels, and so much is habituated and automatic, that even a well-organised and self-aware person typically has only very limited insights into his own attitudes and motivations.

In a group setting people can be helped and stimulated both by their own interaction with other group members, and by watching and listening to other people interacting.

Finally, because groups can stimulate their members they can also be used creatively to generate ideas. An extreme case is a 'brainstorming' session in which the purpose is not so much to describe a situation objectively as to produce as many ideas as possible about it. The creativity of groups can be useful for problem solving; for generating new perspectives and insights; for policy analysis; and so on. Group discussions of experts from the same or from complementary fields can throw fresh light on a problem by focusing collectively on it. In this case one is tapping their expertise rather than studying them as subjects.

So in summary, group discussions have much to commend them:

1   where the social context is important;
2   in 'action research';
3   when understanding and insight are required;
4   where we want to generate new ideas.

The weaknesses of groups

However, group interviews have weaknesses as well as strengths. The main ones are set out below.

First, if you interview people one at a time you have more time and scope to explore their position in breadth and depth. You can get a very rounded picture of their individual beliefs, attitudes, behaviour and personality, and of the interactions between these factors. Groups typically provide less opportunity to follow through with an individual.

Second, in groups there is a risk that social pressures will condition responses in an artificial way. Dominant or articulate characters can influence what is said. People can feel nervous about uttering views opposed to those of the rest of the group. Some people like to play to the gallery, to impress their fellow participants. To some extent these social pressures are realistic, and would be present in the real world too, but also, to some extent, they are artificial offshoots of the particular group situation the researcher has constructed. Group pressures like these cannot be eliminated – although their importance can be minimised by skilled moderation and analysis (see below). In individual interviews this problem does not exist in the same way since there is no-one else present to influence or condition responses – except of course the interviewer, who (however skilled) should not be overlooked as a source of social pressure.

Third, people sometimes feel constrained in what they say in front of their peers. There is a constant desire to 'tidy up' the picture of yourself that you present to the world (or indeed to yourself), perhaps through selection of what you say, sometimes through outright distortion of the truth. Sometimes this will be a deliberate and conscious process, but more often people are unaware that they are trimming the picture – and would very probably reject the suggestion with genuine indignation. These desires are present in any interview, but they can be magnified in a group context because of the pressures mentioned above.

This makes groups generally less suitable for handling sensitive controversial or 'private' topics like personal finance, sexual behaviour, personal hygiene or racial issues. For example, people who have fairly strong racial prejudices may be more inhibited in expressing them in public in front of others whose views are not known. And there are quite a few topics which people are not used to discussing in public. Having said this it is surprising what a good interviewer can get people to talk about in groups. But the more potentially sensitive or embarrassing the topic, the stronger the case for individual interviews.

Groups are not an ideal way of checking on matters of awareness and knowledge – once one group member has given an answer it can be difficult to be sure whether other members would have known it. However there are ways round this, for example getting people to write down key facts privately before going on with general discussion.

Finally, it is organisationally more difficult to get a given number of voluntary participants to one spot at the same time for a group, whereas individual interviews can be conducted in their own homes at times which are (within limits) arranged to suit them. Groups tend to take longer, which can also be a deterrent. This means there must be a greater danger of biases arising through factors like availability and propensity to volunteer in groups than in individual interviews.

In short, both individual and group interview methods have their advantages and disadvantages, and the best choice will often depend on the nature of the problem. For example, confidential topics can argue for individual interviews, but idea generation and penetrating depth of analysis often comes better from groups. However, there is a very great deal of overlap between the two techniques, and either or both can be safely applied to a wide range of problems. Often a mixture of the two will be most revealing.

Groups in practice
How big is a group?

The more people you have in the group the cheaper it is per capita; and the larger the sample you can build up the smaller the risk of atypicality. Unfortunately the quality of the session suffers with larger numbers. The group becomes hard for the interviewer to control. More timid people easily get squeezed out. The group tends to fragment, different sub-groups pursuing their own conversations simultaneously. It takes longer to let everyone have their say on a given issue. The quality of the conversation deteriorates. It is impossible to run a satisfactory group with more than ten people present and there is usually a strong case for getting the numbers down to six or seven participants – normally the optimum size.

With less than six the advantage of reducing numbers often begins to taper off, and the cost per capita advantage of groups tends also to diminish. But there are some purposes for which 'mini-groups' of two to four people may be useful. Sometimes, for example, you may need to collect a great deal of biographical information about each person. Or you may be working with shy or inarticulate people who will not perform well in a big group. Or conversely you may be dealing with people who can become difficult to control in larger numbers (like teenage boys). A small group can then combine some of the advantages of groups and individual interviews.

In practice you can't always be sure how many people there will be at any given session, since you are working with volunteers – often not highly motivated, and sometimes even actively suspicious or nervous about what will happen.

The decision about how many to recruit is always difficult and how far you have to over-recruit depends largely on how good your recruitment is. 'Recruiting' is the trade jargon for contacting people, selecting your sample, inviting them to attend, and (as far as possible) actually inducing them to do so (see Chapter 2). If it is professional and effective you will often get everyone, or only perhaps one or two dropouts per group.

The topic itself and the nature of the target sample also have a bearing on turnout. Some sectors of the population (teenagers, for example) tend to be fairly unreliable, and some subjects can sound more promising or less suspicious than others. Experience is the only guide, and a fair bit of variability must be allowed for. But at the end of the day for most purposes you will probably want to recruit eight or nine people and hope for a turnout of six to eight.

Normally those invited to groups would not know each other (although this is bound to happen by chance from time to time, particularly in small towns). However, sometimes you will deliberately want to work with pre-existing groups – a whole family; a group of workmates; a committee; and so forth. Working with existing groups is usually to be avoided unless there is a real need to talk to them as a unit, since groups of this kind have pre-existing group structures and dynamics of their own, and may be inhibited by the fact that they have to go on functioning as a group after you have gone – which *ad hoc* recruits do not. However, there may sometimes be important reasons for looking at established groups – particularly where you want to study them *as* groups – rather than just as collections of individuals as in most group studies.

Overall sample sizes
All qualitative work is small-scale. How small?

There are rough lower limits. It is hardly ever worth doing one group – just as it is not much use doing two or three depth interviews. The risk of atypicality is too great, and the evidence is simply not very solid. Two groups would be an absolute minimum – and there could hardly be a justification for working on so small a scale, except conceivably as a mere thought-starter at the very beginning of a larger project. In practice four to six groups probably form a reasonable minimum for a serious project. More complex or weighty problems might demand larger numbers of groups.

However, there are also upper limits. Qualitative interviews tend to be expensive per capita, and costs can easily escalate. More particularly there is a limit to the amount of qualitative data which can be usefully absorbed, and going in for massive numbers can produce overkill and stupefaction. For most normal purposes there would need to be a good reason for going much beyond say twelve groups, although there can be no hard and fast rules.

So one is therefore characteristically talking of between (say) four and twelve groups – probably involving between 20 and 100 people.

Interviewing

Quantitative interviewing using structured questionnaires is a highly skilled business, needing considerable training. *Qualitative* interviewing needs very different skills, and is not usually done by the same people.

The quantitative interviewer needs to be able to follow instructions minutely and painstakingly, and to make the inevitable rigidities of a prepared questionnaire acceptable to respondents. Interpretative and judgemental skills are not required during the interview, since the success of the operation depends on interviewers sticking to the precise procedures laid down.

The *qualitative* interviewer (or 'moderator' in the jargon of the trade) needs to be able to receive and understand an often broad or vague brief, and use this as a springboard rather than as something to be slavishly followed. He or she* will have to make decisions throughout the interview as to whether a given line of enquiry is proving useful and worth pursuing, or fruitless and to be headed off – and this has to be done in the light of his understanding of the problem and hence of the possible relevance or irrelevance of particular kinds of information.

This means that the qualitative interviewer also needs to have what we might loosely call 'executive level' skills of interpretation and decision – which means in turn that his time will be expensive.

The moderator will not work from a questionnaire – which would be restrictive and limit the potential value of the qualitative approach – but from a general briefing, designed to make sure he understands what is needed, and therefore will recognise it when he sees it. There will probably also be a 'topic guide', which simply lists the areas thought worth probing. This will often be extremely broad, and will potentially encompass far more ground than could be covered in a single interview. Hence the need for progressive selection and interpretation, not only throughout the group, but throughout the whole series of sessions.

---

* From here on I shall use the masculine pronoun for simplicity but with no gender implications.

The topic guide should normally be prepared by the moderator and agreed by the sponsor. It is the nearest thing in this kind of work to a questionnaire, but it is fundamentally different. It does not attempt to define the form, content or order of individual questions at all, but maps out the purpose of the exercise, the territory which is likely to be relevant, some general idea of priorities, and a broad outline order of events. But the whole topic guide should be subservient to opportunities which arise during the interview itself – the most exciting findings sometimes come from a completely new lead which no-one had even thought about at the time the topic guide was written. Conversely planned lines of enquiry may prove fruitless in the event and ought to be abandoned or modified.

This is why the moderator must be of sufficient calibre and sufficiently well briefed to be able to take decisions of this kind as matters progress. They cannot be referred back, but have to be taken in the heat of the moment – although of course the general drift of the project can and should be reviewed between interviews. So the moderator's understanding of the problem is much more important than the topic guide itself. An experienced moderator may not need or use a topic guide at all with a problem he understands thoroughly, but may prefer to rely on his powers of opportunistic improvisation to pick the best path across the relevant terrain.

He is, in fact, conducting a 'steered conversation' rather than an interview. Respondents must be left as free as possible to express themselves, and the moderator's job is mainly to nudge the conversation progressively into the more fruitful channels.

The general order of approach is probably implicit in the topic guide, but this again may be varied opportunistically. The normal process is to funnel gently from the general to the particular. For example, a piece of public consultation on motorway building proposals might want to begin by establishing people's general feelings about the environment before looking at their particular attitudes to the road itself.

However, like most general rules affecting the conduct of groups, there may be good reasons for departing from this practice. Discussion of generalities sets a context for considering the specifics you are really interested in, and you may sometimes think it better to start with the latter and then work back out to the general as far as seems useful. There may also sometimes be a reason for not introducing a topic until late in the conversation – because it gives away your interest, or because it may prejudice another area of enquiry which you want to cover first. This is particularly likely to be true if you have stimulus material (see below) to which you want people to react. The material may itself suggest ideas to people, so that you will often want to sound out their existing ideas on the same topics before showing the material.

In any case, participants may spontaneously raise topics before the moderator planned to discuss them. In that case he has various options. He can seize on the opportunity of getting on to another relevant topic without intervention on his part, and without breaking the momentum of the conversation. In this event he will just let the conversation run, or even encourage the turn it has taken. Or he can decide that he really wants to defer consideration of that point until later, in which case he will break in, express interest in the turn of the conversation, promise to return to it later – then re-launch the conversation back to some of the things he wants to cover first.

Styles of group interviewing are highly personal: some moderators are active and interventionist in their approach; others deliberately more passive in style. There is room for debate about the theoretical correctness of these different approaches, but the most important thing is that moderators should adopt a style with which they feel conversationally comfortable and which comes naturally to them. Providing you are aware of the implications of your style, and make due allowances for it in analysis, it is (within fairly broad limits) more important to be natural than correct.

Getting started. The first duty of the moderator is to get people relaxed and confident, talking as freely as possible. However, the process of relaxation needs to begin right from first contact with respondents – typically the recruiting interviewer will attend to check people off, settle them down, give them drinks etc.

In many ways it is best for the moderator not to meet them until the session starts, although this is a matter of personal style – some moderators are better than others at sustaining casual chit-chat. Inevitably respondents will want to know what it's all about, in which case the moderator has either to give repeated piecemeal explanations, or fend them off at the risk of seeming secretive. It is probably better where possible for the hostess to collect respondents in an adjacent room and bring them in together when the session is about to start.

You then need to start by giving a quick, simple, reassuring and convincing explanation of what the whole thing is about, what is going to happen, and what you want people to do. You need to explain that the session is being taped (and why), and to clarify the status of the information in terms of confidentiality versus attributable reporting. You must also say enough about the object of the study to stop people worrying about it, although you will not always disclose the full objective immediately, for example where you want to see how salient the topic of interest is within a wider context.

Then it is usually a good idea to go round the group with a few very simple questions. The need to be simple is because nothing is more off-putting to a nèrvous new group than to be immediately confronted with big, complex, abstract or sensitive issues, which only serve to confirm their worst fears. If you begin by asking something like 'Please tell me what you think should be done tó improve the environment in your neighbourhood' you will immediately make most people feel they are not going to be able to cope. They will almost certainly have things to say on such a subject, but not if plunged suddenly into the subject with nothing to hold on to or get conversation going.

Similarly if you begin by asking people how often they clean their teeth or how much they paid for their house they will probably feel embarrassed or shy at the prospect of having to parade their private lives in front of others, and this can easily make them more inhibited or even prickly and defensive. However, they will very probably give you both pieces of information quite happily once a confident and lively conversation is well under way.

Start with something simple, concrete, non-controversial, and unembarrassing, something that everyone can answer. For example, it will be useful in any survey to do with the neighbourhood or environment to have some brief background on their history of residence and acquaintance with the area. So a question like 'How long have you been living where you live now?' makes a good simple starter, and furnishes a useful bit of background data as well. A survey on town centre planning might well start with some simple factual questions about current behaviour like 'How often do you normally go shopping for groceries?'

It can even be worth asking preliminary 'warm-up' questions which are not particularly germane to the enquiry, if they give people a good footing and get them talking easily. One needs to consider the first ten minutes or so of a group as designed more to get people talking than to elicit information. It is hoped that you can do both at once, but the time will have been well spent if you do nothing more than get people conversing freely, easily, confidently and frankly.

Perhaps the simplest and best question to start with is 'What is your name?' The moderator should introduce him or herself, and then ask those in the group to give their names. This not only gets everyone's vocal cords working very quickly; it is also very useful for analysis purposes: it makes it possible to use the classification information on the recruitment questionnaire to relate to what is said during the groups. It also gives the transcript typist a good opportunity to place and identify the voices from the outset.

The first few questions should probably go systematically round the circle so that everyone talks. Otherwise the most articulate will jump in, and the shyer ones will find their vocal cords freeze harder as every minute goes by without having spoken. Anyone who sits for 15 minutes without ever having said a word is likely to have locked up mentally and vocally, and will then find it very difficult indeed to break in.

Structuring the first few minutes of a group can get the less articulate used to the temperature of the conversational water. Once they plunge things become easier. They almost invariably find not only that it is not as difficult as they feared, but that talking about things in this way is actually pleasurable, and even therapeutic.

Encouraging talk. It is important not to carry this structuring too far. You can easily set up the expectation that the session is a series of individual interviews carried out in parallel – which is emphatically not what a group discussion is meant to be. People must be encouraged to chip in freely, and to talk to each other as well as to the moderator.

The moderator will typically want to do as little talking as possible, and once things are under way to avoid asking questions more than he has to. Where possible he will simply nudge the conversation along by using non-committal conversational techniques. For example 'playback' – just repeating the last part of what someone said with an interrogative inflection – is a useful way of getting people to pursue and amplify a statement, without asking a direct question.

Direct questions can sometimes impose a direction on the conversation, where often the moderator will prefer to see which way the conversational ball bounces next. Direct questions can also sometimes put people on the spot. Often you can encourage people to amplify their reasons for saying something by using indirect techniques like playback, but asking a direct question like 'what do you mean by that?', can sometimes stop people in their tracks, and make them feel they have to justify what they have said. Far from helping them to open up it can make them more cautious and inhibited – 'I'd better not say anything unless I can give a reason for it, since he's going to challenge whatever I say'. Most of us do not have ready answers to 'why?' questions about our attitudes and behaviour – and if we do they might well be defensive rationalisations – but people can feel inadequate and embarrassed at not having them when asked.

There are plenty of other indirect ways of encouraging people to keep the conversational ball rolling. Just nodding, smiling, maintaining eye contact or saying, 'Yes' or 'Mmm' or 'That's interesting' from time to time tends to keep someone talking. If you want them to expand or amplify what they have said but without stopping them dead with a 'why?' question, then you can use playback (as above), or simply put a questioning note into your encouragement – 'Yes?', or 'Mmm?', or even an 'interrogative grunt' or a raised eyebrow. But it is important to avoid the impression that what has been said is somehow questionable. Violently raised eyebrows or an expression of amazed disbelief may make the respondent feel that he is on dangerous ground which he had better vacate quickly.

The moderator needs to cultivate a stance of 'passionate neutrality' – at once involved in the group and detached from it. If he is too involved he can start to influence the group; if too detached he can inhibit it by seeming bored or remote. His approval and interest is needed to keep people talking; but approval must be impartial, and not related to the subject matter or to individual viewpoints.

Certainly he must *never* disclose his own feelings by word, gesture or expression – although sometimes people will ask him what he thinks. Of all the 'rules' about moderating this is the only one I can think of no good reason for violating – except conceivably in a brainstorming session in order to provoke ideas, but doubtfully even then.

He must also beware of the dangers of seeming dauntingly expert – and worse still of competing with his respondents to inflate his own ego.

On one level he must be visibly involved with the group, encouraging and developing rapport; yet on another level he must be completely detached, monitoring the conversation objectively, reviewing the ground still to cover in his mind, keeping an eye on the time – and firmly resisting the temptation to join in and argue, even when disagreeing with the points made. It is a great professional challenge for a moderator to remain dispassionate on subjects where he has strong opinions of his own.

Group dynamics. The demands on the interviewer are fairly formidable. He not only has to handle the questioning, continually mapping out the ground still to be covered while trying to remember where they have already been, but also has to handle the dynamics of the group. This refers to the loquacity of the group as a whole and of the individuals in it, and to the influence of the group members on one another. Some groups talk a lot, and tend to rush away with the conversation. They need to be kept on a tighter rein, and need more direction and intervention from the moderator if they are to cover the relevant ground. Other groups are shy and inhibited, and they need to be encouraged, relaxed and allowed to talk.

An important aspect of group dynamics is making sure that dominant characters do not monopolise the conversation, bringing in the quiet members, and ensuring that strong personalities or majorities do not suppress or distort the views of others. This can be a problem, although not normally as insuperable a problem as is commonly thought by laymen. There are some simple conversational techniques which help – not magic solutions, but still useful tools.

Shy people can be brought in by directing particular questions at them; by asking 'What do *you* feel about that?' if they don't contribute; or sometimes just by looking expectantly at them and smiling encouragingly. But it is important not to make them feel that you are putting them under a microscope. Sometimes you can bring them in unobtrusively with a gambit like 'That's a very interesting point, I'd like to get everyone's view on that', then going briefly back to the technique of asking everyone round the circle to comment on that issue.

The same technique can be used to stop an over-locquacious person without offence – picking up something they say as so interesting that you need everyone else's view on it. Before you get to that point you can use eye contact, expression or gesture to encourage the shy or discourage the dominant. Looking at someone while they speak tends to encourage them to continue; looking away is discouraging.

Sometimes it is important to 'legitimise' the point of view of some weak or isolated group member to stop them feeling swamped or threatened by the others. You can make it clear, for example, that you have heard the same ideas expressed in other sessions, even though no one else appears to share them tonight. This can be a useful gambit if one wants minorities to feel they have scope to develop unpopular ideas. However it should never come as the *personal* endorsement of the moderator, who must always stand aloof from controversy. This leaves people free to agree with the idea without feeling pressured to agree with the moderator. On occasion it may even be possible to influence the group dynamics by seating and layout. Strong personalities should be positioned flanking the moderator, and weak personalities facing the moderator, because this helps the moderator to balance contributions.

None of these techniques is foolproof, and there will be occasions where one has to live with a dominant character and just try to aim off in analysis. There may even be occasions (thankfully very rare) when one participant is so objectionably and persistently dominant that the only thing to do is get rid of them as tactfully as possible – or just write off the group.

Stimulus. Sometimes the purpose of the study requires the use of stimulus material – something introduced into the group to precipitate reactions, like product samples, packaging, leaflets, information, advertising and so on. However, stimulus material can be useful even where not central to the purpose. Watching how people react to something can sometimes tell us more than if they simply talk about the subject in the abstract.

In studying political opinions or policy preferences, for example, it will often be found that people's knowledge of the matters under study is very limited. Their reactions in this state of imperfect information can be very important to know, but it can also be useful to give them access to information during the study, to see how they respond, and how they develop and change their opinions. A snapshot of the current state of opinion can be politically useful, although if current opinion is based on ignorance or misinformation it will not be a useful guide to what the public would really want to have done if they knew the facts.

Sometimes stimuli can take the form of objects introduced from outside – concept boards, ads, tapes or films, pieces of information. Sometimes they can simply be dropped in by the interviewer as verbal ideas. In the latter case the moderator again has to be careful to avoid personal endorsement – 'Someone at last night's session was saying ... What do you think of that?'; or 'I've heard it argued that ... ?' It can even be useful to lob in verbal hand grenades – deliberately provocative ideas – to see how people react if you suspect they are being cagey or polite, or to see how strongly held their beliefs are in the face of contrary ideas. If such ideas emerge naturally within the group that is ideal, but sometimes the moderator needs to import them – but again, not as his own opinions. It is important to remember in analysis that this is what you have done, and to be conscious of the possible range of effects.

The sequence of events in each group should be partly determined by the flow of conversation, although the moderator knows what he wants to cover, and has a general 'game plan' in his head, related to the original topic guide, but evolving as experience builds up over succesive groups. Whereas a structured interview aims to replicate as far as possible the identical conditions and sequence every time, this is emphatically not the objective in groups. We want rather to choose the most suitable route for extracting the information we want on that particular occasion, and the moderator's understanding of that is bound to evolve with each group completed.

In any case the game plan may need to be varied from session to session according to the population under study. The preoccupations and dispositions of tonight's group of pregnant women in our survey of attitudes to health care is going to be very different from yesterday's group of pensioners, and the kind of information which will emerge (and the ways in which we can best get at it) will need to vary accordingly. The moderator therefore needs to keep his game plan loose and take advantage of the way subjects arise to lead the group gently over the required territory. Trying to bash through the topics in a rigidly prescribed order merely hamstrings conversation.

The sessions themselves might last about an hour and a half to two hours, depending on the subject and context. If they are longer it will be difficult to get people to come, and difficult to sustain interest. Shorter sessions simply do not have time to do justice to anything but the simplest topics, bearing in mind that:

1   participants need to be kept on a reasonably loose rein, which often makes for discursive conversation; it takes time to let each participant have even a brief crack of the whip on a single topic; and
2   it can take 10 or 15 minutes 'warm-up' time before you really get down to the meat of what you want to know.

Technique is very important in moderating. But while technique is improvable, it is not perfectible, and there are very few definite rights and wrongs. It is largely a matter of evolving an approach and a set of skills which works for you, which you feel comfortable with, and yet which preserves the necessary objectivity and balance outlined above. The skills themselves are largely just the same conversational skills as we all use every day – but group moderators try to handle them more consciously and more skilfully to achieve their particular ends.

There are very few golden rules, and certainly no magic formulae for cutting through to Truth – if indeed there *is* any single monolithic truth, which is not typically the case. Human beings are complex, ambivalent, inconsistent creatures; and not even the brightest and best organised of us lives in a sharp-edged world where we have consciously and consistently sorted out our attitudes and beliefs on all conceivable subjects. It is a mistake to assume that there is a pristine Platonic reality under the muddle of our public utterances to which really sharp research tools can cut unerringly through. Underneath the mess of language lies a mess of thought and a tangle of behaviour. If our research tools cannot recognise ambivalence and inconsistency as real and important they will not help us to a very profound understanding of human thought and behaviour.

So the ultimate limitations in interviewing technique are limitations in the subject matter as well as in the techniques themselves. As human beings we should be thankful that others do *not* ultimately possess the power to dissect and pin down our attitudes and motivations in a definitive and deterministic way – because if they could they might also be able to control us.

Variations on a theme
It is worth considering briefly a few variations on the kind of standard group procedures discussed above.

Extended groups. These are sessions designed to last three or four hours, or even longer, to give scope for very intensive and extended treatment. It is an interesting development, although there must be worries as to whether it does not increase volunteer bias, or induce respondent fatigue.

Reconvened groups. Perhaps more interesting is the idea of getting a group back several times over a matter of weeks. This gives more space for the input of information, and the study of the way attitudes and beliefs evolve. It also gives scope for taking the group on field trips, exposing them to exhibitions and the like.

Combined groups and individual interviews. A further variation on this is where a group is reconvened as a series of individual interviews – or conversely where a series of individuals are reconvened as a group.

Other interview techniques. Group moderating is basically conversational, but there are again supplementary variations. For example:

1   brief self-completion questionnaires can be used in conjunction with the group – to get more complete information on particularly crucial or private issues, or to cover matters of knowledge and awareness;
2   there is typically a short recruitment questionnaire üsed for sample-selection purposes, and this can be extended to supplement the data;
3   a battery of so-called 'projective' techniques can be used to defeat the excessively rational emphasis that any conversation-based interview can have. In real life irrational factors may have a decisive influence on our actions, but it is often difficult to recognise (or admit) this in conversation. These techniques include devices like sentence completion, role playing, card sorting, or getting people to draw or even act out their feelings. This is further discussed in Chapter 7.

Analysis and presentation

The analysis stage is one of the most important, and probably one of the most neglected, parts of the whole process. Thorough analysis increases the yield of information, its reliability and its relevance to the subject in hand.

Commonsense should tell you that you can't remember everything of value that is said during an interview lasting one or two hours. Moreover, first impressions of a discussion group can be misleading. While running a group you have to concentrate on managing the discussion, and eight people flitting from subject to subject can make the session seem like a speeded-up film. The researcher must remain detached, but he is nevertheless very involved with the process of the group. He has little time to subject what people are saying to the kind of detached scrutiny that is necessary for sound analysis. Ideas jump out because:

1 they are interesting;
2 they strike a chord;
3 they confirm (or contradict) his own (or someone else's) theories);
4 they are well expressed or forcefully delivered.

People don't always mean what they say (or say what they mean). When you can play and replay the tape at leisure, you can check your interpretation, and weigh contradictory statements. Analysis helps to guard against 'selective perception' by the interviewer – noticing the things which are dramatic, and/or which interact with your own prejudices. Thorough analysis also helps you to stand back and recognise the effects of what happened at the interviewing stage and the consequences of defects in interviewing technique. There is no such thing as a perfect group and the stimulus always has to be evaluated with the response.

Qualitative analysis poses problems on two levels:

1 *Functional* problems: How do I *cope* with this great mass of formless data? How do I break it down and digest it?
2 *Interpretative* problems: How do I decide what it *means*? Do I take it literally? Do I believe what people say? How do I decide what it all adds up to?

Functional problems

As with interviewing there is a myriad of tools and approaches, and (so long as these are thorough and objective) it is mainly a question of developing personally satisfactory procedures. (Analysis techniques are discussed more fully in Chapter 4.) The best and most thorough way is to tape your interviews; have the tapes transcribed; listen to the tapes with transcripts in front for annotation; make notes as you go, probably organised under topic headings; and finally, pull the whole thing together as a summary.

I myself tend to use a word processor with computerised sorting software, but much the same process can be carried out (more laboriously but probably more cheaply) with a ring-binder and biro. I go through each transcript while listening to the tape, and type into the word processor both my own notes and comments about the material, and a series of possible verbatim quotations for possible use in the report. Both notes and verbatims are coded in a way which enables me to identify the session and the respondent, and to pick notes and/or quotations on any particular topic. These are broad and loose codings – not analytically important like the codings of an open question in a quantitative survey, but just rough tools for handling and getting access to the data. The real data processing goes on inside your own skull.

Analysis of qualitative data is essentially non-numerical. There may be occasions where the researcher should actually tot up the number of people who said different things for his own illumination, but it will rarely be proper to quote such numbers in the report, and certainly not in such a way as to make them seem like mathematically reliable statistics. If that's what you were after, you're doing the wrong kind of research.

Interpretation problems

Analysis is partly a matter of describing what was actually said; but much more a matter of *interpretation*, since the direct semantic content is rarely the whole (or even the most important part) of the story. Interpretation exists on two levels: deducing what people *mean* from what they *say*; and assessing the *implications* of what is said for the problem in hand.

The first level of interpretation is necessary because respondents:

1   are often inarticulate;
2   may be ambivalent and self-contradictory;
3   often don't themselves understand what they think or why they do things;
4   may not want to admit to others (or even themselves) how they feel or behave, and hence may distort or even lie;
5   may be subject to group or other social pressures;
6   are in an artificial situation.

For example, someone may say 'I'm not very keen on that', which on the face of it implies a fairly neutral, perhaps slightly negative, attitude. But someone given to understatement might well use this expression to express fairly strong hostility which might be clear from the context and from intonation. On the other hand someone else might mean that they are in favour, but not highly enthusiastic. Thinking about it intelligently, listening for tones of voice, and looking at the wider context can help to sort out meaning on this level.

Similarly someone might contradict themselves, and we need to try to analyse which is their real belief, or whether they are genuinely ambivalent. These are all problems of the immediate interpretation of the data. There are no magic tools for this – again one uses the same techniques as are used for analysing conversation in ordinary life, but more intensively, more systematically and more consciously; and with the facility of going back repeatedly over tapes and transcripts. These problems are aggravated by the fact that group interviews rarely deal only with the more cut-and-dried areas of attitude and behaviour, and have to cope with intangible or even subconscious attitudes and motivations.

In summary, the sense has to be interpreted by:

1 building up a picture of each individual through the interview;
2 looking at remarks in context, including the input of other group members and the moderator;
3 noting consistencies and inconsistencies;
4 listening to tone of voice, and noting the degree of conviction or enthusiasm with which remarks are made;
5 assessing the effects of dominant personalities or group pressures;
6 just listening hard, and making intelligent judgements about what is said.

The second level of problem, dealing with implications, involves wider judgements. Even once we think we know what people mean, how does that bear on the problem under study? Suppose in a piece of public consultation there is a body of opinion hostile to a proposal on the basis of evident misconceptions about it which for some reason cannot be cleared up during the interviews. The hostility is a fact, but it is less clear whether people are hostile to the real content of the proposal, or only to what they understand of it. Ideally we would give them true information and observe their reactions. Failing that, we have to try to deduce from everything they have said how they *would* react to the proposal if properly expressed – or more importantly still if actually implemented.

Special problems of groups

The distinctive analysis dimension which arises with groups but not individual interviews is the identification of who said what. This is important for three reasons:

1 because otherwise when you see a comment being made frequently you do not know whether everyone is saying it, or one person saying it frequently;
2 because it can be important to be able to relate what a given person says at different points at the interview – was it the

person who complained most about public transport who is now opposing out-of-town shopping centres? If you want to do this intensively you might be better off with individual interviews, but it is nevertheless important to keep *trying* to do it with groups;

3 because you might want to relate what is said in the groups to information on the recruitment questionnaire – is the person who complains about public transport and opposes out-of-town shopping centres classified on the questionnaire as having or not having access to private transport?

Thus the transcript should read as far as possible like a play script, with different participants identified. This demands clear recording, preferably in stereo, which improves clarity and also helps directional identification. It is also easier if (for example) men and women sit alternately rather than in blocks, and if participants are asked to identify themselves sequentially at the beginning. One hundred per cent identification is not always feasible even then, and that has to be recognised as a basic fact. But if it is properly done you can succeed most of the time, and it is certainly worth the attempt.

Thorough analysis is expensive for the client, hard work for the researcher, and time-consuming for both. It is very labour-intensive – an expensive class of labour, which is often under time pressure. It is also largely invisible to the client (who may sit in on some groups, but rarely wants to sweat through tapes or transcripts, and will probably not even think to ask what happens at that point). So analysis is a stage at which there are many incentives to cut corners, and I suspect it is accordingly an often neglected corner of the qualitative field.

Presentation

Qualitative research is direct and vivid. The sounds and very smell of the marketplace come through the interviews, and indeed this is not incidental. Much of its value comes from this vividness and the insight it can give us into the way people think, feel and behave.

This must be transmitted through the report although it can also be valuable for the people who will use the research to attend the sessions and get some first-hand impressions. Verbatim quotations not only make the report more interesting, but often convey the tone and quality of people's thoughts better than the researcher's own descriptions.

However, qualitative reports should not consist merely of a few random scents blown on a formless wind. The researcher is not merely a tape recorder or camera recording impassively what he sees. He is essentially an analyst and interpreter, and his role is to structure his fairly formless data. A good qualitative report has a firm intellectual grip on its material as well as being atmospherically vivid.

Some people would like to believe that the researcher is merely a passive instrument, since this seems to prevent the dangerous serpent of subjectivity from rearing its head. It is true that objectivity and detachment are precious virtues in research, but it does not begin to be true when researching human populations that subjectivity can be banished by proper scientific procedure – even in quantitative research, which appears to be so objective. Scientific rigour has its proper role and its proper limits in sociological investigation. Paradoxically it tends to be the more superficial facets of human thought and activity which are the most readily susceptible to precise and objective measurement. It is one of the aims of qualitative research to take us into fields which are important but not easily measurable, and we cannot in all conscience demand that it should do so while remaining anchored to the laws of incontrovertible evidence.

6 Participant Observation in Social Analysis
Ron Bastin

The use of participant observation as a research method dates from the pioneering ethnographies of Branislaw Malinowski (1922; 1927; 1929; 1935). Malinowski's work differed from that of his predecessors in the critical respect that whereas social anthropologists had previously only visited societies for short periods to record general descriptions and informants' statements about social life, Malinowski lived in the Trobriand Islands for a total of two years and was able not only to record the stated principles of social organisation, but also to observe and to record events at first hand in a scrupulous manner.

This new research method allowed Malinowski to move beyond the static view of human behaviour as governed by a system of timeless rules and beliefs to the view of society as an organic construct in which tension and stress between individuals and groups was mitigated by customs, beliefs and institutions which had the function of promoting social cohesion.

By examining the minutiae of everyday life, Malinowski was able to show precisely how various social institutions contributed to the maintenance of society and to identify conflicting social demands which sometimes caused individuals to act contrary to espoused ideals; thereby providing an objective analysis of the social system and of individual behaviour within the system.

Although there have been major shifts in the subject matter of social anthropology as researchers have increasingly turned to examine social change both abroad and in their own societies, the value of in-depth field research remains unchallenged. Anthropologists seek to obtain an intimate knowledge of their research community (albeit a country village, an urban housing estate or an ethnic minority) through combining data obtained using the more formalised techniques of social surveys, structured interviews and genealogical reconstructions with information obtained through participating in everyday affairs and observing behaviour as it occurs. In so doing, the researcher occupies the complementary role of observer and participant and is able to conduct the analysis by abstracting everyday actions to uncover the principles governing behaviour and by modifying theoretical generalisations to accord with perceived behaviour.

Yet although participant observation has provided the methodological foundation for anthropological analysis since the 1920s, its potential contribution to policy planning has been greatly underutilised. This fault partly lies with the anthropologists themselves who, while concerned to document social change, have invariably fought shy of involvement in applied studies on the grounds that the results of their research are likely to be used for 'social engineering'.

A further factor inhibiting the use of anthropologists by nonacademic organisations has been the insistence on long periods of field research. While social anthropology is historically grounded in the study of rural communities where the agricultural cycle is of critical importance to ethnographic enquiry, it does not necessarily follow that all research must entail a year or longer in the field. Anthropologists involved in consultancy work are seldom called upon to provide full ethnographies but are instead requested to undertake very specific research aimed at achieving defined goals. The researcher will therefore not require an intimate knowledge of the whole society but will only be concerned with factors pertinent to the research focus.

This is not to argue that all anthropological research can be conducted in a short space of time. Different types of projects call for different scales of inputs and a social impact study involving 100,000 people may necessitate several years' research. By comparison, a social investigation into work practices in an office or factory can yield results in a matter of weeks; particularly if the client is able to give the investigator a clear idea of why he is commissioning the research. What is important is that the flexibility inherent in the anthropological method means that the same investigative techniques can be used among sample populations of varying size in a wide variety of social setting.

Participant observation and policy planning

Although its potential has yet to be fully utilised, participant observation has much to offer any organisation interested in social behaviour and is particularly applicable where proposed changes are likely to have a direct influence on people's lives. Unfortunately space does not permit a full enumeration of the possible applications of participant observation but let me provide a hypothetical example to show the likely contribution of anthropological research to policy formation in an urban industrialised setting.

Assume that a local council has a housing estate which is subject to a great deal of vandalism. The council is concerned to reduce the level of damage because of high maintenance costs but has found that increased surveillance has had little effect on the problem. It has therefore decided to commission an anthropologist to investigate the problem and to outline solutions.

The council will in all probability be reluctant to fund a full-scale research project without some idea of the likely success and will therefore require that a pilot study be undertaken. The time allowed for exploratory research is generally short and investigations at this stage will be designed to define the field of enquiry. The anthropologist will interview as many affected parties as possible including estate residents, council officials, the police and, if possible, the vandals themselves with a view to outlining the system of interaction between groups which may be influencing some individuals to commit acts of vandalism. In so doing, the researcher is not interested in the vandalism *per se* but is more concerned to identify the social circumstances within which the act takes place.

At the end of the pilot study the anthropologist will be aware of the main social components and will produce a report outlining initial findings and identifying areas of further investigation. It is worth noting that this report is largely based on the results of interviews and that the researcher will not have established the depth of contact necessary for participant observation.

Assuming that the pilot study produces some potentially fruitful avenues of research, the anthropologist will proceed to the full study. It is at this stage that the researcher seeks to gain acceptance among the estate community and to examine people's behaviour. While the researcher may not actually witness acts of vandalism, he will become aware of their execution and through getting to know the culprits will be able to analyse the motivation behind the act.

This is not to argue any easy solution to the problem. Individuals act for a variety of reasons and it may well be that vandalism is the manifestation of numerous sources of discontent. It could be, for example, that specific residents are the target of vandalism or that vandalism is committed as an act of defiance against authority (the police or the council); while unemployment and boredom may be further contributory factors.

By the end of the fieldwork period the participant observer will have obtained first-hand knowledge of the social circumstances prevailing on the estate and will have witnessed interaction throughout the social system. Furthermore, the anthropologist will have had extensive discussions with respondents and will be able to take account of residents' attitudes, wishes and suggestions for change in the final report.

In making recommendations for change the anthropologist will seek not only to evaluate policy modifications in terms of the direct contribution to a decrease in vandalism, but will also evaluate them in terms of the general effects that they will have on residents' lives. While any actual recommendations would depend on the results of fieldwork, it is possible to outline some hypothetical changes.

It may well be, for example, that vandalism is largely the result of boredom and that the provision of a social centre on the estate would serve as an outlet for potential vandals. The same recommendation may also be made if residents complain of inadequate social facilities and it is felt that increased social interaction on the estate would indirectly contribute to a decrease in vandalism.

Recommendations may also be made for changes in council policy. Residents may feel that the council has little interest in their situation and morale on the estate may be very low. If such is the case, then the anthropologist may feel that the provision of a council 'clinic' for tenants to air their grievances would stimulate a greater interest in conditions on the estate and induce parents to bring pressure to bear if they suspect their children of committing vandalism.

The anthropologist may also feel that there is a need for alterations in the policy of policing. If the observed interaction between the police and young people is such that it is felt to contribute to 'retaliatory' vandalism, then the authorities may be persuaded to adopt a softer, more conciliatory line in their dealings with youngsters.

Which recommendations are adopted depends very much on how the council decides to allocate resources. A change in policing policy has zero cost for the council and the provision of a local 'clinic' may represent a saving in maintenance costs if building defects are identified and remedied at an early stage. The provision of a community centre is however an expensive undertaking in terms of initial capital outlay but part of this will be recouped if vandalism is significantly reduced.

The final stage at which participant observation can make a significant contribution to social policy is in monitoring and evaluation. Although the anthropologist can uncover the reasons behind specific actions, the analysis is of necessity limited to those circumstances prevailing at the time of enquiry. Further, although he may be confident that his recommendations will have the desired effect, he can never be absolutely sure that other factors will not come into play once the changes have been made. The anthropologist will therefore wish to review the situation periodically in order to assess the effects of the new measures and to recommend modifications to the programme in areas where the expected results have not been achieved.

This holds a number of advantages for the client. The council will have committed resources to the programme and will be concerned to know both the success of the policy and ways in which it can be improved. If, for example, it is found that a social club significantly reduces vandalism, then the incorporation of a community centre as a standard design feature in future estates will not only reduce the likelihood of damage but will contribute to an improvement in the quality of life for tenants.

Field research methods

Having illustrated how the insights into social organisation obtained through participant observation can contribute to social policy, it is now possible to examine the various research techniques employed by anthropologists.

While participant observation lies at the heart of field investigation, unobtrusive research is only part of the anthropologist's toolbag and occurs alongside the systematic collection of data obtained through conducting interviews and social surveys and through the examination of documentary material.

To take documentary sources first, the anthropologist will need to find out as much about the proposed research community as possible before entering the field and will therefore try to examine all available background material. This may include ethnographies written about the society itself or about similar social groups and will entail the examination of historical records kept by governments or missionary agencies. Hence the anthropologist begins to build up a mental picture of the social group and to develop possible avenues of investigation.

Documentary material may also form an integral part of the anthropologist's research data. This is particularly the case where the researcher is investigating interaction between the subject community and the wider society and where it is necessary to establish how both parties regard each other. To return briefly to our case study, the researcher would seek to define official policy towards vandalism by reviewing council records about the estate and through analysing police reports of investigations. This would provide base data for comparison with informants' interpretations of council policy and of the attitudes of the police.

On arrival in the field the anthropologist will need to define the population under investigation and it is usual for the investigator to conduct a social survey during the early stages of research. The type of questions contained in the survey will obviously vary according to the research focus but in terms of our case study the anthropologist would wish to obtain basic demographic and economic data, as well as gathering information on general social conditions. This would tell the researcher the size and employment status of the potential vandal population and would facilitate an assessment of the social circumstances under which residents live and of the social climate on the estate.

The social survey also provides the opportunity for the anthropologist to explore initial hypotheses and to re-examine first impressions. Such an examination is necessary because the researcher will inevitably have some preconceptions about the subject group prior to fieldwork, particularly where research is being conducted in the anthropologist's own society and the internalisation of rules and values may influence the analysis. In interviewing a wide cross-section of the population the researcher is forced to reconsider early assumptions and is thereby able to achieve greater objectivity.

The social survey is also important in introducing the researcher to the population. The anthropologist will have to explain his presence to each interviewee and people will then have at least some idea why the research is being conducted. This is not to argue any immediate social acceptance. The anthropologist is an outsider and people will undoubtedly be suspicious. Even within their own society anthropologists may be set apart on economic grounds (the ownership of a car or expensive clothes), by social differences (regional accent or style of speech), or by ethnic differences (a number of respondents may be of foreign extraction) and these are all problems which have to be overcome.

Further, despite their best efforts, the presence of anthropologists is frequently misinterpreted and this can give rise to problems. In terms of our case study, the anthropologist will inevitably be associated with the council and certain residents may see him as a broker who can use his presumed influence to provide access to services and benefits.

Clearly, the researcher would not be in a position to obtain favours for specific individuals and it would be ethically improper to believe that he could. Nor indeed can the investigator offer any benefits other than an improvement in the condition of the estate if the research results in a decrease in vandalism. To offer any promises beyond this would result in disappointment and undermine the researcher's credibility.

Identification with the council may also present problems for the anthropologist in dealing with young people because they may suspect him of wishing to identify the vandals and to have them convicted. Any promises that such is not the case will count for very little and the researcher must adopt the longer-term strategy of waiting until he has established a general reputation for impartiality before seeking to gain their confidence.

Suspicion is something that is only overcome by time and familiarity and the task of the anthropologist during the early days of fieldwork is to establish as many social contacts as possible. It is at this stage that the observer begins to become a participant by taking part in community activities; which in our case study would be local dances, discos or, perhaps more importantly, the pub. The anthropologist will over time become known as a 'regular', start to know people on a social footing and through them meet more contacts; thereby, it is hoped, establishing a network encompassing the whole community.

As in all social situations, the anthropologist will get along better with some people than with others and will establish a good rapport with certain individuals. These respondents will be more forthcoming in their answers to questions and will be a good source of local gossip and background to current social events. Yet although the researcher may value both their company and their information, it is necessary to maintain some degree of social distance. To be seen to be strongly allied to one group of respondents may have a detrimental effect by excluding the researcher from other factions and the anthropologist must therefore maintain a neutral stance.

Finally, it is necessary to discuss the process of obtaining and recording data. The anthropologist seeks to be as systematic as possible in recording data and may use a tape recorder, take extensive notes or just jot down one-word notes or key phrases. Which method is used depends very much on social context. The use of a tape recorder or taking extensive notes may be acceptable in a pre-arranged interview but producing a notebook in the middle of a general chat is liable to destroy the conversation completely and the researcher may prefer to rely on memory or to jot down key words or phrases once the discussion has finished.

Notes are written up when the data are still fresh and most researchers record information on a daily basis. While the actual method of organising material is a matter of personal preference, it is advantageous to arrange data in such a way that they can easily be rearranged under new headings as the research begins to take shape and as fresh avenues of investigation are undertaken.

Analysing field data

During the course of fieldwork the participant observer will have compiled a variety of data from different sources and will therefore be in the position to approach the analysis from a number of different standpoints. Where the anthropologist commences examining the material is not of great importance because the analysis will require that all sources of data are eventually considered. The analyst must, however, constantly bear in mind that the data not only originate from different sources but are of distinctly different types.

The anthropologist will, through the use of social surveys, have compiled a considerable amount of information on such areas as population, income, education and marriage patterns. These social facts are readily amenable to numerical interpretation and it is usual for the researcher to begin the analysis by establishing the general characteristics of the society.

A further area where the anthropologist may quantify data is in comparing informants' statements with observed behaviour. This is not undertaken in order to establish a numerical coefficient but to identify all instances where similar disjunctions between statements and actions have been observed. This allows the researcher to review and compare the case material relating to specific incidents and to identify the social and structural reasons underlying types of behaviour.

The analysis of the difference between statements about rules and the way people act also requires the evaluation of two very different levels of information. Statements about behaviour are invariably obtained in response to formal questions and are therefore liable to reflect 'ideal' behaviour which may have little substance in reality. Furthermore, the respondent is a member of the community who occupies specific roles and statuses, and responses and actions associated with the respondent are a reflection of that particular social position.

In the course of analysis the anthropologist therefore constructs a multifaceted model of society in which statements and actions are evaluated according to the social position of the individual and from which organisational principles can be abstracted and the purpose of social behaviour deduced.

While seeking to uncover the internal logic of the social system, the anthropologist is constantly concerned to show how organisational principles have been arrived at and the researcher has frequently to validate deductions by reference to specific social episodes using case studies. The use of case material not only adds richness to an otherwise abstract analysis but also facilitates the presentation of different kinds of data.

Case material is particularly useful where the anthropologist is dealing with change over time. Fieldwork is conducted at a specific moment in time (the ethnographic present) but this temporal dimension is often insufficient to explain current events and a diachronic analysis is required. In terms of our case study, current acts of vandalism may result from events which took place before the researcher was in the field and it will be necessary to undertake retrospective analysis in order to show how present behaviour is part of a continuing sequence of events.

The use of case material is also important in situational analysis where the anthropologist is concerned not with behaviour in relation to social norms but with behaviour in a specific set of circumstances. This approach is useful where the subject group is poly-ethnic and can also be effectively utilised in studies of the adaptation of immigrant groups to new environments through examining their responses to specific circumstances.

Summary

The preceding discussion has sought to outline the relevance of anthropological investigation in modern industrial economies. The approach taken has been to emphasise the practical application of fieldwork methods through an imaginary case study and to show how the resultant data can contribute to social problem solving and to policy formulation.

It has been shown that the combination of formal and informal methods of data collection used by anthropologists can provide a great depth of insight into 'natural' behaviour and that the anthropological method is appropriate in both rural and urban settings.

The fact that anthropology has been slow to react to the challenges of applied research is in part attributable to a reluctance among academics to accept contracts from outside agencies on the grounds that the time budgeted for will not allow for sufficient fieldwork to be undertaken.

While the researcher may not be allowed all the time necessary to produce a full ethnography, the flexibility in anthropolgial methods means that the focus of the research can be scaled down without any major loss of quantitative information. Indeed, the concept of participation is not based on active involvement but on being in the field long enough to merge into the social background and observe events as they occur. All that a shorter research time means is that the anthropologist will not witness quite so many events.

References

Malinowski, B. 1922, *Argonauts of the western Pacific*, London, Routledge and Kegan Paul.
Idem. 1927, *Sex and repression in savage society*, London, Routledge.
Idem. 1929, *The sexual life of savages*, London, Routledge.
Idem. 1935, *Coral gardens and their magic*, London, Routledge.

7 Projective Techniques in Social and Market Research
Alan Branthwaite and Tony Lunn

Suppose, for a moment, the Liberal Party were a restaurant. What sort of place would it be and what sort of food would it serve?

If the Conservative Party were a make of motor car what would it be like?

Could you draw, using shapes and colours, the feelings you have about the Social Democratic Party?

Say the first things that come into mind when I say 'Labour Party'.

In 1988 an election was held and afterwards a coalition government was formed between the Conservative and Labour Party. The first things they did when they came into office were ...... Can you complete this story saying what happened and how things developed?

These are some examples of projective techniques used in recent research on political parties (Lunn et al, 1983). In this chapter, the aim is to look at the uses of projective techniques in market and social research and, in particular, to discuss the theory and rationale behind these techniques, in order to suggest why they are so potentially useful to research.

The theory and rationale for using projective techniques
The term 'projective technique' covers a wide range of procedures, as can be seen from the examples above and the list of techniques at the end of this chapter. What these techniques have in common is that the task is highly ambiguous, novel and sometimes even bizarre. It is unclear what sort of response is expected. In essence, projective techniques involve the presentation of stimuli designed so that their meaning or interpretation is determined by the respondent who has to structure and impose meaning into the task. The basic assumption is that this injection of meaning will reflect the personality, concerns and

interests of the respondent. By this means projective tests circumvent three important barriers to the study of people's motives and attitudes, and their use facilitates the exploration of individuals' psychology at a deeper level than people are conscious of or can articulate. These three barriers to the expression of the individual's inner world are:

1   repression and the unconscious;
2   self-awareness and rationality;
3   social influences.

The barrier of repression and the unconscious

The origins of projective techniques lie in psychoanalysis and personality theory, beginning with Freud. Originally projective techniques were a device for examining repressed experiences in patients' unconsciousness. The techniques are based on three of Freud's theoretical principles. The first principle is the fundamental one of determinism. It is believed that responses to stimuli, however apparently bizarre, are not random, but are *determined* by the individual's personality and structure of thought. All our actions and remarks have mental causes.

Projection, the second principle, is the mechanism by which inner feelings and ideas influence our perception of the outer world. Our subjective beliefs, of which we are often unaware, are given embodiment in objects and people around us. The meaning and value of things around us is determined by our own needs and emotions. In this way ideas that are repressed because they would cause guilt and worry if they were acknowledged, find expression and outlet by being transferred to the external world. In short, things that are important to us, exciting and of concern, but which we are not happy about acknowledging to ourselves or society, we readily perceive in other people and events. By this means we find expression for our self-censored interests. Warren (1934) describes projection as 'the tendency to ascribe to the external world repressed mental processes which are not recognised as being of personal origin and as a result of which the content of these processes is experienced as an outer perception.' It is morally, socially and personally condemned to hate other people, so it causes us less anxiety to maintain, by projection, that it is the other person who hates us. In its turn this justifies our hatred of them.

The third principle underlying projective techniques concerns the role of fantasy in facilitating the expression of repressed ideas. Because of the unrealistic and fantastic nature of the task, responses are not treated seriously and so they escape censorship. In this way, responses escape which would be suppressed if treated more realistically. The humour and joking which often surrounds people's reactions to projective tests is an important and productive feature of the techniques, and is to be encouraged because it helps in the expression of sensitive feelings.

The barrier of self-awareness and rationality
While originally the process of projection related to the attribution of repressed, self-censored impulses, it is important to realise that projection also operates in everyday perception and interpretation of experience on the basis of needs and motives which are not repressed. Projection has for example been demonstrated experimentally by inducing needs such as hunger in starved subjects, who were found to perceive unconsciously more food images in ambiguous stimuli (Sanford, 1937). The significance of these experiments is in demonstrating that internal physiological and psychological motives are revealed in the processes of sensory perception and selective interpretation of events. Projection does not always involve deeply repressed and self-censored needs, in the Freudian sense, but also needs and ideas which we are simply unaware of at the time as the cause of our views. Our everyday perception of the world involves a complex process of decoding and interpreting sensory stimulation, which reflects our internal expectations and personal frame of reference. By and large, we are unaware of the influences which shape our image of the world and therefore unable to report on them directly. This is well known in the perception of visual illusions that are ambiguous figures, such as the drawing of the young and old women (Boring's wife and mother-in-law figure) which can be found in Gregory, 1970. Looking at that drawing we make sense of the lines and shapes by organising them into a meaningful configuration. In looking at the same drawing, different people habitually see one of the women first and sometimes find difficulty in shifting their focus to the other. Which of two ambiguous figures is seen first and which predominates in our perception has been hypothesised to reveal personal biases (Forsyth and Huber, 1976).

Surprisingly, perhaps, recent revelations about the neurophysiology of the brain seem to us to argue for the use of projective techniques as a means of increasing our understanding of the motives for behaviour. There is growing evidence (Ornstein, 1972; Springer and Deutsch, 1981; Blakeslee, 1980) that the two hemispheres of the brain are different in the way they work. This gives rise to two kinds of consciousness in the different hemispheres. The two hemispheres respond differently and process experiences in different fashions. In addition they find expression through different modes and in different styles of behaviour.

The left hemisphere (which in general controls the right side of the body) has the following characteristics:

1 It is analytical in its approach to experience and uses logical modes of thinking and reasoning. The left hemisphere is predominantly involved in processing verbal and mathematical problems. The centre for language and verbal ability is located in the left hemisphere.
2 It operates in a linear mode and processes information sequentially giving rise to ordered, rational thinking.
3 It uses convergent thinking in dissecting problems and finding solutions.
4 It is intellectual and conscious in the normal sense so that the experience of the left hemisphere is more accessible to introspection and communication through language.

The right hemisphere (which controls the left side of the body) functions in a different way:

1 It is holistic in its approach, integrating and relating experiences.
2 It is primarily responsible for our orientation in space, body image and recognition of faces.
3 It is involved with artistic endeavours, physical skills and crafts.
4 Information is processed diffusely and in a non-linear fashion. Different inputs are integrated simultaneously.
5 It is divergent and creative and functions in an intuitive and unaware fashion. The right hemisphere is probably responsible for those creative insights which take place when we suddenly grasp the solution to a problem in a 'eureka' experience.

Some people prefer one mode of thinking over the other, but normally both hemispheres of the brain participate to some extent in most activities, and both process the experiences we have. However, each hemisphere may concentrate on different aspects of that experience such as the appearance of a person and what was said in the conversation.

In conducting research it is relatively easy to gain access to experiences and information through the left hemisphere by asking questions and obtaining reasoned and well justified verbal responses. However, it is less easy to obtain information about the experiences, images and intuitions of the right hemisphere although these may be as important in influencing our ideas and preferences. Certainly we are not always conscious of our reasons for our choices. In an experiment by Nisbett and Wilson (1977) respondents judged four pairs of nylon stockings which were laid out in front of them from left to right. The stockings were actually identical but those in the extreme right position were chosen as being the nicest four times more often than the stockings judged at the extreme left. Respondents gave various rationalisations for their preferences when asked but these were clearly incorrect as the stockings were identical. No subject ever mentioned the position of the stockings as an influence. Their explanations for their preferences would be manifestations of left-brain experience but the real reasons for the choices probably lay in the right hemisphere and they were inaccessible through ordinary verbal questioning. It is not uncommon to do things because of a 'hunch' or make even important decisions, like buying a house, on the basis of a feeling which is difficult to justify or put into words.

Projective tests have a role in facilitating the expression of the right hemisphere mode of consciousness. By not requiring logical, rational answers, projective tests overcome the barrier of rational, logical self-expression. They give more scope for the expression of intuitive images and associations which are part of the right-brain mode of operation. These associations and their effect can be expressed through daydreams, fantasies and images. A rough classification of projective techniques which can facilitate expression of right-hemisphere consciousness is given in the table below. It should be emphasised, however, that almost every task will involve both hemispheres, but to varying degrees according to the nature of the task. In particular, in so far as language is the mode of expression, the left hemisphere will be involved to some degree. Fuller descriptions of the specific techniques are given later in this chapter.

Projective techniques which facilitate expression of:

Left-brain *consciousness*	*Right-brain* *consciousness*
● Sentence completion	● Personal analogies
● Story completion	● Direct analogies
● Obituaries	● Symbolic analogies
● Adjectivisation	● Psycho-drawing
● Role playing	● Free association
	● Personification
	● Psychodrama

The barrier of social influence

It is evident that much of what we do and say is heavily influenced by social factors. The attitudes and opinions we express are grounded in the social context. The social situation, as we perceive and understand it, is influential in the production of individuals' social behaviour and dialogue. A model depicting the influence of social situations on individual actions has been described by Branthwaite (1983) based on recent work by social psychologists.

In summary, social situations influence the social acts and opinions we express by defining rules for appropriate behaviour in each situation and by giving potential roles to enact. In shops, the situation defines rules for buying goods either by self-selection and paying at a checkout, as in supermarkets, or by asking a shopkeeper for the articles. The roles that are available in these situations are varied but include, for instance, efficient shopper, browsing shopper and thief. Mostly we achieve our plans and goals through the role of an honest shopper. The interactions and social exchanges are formalised, limited and highly predictable. It would be easy to anticipate the conversation between customer and shopkeeper as the transaction is very largely determined by social influences on behaviour. Even where there seem to be exceptions, as in the gossip of a village store, these actions are superimposed on the basic rules and conform to other rules such as breaking off the conversation to serve other shoppers.

According to this theory of social behaviour, individuals are independent agents with plans and purposes but they achieve these through socially constrained means. Often too, the plans and goals themselves are strongly influenced by social factors such as the suggestions of others, the needs and expectations of others and the general cultural values we absorb.

Similarly in accounting for our social acts, we explain ourselves in socially meaningful and established expressions. We draw upon the common currency of social exchange to justify ourselves in ways that will be understandable, meaningful and intelligible to other people. For example, after a car collision there is a range of social responses available, including crying, being angry and abusive, etc. These are stereotyped, socially normal reactions we can adopt in the situation. It would be much harder to understand the behaviour of an innocent party in the collision who shrugged their shoulders and drove off. We would be puzzled as to their motives and this would be seen as truly individual and eccentric behaviour. In general our actions in situations are chosen from the repertoire of socially prescribed actions for the circumstance. We express love, pity, guilt, anger in situations where it is warranted and intelligible. It is the social situation which influences our personal state of mind and the views we express. This has been demonstrated in research studies. Schacter and Singer (1962) found that subjects' descriptions of their feelings after being given an injection were a reflection of the behaviour of a confederate who had been in the waiting room with the subject. Where the confederate had been euphoric, then the subjects described themselves as happy.

Bem (1972) has argued that attitudes are inferred from behaviour rather than being the cause of the behaviour. Someone knows he has a favourable attitude to Chinese take-away food because he has bought it frequently in the past. The reasons for buying it may have been situational, but we explain our behaviour by reference to attitudes which we infer from our own behaviour.

In collecting data by means of questionnaires and interviews, many of the responses will be at the level of social stereotypes. Society places a high premium on sensible, rational and logical behaviour, and in interviews respondents seek to be polite and present themselves in socially acceptable ways. People explain their choice of a bank in terms of convenience, while not having a bank account is justified in terms of restricted opening hours. Cinema-goers used to say they like Kung-fu films because of the 'action' and avoid mentioning directly the violence and aggression. People draw on socially acceptable explanations to account for their behaviour, and use socially meaningful influences to account for their acts, such as the recommendation of friends or the desire for status and prestige, or even echo the suggestions of advertising. It is important to recognise that this ethnogenic (or socially generated) level of response is an important indicator of real influences on behaviour.

However, to obtain in addition more personal, individual and idiosyncratic explanations, we need techniques which release the constraints for socially acceptable and intelligible behaviour in interview situations. Projective techniques break down these social constraints for acceptable behaviour by defining a task which is arbitrary and bizarre. In this way projective techniques help to break through and release more personal, idiosyncratic responses. In effect the interviewer, by means of his position and authority over the interview situation, redefines the rules of social conduct in a way which throws the respondent onto more personal, private feelings to make responses. This can be observed in the interview when the introduction of projective techniques creates disbelief, embarrassment and self-consciousness on the part of the respondent. In a group interview, the respondents look to each other for support and, once their incredulity is overcome, they help to establish and endorse the new rules for how to act using projective techniques. The presence of a group embarking on the same unusual projective task facilitates responses so that, paradoxically, groups are often more successful in penetrating to personal levels of response. It is important, in setting up the new rules and terms for responding to projective tests, that the interviewer does not weaken and become socially embarrassed so that the *mores* of the normal society reassert themselves. The rule 'to say the first thing that comes into your head' in a word association test is diametrically opposed to the normal, implicit social rule of 'think before you speak', i.e. consider the impact and implications of what you are going to say before you commit yourself verbally in public.

Projective techniques, then, are useful in breaking down social levels of responding and revealing more personal idiosyncratic ideas (although both are important for understanding individuals' public behaviour). Projective techniques overcome the barriers of social influence by creating a social vacuum in the interview by defining tasks for which there are few or no social resources to fall back on. For example: what would a Hotpoint Bank be like? Respondents' reactions in this vacuum reveal their individual, unconscious and personal psychodynamics. For this reason it is important that the precise techniques employed should be kept novel and challenging.

Nevertheless, in some projective techniques, respondents may be able to fall back on social stereotypes and social frames of responding. Projective techniques are still useful in these cases because here the techniques reveal the typical, habitual social stereotypes of the person. They demonstrate their particular characteristic style of responding. This may be true of techniques like story or sentence completion, such as in the scenario relating to a 1988 election given in the introduction to this chapter. In these cases respondents may use their predominant or habitual levels of social accounting to structure the ambiguous situation in terms of a favourite social paradigm. This might reveal preferences for guilt-reducing scenarios, wishfulness to believe in happy endings and social harmony, aggressive responses, etc. that are typical of the respondents' outlook on life.

Types of projective technique

While one could provide a straightforward listing of projective techniques (see Appendix) it is unlikely to be comprehensive or exhaustive, because the range and number of variations is prolific. There is a limited range of standardised projective tests used popularly in clinical psychology to assess personality (such as the Rorschach Ink Blot Test, The Thematic Apperception Test, the Rosenzweig Picture-Frustration Test). Here a degree of control and standardisation is necessary to make comparisons between individuals. However these standardised tests have not been the most useful in social or market research because they aim to be measures of an individual's basic or fundamental personality independent of any specific context. In market research we usually want to know a person's reactions in relation to a specific product field. So the underlying principles of these standard projective tests have been borrowed and adapted to make tests that fit social or marketing problems being investigated.

It is surprisingly difficult to offer a useful classification of the techniques that are employed, as all of the specific techniques do very similar things. They have the same elements (but to varying degrees) that are integral to the definition of projective techniques:

1 overcome self-censorship and self-consciousness;
2 encourage expression and fantasy;
3 change perspective;
4 inhibit rationalisation and cognitive responses;
5 encourage expression of personal emotion.

Attempts to classify the techniques have focused on rather superficial features which are largely irrelevant to the use and practice of the techniques. There are classifications (Lindzey, 1959) based on the nature of the stimuli (verbal/pictorial, abstract/ concrete), the method of administration, or the mode of response (associative techniques, construction procedures, completion tasks, choice or ordering devices, expressive methods). But whether the technique requires a story to be composed about a line drawing or a set of associations and images to be given, has very little bearing on the function of the technique in the research. Consequently rather than give a classification of tests, we propose to give examples of the techniques to illustrate their various functions and the contributions that they can make to the data. However, it should be emphasised that we do not mean to suggest that the particular tests used to illustrate a particular function are the only tests which will perform that function. As we have said before, most of the tests can potentially give rise to any of these revelations.

Projective techniques revealing the unconscious

Word association. The following words with double meanings were used in research on aggression and violence. These homographs have one connotation which is aggressive and another neutral meaning. Respondents were asked to write against each word other words that came to mind. Responses were analysed as to whether they revealed any bias selectively to perceive, or avoid, the aggressive connotation. The words used included: barrel, ring, bang, bow.

Psychodrawings. In research on the Social Democratic Party, respondents were asked to draw their feelings about this political party. In psychodrawings, respondents are first given instructions about how to use shapes, colours, symbols to express feelings. They are given practice and reassurance using initial exercises. A major strength of the psychodrawing procedure is that it obliges people to express themselves non-verbally. The drawings shown in Figure 7.1 express feelings and ideas about 'life today', 'politics today' and the Social Democratic Party. The drawing of the S.D.P. in its formative phase is one expression of unconscious feelings. The obvious phallic imagery and expression of vigour and assertiveness (which is more impressive in the coloured original) would have been very difficult to obtain through straightforward questioning.

Disillusion with 'life today'

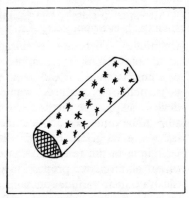

Politics as the 'icy tunnel'

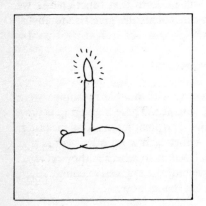

S.D.P. in formative phase
'the shining beacon'

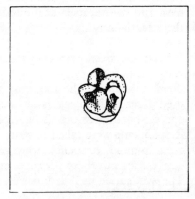

S.D.P. one year later
'ugly and stunted'

Fig. 7.1 *Four illustrations of 'spontaneous projection'.*

Projective techniques overcoming self-consciousness

Idealisation and fantasy solutions. In a study into the benefits of hair shampoos, respondents were asked to describe what ideally their hair would be like after washing in a perfect shampoo. To help overcome the embarrassment and self-consciousness of describing this fantasy self-image in a group discussion, respondents were given a 'magic' shower hat to wear. This trick of masking current reality (if only temporarily) had a remarkable effect in releasing inhibitions about describing their ideal self. Even the seasoned researchers conducting the study were impressed by the eagerness with which the women in the group sought to be the next in turn to put on the magic hat: it was almost as if everyone temporarily believed their fantasies might come true when they took off the hat.

Role playing. A well used task to overcome self-consciousness and social inhibitions in expressing personal feelings is to ask the respondent to role play. In getting the respondent to voice the opinions of an anonymous other, they fall back on their own ideas to perform the task and put their own words into the mouths of other people. The task can be facilitated by acting out the roles, or using pictures or line drawings to focus attention on the role to be taken. In a simple use of role playing techniques, respondents were asked to say how their neighbours might comment on their washing hung out on the line. In a more elaborate example, respondents actually played out a scene of a petrol pump attendant filling their car. They were encouraged to elaborate on what the pump attendant thought and might say about their car, the way they looked after it and serviced it, and their petrol buying.

Projective techniques releasing personal images and intuitions

Analogies and metaphors. The principle of this technique is to transform objects and brands into something else so as to get at their inner properties. By drawing analogies and metaphors, the technique reveals the images, feelings and associations of the concept. There are three types of analogy although the distinctions are not very important. They are:

1   *Personal analogies* where the respondent imagines himself as the object and 'feels' like the object. Respondents in a group might take on the characteristics of kettles or the pieces of a Wedgwood tea service and examine what it would be like, and how it would feel to be used in a home.

2   *Direct analogies* are made between different objects and concepts. In general organic analogies for inorganic problems or *vice versa* are more effective than analogies from the same realm. For example respondents might suppose that political parties were like restaurants and decide what the food and ambience would be like in an S.D.P. restaurant. Other analogies used in the research on political parties were beds ('what would the Labour Party be like to sleep on?') and cars ('what would it be like to travel in a Conservative car?'). Some of the responses to the S.D.P. were that it served plain cooking, is wholesome, likes to holiday in Venice, is good at team games, shops at Safeways ('more choice than Sainsbury's'), and so on.

3   *Symbolic analogies.* Symbolic or poetic metaphors are used to describe the essentials of the problem or object. Making associations between music, colour, textures or objects in the room have proved useful analogies. Some drugs sounded to G.P.s like noisy pop music (with little in the way of harmony or sophistication) while others were more like classical pieces sometimes strident and confident and in other cases soothing but rich and complex.

Projective techniques overcoming conventional thinking

Personification. In this technique, the object is brought to life and the respondent is asked to imagine it as a person (or animal) and describe how it would look and behave as a person. By casting the task of describing and evaluating common objects into a novel frame of reference, the technique avoids the use of conventional ideas drawn from the media and conventional wisdom. In one study (Cooper and Pawle, 1982), doctors were asked to personify drugs as if they were people. Some drugs were seen as 'young, in their prime of adolescence, vigorous but a bit unpredictable' while others were seen as 'Harley Street doctors, staid, wise, reliable and prestigious, though sometimes a little out of date'. These revelations of the meaning and value of drugs to individual doctors could probably not have been obtained in any other way than through projective tests which stripped away the technical language and jargon.

Projective techniques overcoming social constraints

Construction or completion tasks. There is a group of projective techniques which involve completing stories or sentences for which the beginning is supplied, or constructing stories around a theme or drawing. The following example illustrates how these techniques can overcome social constraints on responses because of social norms for politeness and self-consistency where by the individual presents himself as a competent, rational and admirable person. This example comes from the research on the S.D.P. Converts to the S.D.P. were asked to complete statements supposedly spoken by cartoon characters, beginning 'I voted S.D.P. because ......' One previously loyal Tory voter constructed very emotional arguments attacking the hypothetical S.D.P. voter as a traitor and deserter from other parties. In her description and comments on this exercise it became fully apparent that it was herself she was really attacking in these terms, although there had previously been no indication in the interview that she had ambivalent feelings about supporting the S.D.P. The strength of these feelings, which were exposed here by the projective technique, can be judged in this case because respondents were contacted in a follow-up by telephone. At this stage, the particular respondent denied ever having supported the S.D.P.

As a second example of a construction task being used to overcome social constraints, consider the now classic research study of instant coffee conducted by Haire (1950). The straightforward question was put to people who did not use instant coffee: 'What do you dislike about it?' This question produced a social cliché in that answers were very stereotyped in terms of: 'I don't like the flavour'. To probe more deeply for a more convincing explanation, projective techniques were used. Two shopping lists were constructed for two hypothetical housewives. The lists were identical except that one contained instant coffee and the other included ground coffee. Respondents were asked to describe the type of woman who would have prepared each list. This technique revealed that the housewife who used instant coffee was perceived as lazy, disorganised and a poor wife.

Writing *obituaries* is another example of construction tasks. Respondents are asked to write an obituary notice for a favourite product describing its successes and achievements but also its weaknesses and ultimate failings. In this way, both the good and bad aspects are forced, and positive commitments, or a reluctance to be critical, are put into perspective. Consider the following two obituaries from doctors about a favoured and currently successful drug (Cooper and Pawle, 1982):

> It never stood out ... it was always a bit shy. But a useful old friend, and a 'good night's sleep' in my bag.

> On looking back over its life we remember its infancy when, as normal, the medical profession approached this drug with care and caution, thinking it expensive and a relative luxury. In later life, it became a friendly and familiar name in the surgery, loved by many adults and children alike.

Evaluating the data from projective techniques

Approaches vary to the analysis of projective data. Some approaches attempt to formalise the procedure by carrying out a content analysis of the themes produced. The limitation of this approach on its own is that it encourages overly superficial processing and merely descriptive analyses. In much practical social research, projective data are analysed like other qualitative data from interviews (Cooper and Branthwaite, 1978). The data are examined for the insights they can suggest into the underlying attitudes, needs, motives and cultural influences. This procedure is inductive on the part of the researcher and draws upon a wide background of psychological knowledge and theories to recognise and reveal the processes at work.

It is very difficult to separate the analysis of projective data from the role and input of the researcher who uses them. It is in the very nature of projective tests, which are creative and divergent in their procedure, that no mechanical assessment of the responses is satisfactory. The responses cannot easily be aggregated and a summary obtained in the way that totals and averages can be used to summarise data from more objective measuring scales. The processing and integration of projective responses necessarily involve a degree of subjectivity on the part of the researcher. In analysing projective responses, the researcher must weigh up what part of the response reflects personal attitudes, unconscious motives or social cliché. For example, the most common word association to the stimulus 'bread' is 'butter'. The frequency of this first association in a group of respondents would suggest something about the social culture in which they all share. It would be the second and third associations which told more about the individuals' images and ideas.

Subjectivity of analysis is an integral feature in the interpretation of projective data as they will be influenced by the biases, or the particular interests, of the researcher. There is also the need for judgement on the part of the researcher in deciding which are fundamental responses. Again there is no independent yardstick for monitoring the depth of responses. Consequently, it would seem that the proper perspective for evaluating projective tests is as a tool for the researcher to increase his contact and insight into the problem in hand. According to this view, their use is rather analogous to the way an experienced gynaecologist learns to prod and feel the foetus with his hands on the mother's abdomen, and to diagnose what is happening inside from his impressions. It would be difficult to get a scientific instrument to make the same measurements and inferences.

Reviews of projective techniques in, for example, textbooks of market research focus unduly, it seems to us, on criticisms of these tests. We believe this is based on a misunderstanding of the role of projective techniques in research. There are undoubtedly problems in formally assessing the reliability and validity of projective tasks. A great deal of effort has been expended in evaluating their use in clinical psychology but without reaching an unequivocal conclusion (Kassarjian, 1974). However, much of the problem is knowing what standards and criteria to apply (Murstein, 1965).

In practice, within a particular study, there is often considerable consistency in the projective responses of individuals, which draws attention to predominating themes or ideas. Alongside this, there is often a diverse range of other responses. An unusual response by an individual in a group may resonate with the other people who instantly recognise the meaning and relevance of the projection, although they had not produced it themselves at the time. In analysing the data, both the common and the odd responses can illuminate the underlying psychological mechanisms. However, there is little reason to expect reliability by specific individuals on a second occasion (which is the usual paradigm for measuring reliability) because of the fluidity of human thinking. There is little in human mental life that is static and enduring, and unaltered by the circumstances and occasion surrounding production (Semeonoff, 1973). However, because a particular insight is not reproducible by the same person on another occasion, is it any the less of an insight? This must rest on the judgement of the researcher. Sometimes it is not possible to recreate the atmosphere or chain of associations which encouraged a particular depth of responding. Similarly with measures of validity, the problem is to know by what yardstick to compare and assess the data yielded from projective tests. To make a more superficial and mechanical test the criterion would seem to disregard the values and advantages of using projective techniques in the first place.

This is not to disregard the importance of establishing reliability and validity in the assessment of measuring techniques. But projective tests should not be judged simply by the criteria of objective scientific research. Projective techniques used in qualitative applied research are primarily a device for increasing the depth of understanding and insight of the researcher. It is on the basis of these data that the researcher's judgements and recommendations will be based. The ultimate test of their validity lies in the success or failure of those judgements in the market place. Jameson (1971) suggests this is the appropriate criterion for assessing instrumental research as opposed to empirical scientific research. The best use of projective techniques is in suggesting ideas (hypotheses) to the researcher, and leads for further exploration and testing in order to gain more knowledge and understanding. The test used of the data is essentially whether the lead bears up and is supported by other data. The shrewd researcher looks to see whether the results of projective techniques make coherent sense in terms of other information that has been gleaned.

One of the main problems in critically evaluating the contribution of projective tests in applied research is the variety and range of tests used. In clinical practice, there is a well used range of standard tests for assessing personality including such well known examples as the Rorschach Ink Blot test and the Thematic Apperception Test (TAT). However, in market research, these standard tests have not proved so useful as ones specially constructed with stimulus material specifically related to the product and problem in hand. So a variety of cartoon figures, sentences for completion, analogies, etc. have been constructed in relation to particular projects. The drawers and files of market researchers must be brim-full of examples tailored to the needs of individual studies, many of which show a high level of creativity and inventiveness which is often the hallmark of their success in posing novel and fantastic problems to the respondent. But it is not surprising that this great variety of projective stimuli has not been subjected to rigorous scrutiny to assess their value and efficiency. Individual qualitative researchers can give many examples of successful and favourite projective tests which they have found personally beneficial in gaining insight into a problem. This level of testimonial may be to date the most appropriate means of evaluating the usefulness of projective tests. However, there would seem to be scope for a more systematic research study into the advantages and limitations of *particular* projective techniques. It would be desirable to establish which techniques were most useful, if only in the opinion of experienced researchers, in obtaining specific types of data and overcoming particular barriers. Ideally, there should be some attempt to investigate the depth of response which these tests achieve, but it is difficult to envisage how this could be adequately measured at present.

Conclusion

Projective techniques are devices for diverting attention in interviews, so they appear not to be asking for a personal reaction. Attention is diverted in a number of ways: by asking for immediate responses, by taking the role of other people, by the humorous and often trivial appearance of the tasks which seem not to call for a serious, considered response. But such is the nature of our thinking that we are incapable of producing a genuinely random reaction. So the responses that are made are based on personal experience and determined by subjective factors which are revealed through these procedures. Projective techniques are also an aid to expression and communication in research, so that ideas and feelings can be articulated that would not be easy to express through language or which do not fit with the social conventions of conversations. A useful way of summarising the role of projective techniques in facilitating interviewing is shown in Figure 7.2.

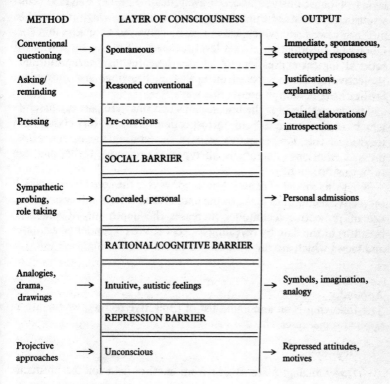

Fig. 7.2 *Uses of projective techniques to release different layers of consciousness.*

As indicated in the figure, different methods in interviewing achieve responses at different levels of consciousness. Normal methods of verbal questioning, reminding and pressing respondents will elicit data at the conscious level of social exchange; that is opinions and views which the respondent is aware of holding, which can be conveyed by language and which are part of the self publicly displayed, including our socially acceptable views. Sympathetic probing and listening in the interview will achieve the next lower level of consciousness which are those ideas and feelings that are privately held and not normally publicly displayed. This level of revelation requires good rapport between interviewer and respondent. Projective tests, especially those based on taking the role or point of view of others, are useful in penetrating to this layer of consciousness. However, the data are still conveyed using language and are, in principle, part of respondents' self awareness.

Projective techniques have a major role in penetrating to deeper layers of consciousness and self-awareness. The next layer of consciousness consists of those feelings and intuitions which it is hard to put into words and which are not easily conveyed through language. Obtaining information at this level means penetrating the barrier of rational logical expression to release these feelings and intuitions. Projective techniques based on analogies, drawings and movement facilitate expression in non-verbal ways.

The deepest level is the unconscious and unaware part of ourselves which is not amenable to introspection. This is the classic and traditional role for projective tests in penetrating the barrier of repressed emotions. Potentially all types of projective techniques can fulfil this function.

What this model of consciousness conveys is the contribution which projective techniques make to the data obtained from interviews. The use of projective techniques increases the depth (or, if you like, breadth) of the data by revealing aspects of the respondents' attitudes and views which are not available to verbal questioning.

Appendix
The following is an annotated list of projective techniques for use in applied social research.

1 *Analogies.*

Direct analogies are sought from another field for the products, objects and companies being investigated. Analogies can be made with any other object but common examples might be animals, restaurants, holidays or cars.

Symbolic analogies are analogies or metaphors drawn from abstract things, such as music, sound, texture, smell, colour. The task is to find appropriate metaphors to represent the products being investigated.

Personal analogies involve the respondent imagining that they are the object (sometimes taking an appropriate posture) and describing how the object 'feels'. This involves depicting the facts, emotions and values of the object's life.

2 *Cartoon tests.* Cartoon figures are shown representing a situation or conversation of interest. The figures have 'bubbles' which

respondents are invited to fill in. Sometimes two bubbles are used, one to write in what the character says, the other what the character 'really' thinks.

3 *Dreams*. Respondents make up a dream relevant to the topic under investigation. In essence this is a variation on story construction tasks (see below) but the advantage is that by placing the task in the context of a dream, the 'rules' about dreaming are brought into play. Thus the story does not have to be logical; it can be fantastic and anything can happen which gives greater expression of the irrational and emotional.

4 *Future scenarios*. The respondent is encouraged to describe the future as it might be in five or ten years' time, and to say how lifestyles and products might have developed and changed. The technique promotes fantasy and wish-fulfilment.

5 *Personification*. This is a way of bringing objects to life and describing their character and how they might feel, live, act, go on holiday, etc.

6 *Picture association*. This is similar to word association but involves collages of pictures to find appropriate associates for the object or brand being studied. The pictures typically show ranges of faces (male and female), houses, cars and perhaps clothes. It is often true that no single face or image quite fits with respondents' mental associations, but the pictures encourage respondents to suggest combinations and compromises. The technique has the advantage of making subjective images more explicit and concrete, which leads to greater exactness and detail in conveying what is in mind.

7 *Psychodoodling, psychodrawing, 'psycholumps'*. Respondents are given instruction in the use of shapes, colours and symbols to express feelings and emotions. Practice on feelings like 'love' and 'anger' is usually helpful and found to be fairly easy to do. In psychodoodles, respondents are encouraged to make a doodle. In some cases they are given an initial shape to turn into a relevant pattern. In psychodrawing the emphasis is on symbols or scenes. Psycholumps use modelling clay to form three-dimensional shapes. The way in which all these drawings and models take progressive shape is instructive, and respondents should be encouraged to describe what they are doing as they progress.

8 *Role playing*. Respondents are given roles to act out a scene. If the scene is an unfamiliar one, time should be given for the 'charac-

ters' to work out the play and sequence of action. It is important to emphasise improvisation and encourage participants to think themselves into their roles. *Psychodrama* is a variation on role playing, where respondents bring inanimate objects (such as products, household equipment and even specific parts of the body such as the hair or skin) to life and enact their feelings and interactions as in, for example, the conversations which might take place between hair care products on the supermarket shelves after the shop has closed.

9 *Sentence completion.* The beginning of a sentence is given for respondents to complete.

10 *Story completion/construction.* A few sentences are presented outlining an event. The respondent then develops the scenario and completes the story. Pictures and drawings are also used to set the scene for the creation of a story (as in the standard Thematic Apperception Test of personality).

11 *Word association.* Respondents say, or write down, all the words which come to mind in response to stimulus words. The instructions usually emphasise speed in responding and the importance of saying everything that comes straight to mind. A few practice words are usually given before the critical words.

References and further reading

Bem, D.J. (1972), 'Self-perception theory'. In L. Berkowitz (ed.), *Advances in experimental social psychology*, vol. 6, New York, Academic Press.

Blakeslee, T.R. (1980), *The right brain*, London, Macmillan.

Branthwaite, A. (1983), 'Situations and social actions: applications for marketing of recent theories in social psychology', *J. of the Market Research Society*, vol. 25, pp. 19–28.

Cooper, P., Branthwaite, A. (1978), 'Value for money of qualitative research', *Proceedings of ESOMAR*, pp. 45–66.

Cooper, P., Pawle, J. (1982), 'Brand personality', *Proceedings of the BPMRG symposium*, Bristol.

Forsyth, G.A., Huber, R.J. (1976), 'Selective attention in ambiguous figure perception', *Bulletin of the Psychonomic Society*, vol. 7, pp. 498–500.

Gregory, R.L. (1970), *The intelligent eye*, London, Weidenfeld and Nicolson.

Haire, M. (1950), 'Projective techniques in marketing research', *Journal of Marketing*, vol. 14, no. 5.

Jameson, C. (1971), 'The human specification in architecture: Manifesto for a new research approach', *The Architects' Journal Information Library*, 27th October, pp. 919–941.

Kassarjian, H.H. (1974), 'Projective methods'. In Ferber (ed.), *Handbook of marketing research*, New York, McGraw Hill.

Lindzey, G. (1959), 'On the classification of projective techniques', *Psychological Bulletin*, vol. 56, pp. 158–168.

Lunn, T., Cooper, P., Murphy, O. (1983), 'The fluctuating fortunes of the U.K. Social Democratic Party', *Proceedings of ESOMAR*, pp. 151–179.

Murstein, B.I. (ed.) (1965), *Handbook of projecture techniques*, New York, Basic Books.

Nisbett, R.E., Wilson, T.D. (1977), 'Telling more than we can know: verbal reports on mental processes', *Psychological Review*, vol. 84, pp. 231–259.

Ornstein, R.E. (1972), *The psychology of consciousness*, Harmondsworth, Penguin.

Sanford, R.N. (1937), 'The effects of abstinence from food upon imaginal processes', *Journal of Psychology*, vol. 3, pp. 145–149.

Schacter, J., Singer, J.E. (1962), 'Cognitive, social and physiological determinants of emotional state', *Psychological Review*, vol. 69, pp. 379–399.

Semeonoff, P.D. (1973), 'New developments in projective testing'. In Kline, P. (ed.), *New approaches in psychological measurement*, London, Wiley.

Springer, S.P., Deutsch, G. (1981), *Left brain, right brain*, San Francisco, Freeman.

Warren, H.C. (1934), *Dictionary of psychology*, Boston, Houghton Mifflin.

PART III

The Practice

Drawn and scripted by an executive officer (female, mid 30s) in a DHSS local office.

Introduction

The policy process consists of a number of stages. These have been variously described, but Stokey and Zeckhauser (1978) suggest seven stages: system definition, problem formulation, consideration of policy options, predicting consequences, evaluation, implementation and monitoring. The first two stages are roughly analogous to the preliminary phase of a research project while the last three correspond to the validation phase (see Chapter 1).

The three examples of qualitative research included in this section inform different stages of the policy process. The examples also illustrate the use of different methods and combinations of methods and vary in analytic and presentational style, in the reason for adopting a qualitative approach and in the relationship between qualitative and quantitative data. However, to select just three examples of applied qualitative research is a pernicious task and readers are urged to explore the literature more fully (see page 197).

The first example, 'Problem definition: attitudes to benefits', is taken from an exclusively qualitative study by Jane Ritchie and Alison Matthews, which was designed to elucidate why some people claim welfare benefits and others, although eligible, do not. This information was needed if new and improved promotional strategies were to be evolved and the research might, perhaps, be best described as concerning *problem formulation*. Significantly, numerous large-scale attitude surveys had already addressed the same question but had proved largely inconclusive with respect to:

- the key factors which discriminate between claimants and non-claimants
- the nature and relationship of the key elements involved in the decision to claim
- the underlying attitudes which affect the receptiveness of potential claimant to information about the scope and nature of the scheme (Ritchie and Matthews, 1982, pp. 3–4).

The primary aim of the study was to *explore* attitudes and behaviour in an attempt to understand more fully the reasons for not claiming rent allowances. This led naturally to the choice of an in-depth approach with three specific objectives:

- to allow tenants to describe in their own way the factors involved in their 'decisions' to apply or not to apply for an allowance. It was hoped that this would provide further information about the nature of the decision making process and its key elements.
- to allow tenants to introduce and describe the attitudes which underlie or are connected with the decisions involved without undue direction on the part of the researchers. It was felt that this would enable some identification or confirmation of the attitudinal factors involved and hopefully those which differentiate between claimants and nonclaimants.

● to provide an opportunity to explore how the related attitudes might affect the receipt and utilisation of information about the scheme (op. cit. p. 4).

The research, therefore, aimed not only to be exploratory and descriptive, but also to identify explanatory relationships and to confirm (or, presumably, to reject) *a priori* explanatory factors gleaned from previous research.

The study involved group work and depth interviews with claimants, followed by depth interviews with non-claimants. The choice of comparison groups followed naturally from the study objectives, while the definition of the quota sample of claimants (by age, family composition, ethnic origin and type of accommodation, e.g. furnished /unfurnished) was such as to be likely to embrace a wide range of different claiming experiences. The sample of non-claimants was more constrained: they were identified after a screening survey mounted in groups of streets with high concentrations of private tenants. Fifty-three of the 91 eligible non-claimants identified were selected purposively to represent a range of circumstances and 44 were successfully interviewed although not all proved to be eligible. Clearly, a practical limitation on undertaking a traditional survey of non-claimants would be the difficulty of obtaining a sufficiently large and representative sample of non-claimants.

Ritchie and Matthews' analytic style is commendably transparent and creative. Parts of their analysis are recognisably akin to the methods of grounded theory (Glaser and Strauss, 1967; see also Chapters 1, 4 and 11); but there are also examples of content analysis and the careful and persuasive use of incidence tables to explore the relationships between the concepts identified, and also to 'test' hypotheses concerning the links between the concepts and views about claiming behaviour.

The second study, 'Monitoring policy: observing the police in action', is taken from a large programme of research designed by David Smith and Jeremy Gray to *monitor* policing policy, practice and organisation in London and to provide a new understanding of relations between police and people. The perspectives of different actors were examined in different ways. First two surveys were mounted, one to ascertain the extent and nature of contact between Londoners and the police and to establish how people's views of the police are influenced by their own experience; and the second to describe police work from the officers' point of view. Then, in order to better understand the value systems of a key group – young black people – participant observation was carried out in a self-help hostel. Finally, it was necessary to ask how the different perspectives come together and are worked out in the practice of police work. To answer this question the researchers accompanied police officers over a two-year period and Chapter 9 reports two separate incidents which were observed. Observation is perhaps the only means of learning what actually happens between a police officer and, say, a suspect particularly if the behaviour would be widely recognised as illegitimate. However, observation is not without its problems (see Chapter 6) and Smith and Gray point out that the presence of an observer could well influence the police officer in his choice of activity and in refraining from 'some things that he would otherwise do because he thinks it is too dangerous to let the observer see them' (Smith and Gray, 1983, p. 11). On the other hand a policeman 'has to achieve certain goals and only knows certain ways of doing it, and he is simply not capable of acting a part for hours on end' (ibid.).

Partly to lessen these problems Smith and Gray tried to become accepted as temporary and honorary members of the group. As it happened their approaches had to be somewhat different because Gray, being younger and strongly built, was viewed by some officers as a potential competitor. He had, therefore, 'to become more fully a member of the group on equal terms if he was to be acceptable at all' (op. cit., p. 15). The result was to facilitate the possibility of triangulation by observer (see Chapter 1). The researchers were prevented, by the objective of gaining acceptance, from taking notes or using tape recorders. The fieldwork was written up as soon as possible after observation, but this was sometimes several days later. Smith and Gray believe that virtually all the incidents witnessed were recorded, but some of the initial filtering and analysis of the data – in remembering what was significant – was necessarily unconscious. Consequently certain limits are placed on the form of analysis and presentation.

Smith and Gray's report runs to 315 pages and no extract can be representative or adequately convey the richness of the material which they gathered. Their presentation is thematic: each theme is stated in bare outline and then supported by a mass of detailed incidents. The incidents reported in Chapter 9 show the police officers concerned in very different lights; the first is an example of policing at its best; the latter is much more disturbing and would probably have been 'invisible' to research techniques that offered the actors the possibility of *post facto* rationalisation. More important, as a reason for including them in this volume, is the way in which the careful accumulation of detail adds to the authenticity of the reporting and yet does not preclude the possibility of drawing conclusions that are pregnant with policy implications.

In suggesting changes in policy, as Smith and Gray do on the basis of the research as a whole, they are forced to 'try and balance the sometimes conflicting experience, views and objectives that exist' (op. cit., p. 318). But, an essential aspect of their approach is 'that such commendations should be publicly discussed, together with the argument and information on which they are based' (ibid.). Giving the reader access to data in this way enables the burden of interpretation to be shared and can also serve to protect the interests of those researched (see Chapter 11). Moreover, Smith and Gray insisted on a guarantee of unfettered publication from the research sponsors, the Metropolitan Police, which further guaranteed the independence of the research.

Chapter 10 was specially written for this volume. Drawing on an *evaluative* study of a psychogeriatric service, Gilbert Smith and Caroline Cantley persuasively argue the case for 'pluralistic evaluation' of policy initiatives.

In common with Smith and Gray, they point to the importance of understanding the different perspectives of those effecting and affected by policy. Traditional evaluation studies frequently overlook the fact that services may mean different things to different people. In part this is because the criteria of 'success' employed in evaluation are generally restricted to those held by the sponsors. But, equally, the reliance of rationalistic assessment of output on hard quantitative data may also be important in that the techniques that yield them cannot generally handle subjective assessments, or multiple measures of outcome.

Gilbert Smith and Caroline Cantley demonstrate that by the judicious use of qualitative material (though not to the exclusion of quantitative data) it is possible to identify different expectations and interests and to evaluate across them. Moreover, because of a focus on process, as much as on outcome, they are able to offer explanations for the success or failure that they identify and thereby to provide a framework for advancing policy alternatives. Pluralistic evaluation also focuses attention on the nature and perception of the policy problem which is frequently obscured in highly quantified accounts of organisational inputs and outputs.

Finally, it is appropriate to draw attention to the pictorial products of projective techniques that pepper this book. The drawings were all produced in informal group situations on developmental training courses involving the editor. In each case the objective was to encourage in practitioners a self-awareness about certain aspects of their work. In a rather unstructured way, and through a process of comparing each of the drawings produced, the 'artists' were asked to elucidate the 'meaning' of their drawings, to offer explanations as to why they portrayed things as they did, and to suggest what, if anything, might be learned from the exercise that was relevant to understanding the problem at hand including their own response to it. Sometimes a single projective exercise in a group of six to eight persons can generate several hours of productive discussion.

References

Glaser, B.G., Strauss, A.L. 1967, *The discovery of grounded theory : Strategies for qualitative research*, Chicago, Aldine.

Ritchie, J., Matthews, A. 1982, *Take-up of rent allowances: an in-depth study*, London, SCPR Survey Research Centre.

Smith, D.J., Gray, J. 1983, *Police and people in London, Part IV, The police in action*, London, Policy Studies Institute.

Stokey, E., Zeckhauser, R. 1978, *A primer for policy analysis*, New York, Norton.

8 Problem Definition: Attitudes to Benefits
Jane Ritchie and Alison Matthews

Editor's introduction

Rent allowances were and remain, although in modified form, a means-tested supplement available to private tenants. Since the scheme was introduced in 1973 there has been concern about the large proportion of eligible tenants not claiming benefit. Large-scale surveys have revealed the extent of non take-up and have provided a wide range of explanations of people's reasons for not claiming. However, as Jane Ritchie and Alison Matthews explain, it was felt that 'there was a need for further understanding of the decision processes involved in claiming which would explain the patterns revealed and provide information on which to base new or improved promotion strategies' (Ritchie and Matthews 1982, p. 1).

The research was undertaken in three stages and was designed to build upon the available evidence on benefit take-up. First, a review of existing research was prepared and subsequently discussed with consultants who were asked to contribute written suggestions for indepth research. Second, five group discussions and ten individual interviews were held with rent allowance claimants. Two of the groups consisted of elderly claimants, two comprised claimants with families and one mainly consisted of young people living in furnished accommodation. Finally, 36 eligible non-claimants, identified by means of a special screening exercise, were interviewed in depth.

All the interviews and discussions were held in London or Liverpool.

Attitudes to benefits

Previous studies on issues of take-up have shown the complexity of attitudes towards benefits and this study certainly confirms this picture. The material collected shows a maze of interwoven beliefs, emotions and images, which display both consistent themes and contradictions.

As an initial attempt to understand the underlying elements involved, we sought the key words or phrases mentioned when people were describing how they felt about benefits. The following list represents those most commonly appearing.

'independence'	*'grateful'*
'pride'	*'need'*
'charity'	*'eligible'*
'something for nothing'	*'entitled'*
'stand on own feet'	*'guilt'*
'ask for help'	*'right'*
'scrounger'	*'freedom'*
'can manage without'	*'control'*
'stigma'	*'personal affairs'*
	'these other people'

The context for these or similar phrases could be illustrated by numerous quotations from the interviews and discussions. As just one example we show some extracts below from the discussion which took place in the elderly claimant group in Camden, when in this particular case, they were discussing their claims for rent allowances.

M. *Well we saw it – I mean we'd been thinking about it but we thought well that's not for us. That's all – then we applied and found it was for us.*

F. *So simple really.*

M. *I know all about it but I didn't want charity. As I'd lost my wife and was on my own therefore I'd got to have something. Just a necessity . . .*

F. *Our mother always brought us up that way that you don't ask for anything – you do it whether you've got money or not, you don't let anyone. . . .*

F. *It's letting people know what you've got that I think stops a lot of people applying.*

M. *. . . you expect after you've been working and you've earned your living and then suddenly you've got to ask somebody for something even though generally he pays in for it – but you've still got to ask for it.*

F. *But surely you're grateful.*

M. *Oh, don't think for one moment I'm not grateful because we couldn't manage without it . . .*

M. *I'm trying to answer your questions as regards as to how you feel when you receive it. And I feel degraded. If the country gives me a pension that I can live on according to the cost, then we should be happy . . .*

F. *Well these forms you fill out – it's more like a means test isn't it? What have you got, what haven't you got? . . .*

F. *They have a right to know before they dish out money, they have a right to know . . .*

F. *Well to me, it's an indignity having to answer all these questions . . .*

M. *Well this lady said that she didn't feel bad about it, nor did I afterwards because I dare say there's other gentlemen in the room have worked quite as many years as I have . . . never had a day off from work and I never took a penny unemployment . . . so I think that I was entitled to it.*

So there's one view of entitlement – it's something that you feel that you earned . . .

M.   *When you see some of these youngsters going about today – I know some of them are unlucky but some of them don't want to work and when you see what they get I don't think I'm cadging – I think I'm entitled to what I get.*
Why should anybody feel that they're cadging?

M.   *. . . and the older you are the more you feel it. I think it's age – it's definitely age. I think once you get to a certain age you want to be independent as much as . . .*
Do you not feel then that you are entitled to it in the same way? Because you have earned it or not?

M.   *I think I'm entitled to it because I was paying for the last two years I was paying £5 a week in stamps for benefit and pension it was coming to £5 being taken from my wages, plus the income tax which was also taken and so I think that I was paying for everybody to have a better old age . . .*

F.   *But even if they don't work – many of them – their circumstances prevent them – you know you can't be sure of having a job.*

M.   *Don't think I'm running a person down because he's been ill I mean as I've just told you I'm very lucky – I'd sooner be as I am than someone who's very ill.*

F.   *But I feel you can't let people simply starve – you simply have to do something.*

F.   *No I don't think they apply for it unless they're really hard up.*

F.   *No I think they have to need it most people . . .*

M.   *. . . when I was drawing my pension, in front of me stood a big negro . . . He spoke in an American accent . . . it turned out that he was sent from America to draw the dole and public allowance . . . he has children – across the road lives his so-called wife, she's also claiming for children and he's drawing £50 a week.*

M.   *As the book stands, he's entitled to it. That's all.*

M.   *But he hasn't paid in for it.*

F.   *That's the welfare state – if you want to change that you'll have to change the whole system.*

M.   *As the law stands . . .*

M.   *But he's an American . . .*

F.   *I don't see why one minds what other people have – you see what I have I'm very grateful for and it helps me, why should I worry about my neighbour – it's no good is it, it doesn't help me.*

(Camden elderly group: claimants)

For reasons we shall attempt to show, we would suggest that many of the views and feelings expressed about benefits link back to two dominant themes. The first concerns *entitlement* and what makes it legitimate for a person to claim or receive benefits. The second concerns *dependency* and the effect that claiming a benefit has on freedom and independence.

By identifying these two themes we do not mean to suggest that they are the only factors involved. It does seem however that other views or elements are often associated with a particular view on one or other of these themes. In addition the way in which different views on independence and entitlement interact seems to be associated with differences in 'take-up' behaviour. In other words, we are suggesting there are certain attitudinal packages and that it is the whole of the package, rather than any one part of it, that is important in the explanation of behaviour.

There are certain difficulties in presenting these 'whole' views since their descriptions could well appear as confused and complicated as the original material from which they are drawn. We have therefore chosen to describe the attitudes emerging in terms of the common 'scripts' presented on entitlement and independence. With each 'script' we attempt to identify the other issues which are commonly associated.

The material which follows is based exclusively on the depth interviews with non-claimants since these provided an opportunity to explore all the main issues with each individual.

Entitlement

The evidence collected suggests there are four common scripts on 'entitlement' to benefits. These involve themes around:

> *'it's a right'*
> *'only if you need it'*
> *'only if you earn it'*
> *'everyone else is doing it'.*

Before examining each of these we need to emphasise that our summaries of the scripts, and the allocation of individuals to them, inevitably oversimplify the situation. The ways in which views were expressed obviously varied in form and their portrayal often contained inconsistencies and overlap with other themes. Our purpose, however, is to identify the dominant ideas which appear to be central to certain views and, in particular, the kind of attitudes and feelings which are most frequently associated with them.

'It's a right'

Benefits are a right as part of the welfare system of this society provided for by taxes, stamps, rates, etc. Thus everyone is entitled to apply for them, either by virtue of having paid taxes etc. or merely by being a citizen of this country.

In its purest form such a view is marked by very matter of fact and unemotive statements about benefits. There is a lack of reference to stigma, very little anxiety about claiming anything and virtually no critical comments about other claimants. In its more rationalised form the idea that some people might just have more 'right' than others begins to be introduced and there appears to be marginally more vulnerability about being a claimant. These views do not, however, override the basic feeling of benefits being a right as part of the welfare system.

> *... which I will do, I wouldn't hesitate to go.* (Some people say that they don't, they wouldn't claim something like social security or whatever.) *Oh I would, I believe I have paid my money in, haven't you if you have been working, insurance stamp and tax, it's only your own money that you get back.* (Why do you think people have that attitude though – there are a lot of people who do?) *I think it must be a bit of pride, but if you have earned it and you know, if you have paid your whack like, you should get something out of it because that's what it's there for you know. ...*
>
> (Liverpool family: male)

> (How do you feel about the existence of these sorts of benefits?) *There again, very good.* (In what way?) *Again with high unemployment, it is some help, and again if you are unfortunate to become ill.* (How would you feel about claiming any of those benefits – if you were in the situation?) *Oh, I'd feel free to claim.* (You said 'free'?) *Well I wouldn't feel no malice or apprehension going and claiming them 'cause it's your right to go and claim them. It wouldn't bother me to go and claim.* (Do you think it would bother some people?) *Oh, I should think so yes ... even if they're entitled to it ... Well, if you pay in for it, you're entitled to it, like health service treatment. Everyone pays their NHS, each employer pays their NHS, so they're entitled to claim on it.* (You talked about scroungers, who were you referring to?) *Well some people do scrounge on the state, people try to fiddle the state ... Well no, all the benefits they give, they should be there, I'm in full agreement with that, but some people need them more than others.* (And you say some of them 'scrounge'?) *Some people do scrounge off the state, yes, I suppose they do. You read in the paper people are better off on the dole than at work, you read that several times, you can only go on what you read, what you hear on the news and read.*
>
> (single male: Camden)

'Only if you need it'

Entitlement is based on need, and, by definition, anyone who really needs supplementary income should have it, and anyone who does not need it, should not.

This is the most common script of all and takes a number of different forms. Part of the reason for this is that what people mean by 'need' is very variable, as we shall see in the next chapter. The important distinction of relevance here is whether need is defined through 'circumstance' or whether it is connected with 'not managing'. In their extreme forms, these two kinds of cases are illustrated by the quotations below.

> Do you see groups, particular groups of people for whom it is legitimate to provide social security and others for whom you think it isn't quite legitimate?

I do see them, yes, mainly for the ones for whom it is fair; I think it is fair for any single parent family if they come up to the nursery with their kids. So for instance, all women who have to cope with kids and are single. Because if they can't work and they have to look after their children what do they do? They need money. Then take all the people who are made redundant, they must eat and keep their families going on. This is the problem today, very hard, very strong. Now I know, though, that there are groups of people who think it is better for me not to do anything during the day and not to work and get social security, because if I did work I would get very little more than social security gives me. In that case there are two sides of it. On the one hand it's a dreadful attitude, on the other it's true wages should be higher, definitely and people should get more money for what they do ...

(Family: Female: Camden)

I don't want to cheat the government, because I'm managing. (Why cheat? Why do you feel you are cheating?) *Because if you are managing, then why are you claiming for it? ... If we can't manage, then we apply, that's alright, that's not cheating or nothing.*

(Family: Female: Camden)

As can be envisaged, these different definitions of need have very different implications for when the people concerned would claim benefits themselves. For the former 'circumstance' group, the whole thing is much more clearly defined, and there is much greater certainty about when they would or would not be entitled to claim. In addition there was little allusion to abuse other than through people choosing to place themselves in disadvantageous circumstances.

For the group who feel the need exists when they are 'not managing' the entitlement issue is surrounded by uncertainty and hesitancy. In addition, this group is much more likely to see some stigma attached to claiming benefits since, by definition, this is an admission of not being able to cope, a point we return to in the next chapter.

Another view associated with the 'need' script was the feeling that if people claim benefits which they do not really 'need', then there will be less money for those who really do need additional income. This view is clearly illustrated by the following answer:

It all comes down in the end, I think, I suppose it is probably pride or just thinking do I really need it, do I myself feel, deep down, right I do deserve that ... it's just something in my conscience, same as in a shop, someone gives me too much change, then I'd give it back. OK so it is a big store and they probably wouldn't miss £4 and I probably could do a great deal with it, but it is a matter of conscience. I'd feel in my own mind that if I couldn't justify my having that money then I wouldn't be able to accept it, I'd feel guilty about getting it. I'd think 'Christ that poor woman down there, all her kids, and I'm having this money'. (And yet the woman down there wouldn't get any more because you didn't do that, she'd get whatever she was entitled to get?) *I know it is stupid; I know it doesn't make any difference whether she gets the money.* (So having registered that, how do you feel about it? *I've registered that all the time, but it is just a thought pattern really. It is just the way you think about things. Probably I think that if I didn't get it OK, so the woman downstairs wouldn't have any more, but probably there would be more money about for putting into schools . . . I wouldn't have thought that if they don't claim it then it still stays there. Obviously that money must be re-employed into doing something else.*

(Female student: Camden)

This quotation also introduces ideas of 'deservedness' and 'guilt' which were not uncommon among the younger non-claimants who felt they had some choice in their life pattern which could not be compromised with 'need'. We shall again examine this in more detail in a later chapter.

With some of the scripts based on 'not managing' negative comments about other claimants begin to enter the scene. One of the more common criticisms from this group concerned any display of luxury or indulgence by people on benefits. The argument goes that if people can afford to do 'these things' (i.e. smoke, drink, etc.) they cannot really 'need' the money so how come they are getting benefits from the state.

'Only if you earn it'

Entitlement has to be earned in some way and therefore some people quite clearly deserve benefits and others quite clearly do not.

Although initially this may appear to be very similar to the 'right' script, it holds an additional and important component. This component centres around the importance of the 'work ethic', and thus just paying for benefits through taxes is not quite sufficient. It is therefore not simply a welfare right to receive benefits and there must be some additional element of effort to make it justifiable or deserved.

(It seems a pity that people feel that they have to manage as you say when there could be money that you could be entitled to – you said entitled?) *Well entitled in as much as – more so than the people that just haven't worked or contributed anything to the state over the years – if you think that you have never had anything off the state and your husband has always worked all his life, he has never asked for anything, you are entitled to it in that way but the world owes nobody a living as regards to giving the money out, it's the way we feel about it and if we can cope with what we have got, we still feel as though in a way it's charity.* (Why charity?) *Because it's coming from the state, it's something you're not earning, toiling for it either physically or mentally – you're not toiling for that money, it's coming in and it's there regularly and you are not doing anything manually, say digging the street or lifting boxes or sweating like that, whatever your particular job might be . . .* (But is the state wrong to provide benefits for people?' *Not for the infirm and the elderly and the people that can't work – the chronically sick.* (Why not for other people?) *But for the people that can do – as I said before – it's job satisfaction and if they were to be given a decent wage, and I don't mean as much as they get on the Social Security because that way it's not going to mean nothing, I mean a job whereby they can say I've done a day's toil ... cleaning up the environment ... My Dad worked until he was 76 so that her* [sic] *retirement pension was a little larger. Now this is what annoys me – my Dad did that so that when anything happened to him my Mum would get a little bit extra on the retirement pension, but the state now gives it to everybody, so that's wiped out ...* (It's something you feel strongly about – actually working for it – isn't it?) *Oh yes – working for your cash – because my Dad always used to say, 'This family will get nothing, only what it's worked for', and we have always been brought up with that instilled in our minds, and my husband's family the same.*

(Married couple (50s): Liverpool)

As with some of the previous group, critical comments about other claimants are likely to accompany such views. The most fundamental criticism which tends to arise with the 'earn' script is that some claimants just live off the state as an easy option.

(You said before that when you claim benefits it affects your pride. Do you think there is any reason to feel like that or not?) *I really don't know. I know it is not like it used to be when I see these young layabouts getting it,* (How do you mean, young layabouts?) *Well young fellas because they don't get well paid jobs they won't work and they're on the social security aren't they so they must be able to live on it. That new property over there, there's a lot of them over there, with high rent £18 a week and they've got two children so let's face it it must be good on the social security to live like that, I mean I see them coming out of the betting shop, I see them coming out of the pub ... There's young people what's never paid in and here's me that's paid me stamp all me life worrying about when I've got to go.* (Do you think, then, it's alright for some people to go?) *Well it's alright for elderly people to go.* (Anyone else?) *Well of course these have got kiddies, they get their family allowance. But they've got to be kept no matter where they are.* (Do you think there is any difference between different groups? Do you see some groups being more entitled than other groups?) *Well I don't see how you can make that really – there's not groups, there are all the people that's on social security – there are either those that's never worked that's come out of school, never been able to get a job, there's no work about now, and there's those that got jobs and they get more on social security so why go to work for it.* (What do you think of people who do that?) *I'm bloody annoyed about that and, of course, they've still got to be kept, haven't they?*

(Retirement pensioner: Liverpool)

It is worth noting in this context that people who had very negative views about other claimants may be in a difficult position when it comes to claiming themselves. There is, for example, the fear of being identified with a group who they themselves have openly condemned. There is also the perceived danger of scrutiny from others asking, as they may have done, does he/she really 'need' or 'deserve' the money?

In order to stand up to such scrutiny they may have to be very certain of their own grounds for a claim under their terms of entitlement.

'Everyone else is doing it'

Entitlement is based on what other people can get and if they can get it, why should others make sacrifices or be deprived?

Although this view is often accompanied by comments like 'We've paid for it like everyone else' this does not appear to be its main justification. It seems to be based more on a feeling of irritation or even envy that other people are getting something which they are not. This seems to be particularly galling when the 'others' seem to be able to do things which they cannot.

> Do you think your income would be about average for people of your age?
>
> Wife: *I don't know what other people's incomes are, but I mean when I talk to other girls, they seem to be able to go to the bingo, you know, they can go out with their husbands on a Saturday, their husband can take them out twice a week.*
>
> Husband: *I think you are better off on the dole, because there's a fella over the road where we used to live, he's on the dole, and how old is he, about 40 I would think, and you see him in the pub waiting for the pub to open in the morning, he's last out when they shut at dinner time, the same thing of a night time, he's in the betting shop all day Saturday and all through the week, we can't do that.*
>
> Wife: *Most people I know their husbands are on the dole, you know it sounds stupid, but they can afford to go out.*
>
> Husband: *We can't afford to go out.*
>
> Wife *You see them going out on a Saturday night ... (How do you feel about that?) It makes you mad, because we were on the verge three weeks ago, ... feeling depressed and what have you, and I was on the verge of telling him to pack up and go on the dole, because they just seem to manage, I mean, I don't know what they have on the table, maybe the food or something goes short, but the kids are better dressed, they can go out, you know the girls can go to bingo, it does make you mad. (So what stopped your husband a few weeks ago?)*
>
> Husband: *I'd be bad tempered if I was at home.*
>
> Do you find that you resent these people or not, or is it just the ...?
>
> Wife: *I don't actually resent the people, but I get jealous of the money they get ... I mean personally if he had the chance, I would like him to do it for two months, just to see if it is true that they get all these things, you know, what they say they get ...*
>
> Husband: *I wouldn't go on the dole.*
>
> Wife: *He wouldn't go on the dole.*
>
> Husband: *I wouldn't go on the dole.*
>
> Husband: *Well I don't think it is degrading, I mean to me, I worked, my parents have worked, my grandparents have worked, my aunties have worked,*

they have all worked, now to me it's not degrading, because it's only what my family have paid into it you know, and what my husband has paid in while he is working, but it does make you mad when you hear people living on it, you know, you think, well why doesn't he pack working . . .
(Family: Liverpool)

It is evident that in this family, the wife held this view particularly strongly, although to some extent supported by the husband. This is probably not coincidental, since as we mention later the women did appear to be more willing to consider claiming benefits than the men, probably because of their greater involvement in household budgeting.

It will come as no surprise to find that the four main entitlement scripts were not evenly distributed amongst the different groups of non-claimants. As Table 8.1 shows, just under half of the non-claimants felt entitlement was based on need but there were proportionately more who held this script among families or people in the 50s. The younger singles were most likely to define entitlement by right while, for pensioners, the most dominant script centred around benefits being earned.

Table 8.1
Entitlement 'scripts'

	Younger singles	Families	Older couples, singles (50s)	Retirement pensioners	Total
Right	4	4	1	2	11
Need	2	5	5	4	16
To be earned	1	–	–	5	6
Comparison with others	–	3	–	–	3
Base	7	12	6	11	36

Independence

The interviews with both claimants and non-claimants leave very little doubt that independence is generally felt to be a good thing. Virtually all the people interviewed said something like 'people should be able to support themselves if they can', 'should be able to stand on their own feet', 'nobody wants to ask anybody for anything' at some point in the interviews. While many people were talking specifically about financial independence, it was clear that this often related to a more general idea of freedom and independence of action. We consider in the next chapter [see original report] why independence is so important, but at this stage it is necessary to understand how and why it is affected by claiming benefits.

The first thing to say is that not all the non-claimants saw independence as negatively affected by claiming benefits. For some it was not an issue at all while others defined the important elements of independence differently. For this latter group, claiming benefits could be a means of increasing independence or freedom in regards to aspects of lifestyle which were valued.

> ... *But if I lost my job and I kept this place on and I wanted to, because I don't see why I should lower my standard of living, you know, just because I was made redundant, then I'd be really pushed, I'd have to think hard about how to get some money one way or another* (And what do you think you'd do?) *Well first of all I'd go through absolutely everything about what I could claim, clothing, you know, if I could get any help, a rate rebate within the rate in my rent, I don't know if that's possible, but I mean I'd go through all these things first and claim every single penny I could lay my hands on* ... (You said that you don't think you should take a drop in your standard of living. Is this something you feel strongly about that you, now, that you shouldn't have to?) *Not just for me, but for people in this country generally ... I don't see why people should be forced to lead a miserable life. You know, I mean it's not much fun without money. I mean, you know, there's enough troubles in life as it is without being, you know, oppressed by something completely out of your hands.*
>
> (Single female (20s): Liverpool)

> ... *I think if they* [benefits] *can give you a better standard of living than you've got, you're entitled to anything and everything that you can get if it gives you a better standard of living and you are within the law, obviously you are entitled to everything you can get ... you should claim anything and everything if it will help you ... Well, it's your burden, or life ... well, it's your priorities really, that's the main thing – you've got to get your priorities right ... my social life is affected, but not to the point that I have to stay in all the time. It can drive you mad to stay in all the time ... Pride doesn't come into it. I don't know pride. I've never been a person with much pride. Pride's not going to buy you a loaf or anything is it ... I mean I wouldn't be too proud to do anything, I might be shy but I would not be too proud to take.*
>
> (Family (30s): Liverpool)

The rest of the non-claimants felt that the critical elements of independence were, in some way, negatively affected by claiming benefits. The reasons given for this focused around three main themes:

> 'it's something for nothing'
> 'it removes control'
> 'it affects your pride'

Each of these is considered briefly below.

'*It is something for nothing*'

This could be renamed the 'charity' theme and, on first sight, it may appear to have nothing to do with independence. There were, however, sufficient examples which suggested some connection along the lines of 'If I get something for nothing, then I owe a debt which I can't necessarily repay, which in turn leaves me feeling dependent'. In other words, it is indebtedness without any freedom to repay which poses the threat to independence. This case was very cogently argued by the following non-claimant.

> *I'm independent, I want it that way. Ever since I was 16 years old I've had my own bank account ... we were always brought up to stand on our own feet, always. I have never had to ask anyone for any money ... I do feel sorry for some old people who are living on a fixed income – pensions they thought would be adequate years ago but now, with the best will in the world, they can't afford to heat the houses where they live – they are frightened to move because of all problems attached to selling a house and anyway where do they go? So they live in a couple of rooms and survive on pride and what little money they have got. I know three different people in that situation and I feel sorry for them. They are the people that need help but their nature would not let them accept it, they are in a kind of trap, pride – need – offers of help – pride – need it's a vicious circle. I know two who would be able to get social security but they would rather die than apply. I know exactly how they feel, we have talked about it often, the feeling of 'Is this what I have come down to at my time of life?' I would feel exactly the same. No matter how desperate the situation they would always say they could manage. I have problems trying to give help to them but we talked it over sensibly – they said they could not offer anything in return for groceries I take when I go and see them – I say that they give me the company that I lack – they saw the point of that, now I take food and they entertain me – a two-way thing. That's why people like us can't accept benefits because it's all take on the part of the person getting it and no give.*

> (Male pensioner: Liverpool)

'*It removes control*'

This theme centres round the view that if you receive money from the state, then you are no longer solely in charge of your own affairs. This loss of responsibility means that 'someone else' has a right to intervene in your life and thus some control is removed. This loss of control could be connected with others determining how your money is spent or with a loss of freedom to deny them access to your private affairs. People holding this view are therefore likely to be particularly sensitive about the financial scrutiny which accompanies claiming benefits.

> (How would you feel, you know, you keep saying to me you are going to go down and claim Social Security benefit, how will you feel about it?) *Well it's being old fashioned, but I would be a little bit upset about it, I will be honest with you.*

(Upset, what makes you think you would be upset about it?)

Well there's something about this social security business. You know, I don't think your life is your own kind of thing, you know they want to know the ins and outs; I don't know there's something about social security that to me – I think working all my life, I think that's what, you know to me it's a disgrace, which it isn't really, because it's only what we have paid into, so they tell me, I don't know.

(But you said yourself that you would be a bit upset?)

I would, I would, there's no good saying any different, I would be because I'm going back when I was very young and an old uncle of mine went, because it wasn't social security then it was the parish or whatever the name they gave it then, and they said to him sell that and sell that and sell that, well I mean that's terrible.

(How do you mean?)

Sell his furniture, sell his home, so in the end the poor old bugger he took a couple in, let his place off and they broke his heart, you know that stands in my mind.

(And do you still think they do this sort of thing?)

No, that's played out that is, that was the parish that was, it was the UAB. I mean this is . . .

(But you were saying something about your life is not your own?)

Well they are too bloody nosey aren't they really, they want to know the ins and outs.

(What sort of things do you think they are going to want to know the ins and outs?)

Well for kick-off, they are going to ask you how much money you have got in the bank, well you know in your own hands – I know a person going back a few years ago she had £300 and I said you are entitled to something, so she said oh I'm not I'm not, I said they can only say no, so they came and she showed them her Post Office book of £300, they haunted her, if she took money out, what did she take it for; she had a little holiday and she had her place decorated and all that, God Almighty, I thought to myself.

(How do you mean they haunted her, in what way?)

Well what did she do with her money, you know each time a visitor came and looked at the book, what are you doing with this and what are you doing with that. I hope the end comes before I go on the social security.

(Female pensioner: Liverpool)

Yes, I feel that. I think I feel strongly that way. Whatever you do you must take responsibility. Whatever it is. If I dropped a cup on the floor, for example, I must take responsibility. That is my clumsiness that's why I dropped the cup. Just an example. So I think in most things, I think like that . . .

(Do you feel that your independence is taken away from you by claiming benefits?)

Yes in a way that. One hasn't got that kind of responsibility or not having that responsibility – is that the right way to say it?

(Maybe this was the thing – 'taking away'?)

A responsibility, yes – which one holds . . .

(Single male: Camden)

'*It affects your pride*'

It is difficult to amplify around this theme because it appears that it is simply the admission of dependence which causes the problem.

> *... perhaps it is just pride ... well, I suppose it is quite difficult to admit how dependent you are financially ... I feel that my position isn't actually very honourable because I'm so dependent on _____ (father of child) ... I mean a lot of my friends, including myself, feel that women's financial independence is, it's something to fight for and I'm not, I'm sort of mixed about it.*
> (And yet, so how would you feel about being more dependent on ... ?)
> *The state.*
> (The state, yes.)
> *Well I think it's the same thing really except that you don't have to, you don't have to have a personal relationship as well, you don't have to be grateful.*
> (Single parent family: Camden)

It is clear that this is not an explanation of why claiming benefits affects independence but merely a restatement of the fact that it does. The reason for choosing to mention pride in this context is that it appears to mean being 'proud' of maintaining independence to many of the non-claimants. We are therefore back to the question of why it is so important to be able to cope without help.

Views on how independence can be affected by claiming benefits are not mutually exclusive in the same way as most of the entitlement scripts. For many of the non-claimants, we cannot assign one particular view since two or three of them may co-exist. It is possible, however, to distinguish between those who feel independence is not negatively affected by claiming benefits and those who do. They are distributed between the different groups as in Table 8.2.

Table 8.2

	Independence affected	Independence not affected
Age/family groups		
Younger singles	4	3
Families	7	5
Older single/couples (50s)	5	1
Retirement pensioners	8	3
Total	24	12

Thus two out of three non-claimants felt independence was adversely affected by claiming or receiving benefits, although inevitably the strength with which this view was held varied considerably. Younger non-claimants were less likely than the older groups to feel independence was affected and this was particularly so among the families. Nevertheless, in èach group the people who felt that there were some negative effects were in a majority.

As might be expected views on independence relate to the main entitlement scripts. The composition was as shown in Table 8.3.

Table 8.3

	Independence affected	Independence not affected
Entitlement based on:		
Right	3	8
Need	14	2
To be earned	6	–
Comparison with others	2	1

The group who are least likely to feel independence is affected are those who believe entitlement is a right. The only group who without exception saw independence as affected by benefit support were those who believed it had to be earned. These composite attitudes can therefore add up to very polarised views about benefit support. At one extreme there is a fairly neutral view about the whole thing with entitlement based on right, independence unaffected and very few unfavourable perceptions of the system or its clients. At the other extreme there is a package of attitudes, based on entitlement being earned, negative attitudes towards other claimants and independence being adversely affected, which can add to a very serious deterrent to a claim.

Reference

Ritchie, J. and Matthews, A. 1982, *Take-up of rent allowances: an in depth study*, London, Social and Community Planning Research.

9 Monitoring Policy: Observing the Police in Action
David J. Smith and Jeremy Gray

Editor's introduction

In 1983 David Smith and Jeremy Gray published the results of a large-scale research programme concerned to study 'relations between the Metropolitan Police and the community it serves'. Not surprisingly the results attracted considerable media attention and the fact that they were published at all is significant. The research was initiated and funded by the Metropolitan Police with the assistance of the City Parochial Foundation, but was to be independent and this was guaranteed by an agreement that 'the findings would be published in full and that, while the drafts of the reports would be discussed with the Met in advance of publication, the final decision on drafting would rest with PSI [Policy Studies Institute]' (Smith and Gray, *Police and People in London*, PSI, 1983, pp. 316–317).

The research programme comprised two surveys, one of 2,550 adult Londoners and the other of 1,770 police officers up to inspector rank; an intensive participant observation study of young black people at a self-help hostel; and, finally, an observational study undertaken over two years of police at work from which the following extract is taken.

The first objective of the observational study was to complement the survey of police officers by providing a more detailed description of selected groups of officers 'filling in the full background: the motivations and personal characteristics of the officers involved, what they think they are trying to achieve, how their objectives and activities relate to the wider structure of the Force' (op. cit., p. 2).

The second objective was 'to describe and analyse the psychology of working groups of police officers: to show how individuals develop through the group ideas about what counts as success, attitudes towards certain types of person and models of the way in which a police officer should behave' (ibid.).

Third, the researchers 'set out to describe how the pattern of policing and the behaviour of police officers is shaped by the internal structure of the organisation in which they work and by the legal and procedural rules imposed from outside' (ibid.).

Most of the information 'was obtained in one of two ways: by accompanying, observing and talking to police officers over long periods while they were doing their job; and by carying out informal interviews, mostly with senior òfficers. Various other methods were also used, but to a lesser extent: silent observation of classes and selection boards, formal interviews with recruits during their initial training, and study of internal documents (files on policy changes and Force Inspectorate Reports)' (op. cit., p. 3).

The two incidents reported are two of three included in the research report where police behaviour might have been affected by the race of the suspects involved. As such they constitute only part of the evidence presented by Smith and Gray in a much more extensive analysis of the impact of race and class on police behaviour. They are included primarily to illustrate how the careful accumulation of data can add authenticity to reporting, but they also exemplify the way that grounded observations – here concerning the handling of the incident by police officers – may have self-evident policy implications (in this case with respect to police management, training procedures and even, recruitment policies).

The term 'relief' in the text requires explanation. Each police division is divided into four groups (reliefs) of uniformed officers under the command of an inspector. Each 24-hour period is divided into three shifts operated by a different relief with the fourth relief on weekly leave. The initials 'DJS' refer to David Smith, 'JG' to Jeremy Gray. Asterisked headings have been inserted by the editor.

An excellent piece of police work *

The first incident occurred during a night shift that DJS spent in a van with the driver and a probationer. The division was one with a large Asian and smaller West Indian population. At about 3 a.m. the van answered a call for urgent assistance in a mainly Asian area. When the crew arrived, all the other officers on patrol from the relief were already there (about a dozen in all) together with the inspector. There was a lorry parked outside a club with about five black people standing in the back and looking out over the tailboard. About ten more black people were spilling out of the club onto the pavement and were arguing with the group in the lorry. A number of the black people involved had dreadlocks, most were men, few were older than 25. As matters developed, more people came out of the club and others went back into it. The inspector was talking to a black man who appeared to be the spokesman for those in the club. The rest of the police officers present were standing well back (the inspector later said this was at his orders). There was quite a commotion, with people talking in loud voices or shouting. It was raining hard. It became clear that the man from the club accused those on the lorry of taking some of his equipment (a loudspeaker). The people on the lorry implied they didn't have it without actually saying so.

The inspector remained completely calm, though his manner was very firm. He spoke in a loud voice, with great emphasis. To the people on the lorry he said, 'He says you have taken his loudspeaker. Will you give it back to him?' In reply, the people on the lorry smiled in a menacing way and said things that were not relevant. To the man in the club the inspector said, 'I'll shine the torch into the lorry and you can get up and look for your equipment'. The man was understandably reluctant to do this, since the people on the lorry seemed very hostile. The inspector told the people on the lorry to put the tailboard down. After some protests, they did so. Then one of them said, 'You're not going to search this lorry. You can't search it without a warrant'. The police would, in fact, have been perfectly entitled to search the lorry, since there was reason to think it was carrying stolen property. However, there was a total of about 15 people who belonged to the party on the lorry, so even with 12 officers, searching the lorry could have been difficult if the people resisted. Besides, the people in the club (probably about 50 of them) might then have joined in against the police. At this point, DJS was scared.

The inspector ignored the man's remark about needing a search warrant to search the lorry. He shone his torch into the back of the lorry and urged the man from the club to search for his equipment. But there was a line of five men standing inside the lorry and peering out, so he could not see in very far, and he would have had to get up onto the lorry to search it. He was not willing to do so. After the torch had been shone for a minute or two, the man from the club may have caught a glimpse of his loudspeaker. In any case, those in the lorry suddenly disappeared to the back and roughly bundled a loudspeaker out. It was quickly taken into the club by a group including the spokesman, who shortly came out again, saying, 'Wait, I think they've got our record box'. At this, the people on the lorry said, 'Right, we'll be off, then'. The inspector quickly stepped in and said, 'No, you bloody well won't. You're not going anywhere until I say so'. At this point DJS realised that he had taken possession of the keys of the lorry on arriving (about one minute before the van and DJS). After about a minute, people spilled out of the club, saying, 'Yes, they've got our record box'. Again, the people on the lorry denied it by implication.

The inspector said to the man from the club, 'Are you prepared to charge these people with the theft of your record box?' The man did not reply. A man with dreadlocks on the lorry said to him, 'Look, what do you mean by calling in the pigs like this? What do you want to do with these supporters of the National Front, they're a load of Nazis'. The inspector ignored this, and said to the man from the club, 'The law says that I can't charge these people with theft unless you are prepared to sign the charge sheet. Tell me yes or no whether you are prepared to sign it'. The man said, 'I suppose so'. The inspector said, 'I'm sorry but that's not good enough for me. Let me make this absolutely clear. If you will say that you will definitely sign the charge sheet, I will take this lorry into the police station and I will arrest everyone on it and charge them all with theft. Is that clear?' There was a pause, during which an Asian man came out of the club – the only man DJS saw on either side who was not black. He started to tell the people on the lorry to give back the record box. At this, a man with dreadlocks on the lorry said, 'Who are you anyway, some kind of Paki bastard? What have you got to do with us? You're some kind of Paki, aren't you?' The inspector said, 'Never mind about that,' very firmly, thus putting an end to this racialist talk for the time being. He turned again to the man from the club, saying, 'Are you willing to sign the charge sheet, yes or no? I've explained to you that if you are, all these people will be arrested'. After a further pause, he said, 'All right, yes'. For a moment, there was another diversion as the man with dread-locks on the lorry saw that the Asian was wearing a badge (probably a 'fight racism' badge) and said, 'Why are you wearing that badge? What does that badge defend?'. Ignoring this, the inspector said, 'Freddie,' and the area car driver came running forward, 'take it in'. The inspector tossed the keys to Freddie, who went forward to sit in the driver's seat of the lorry. At this, the men on the back of the lorry suddenly disappeared into the darkness behind and then re-emerged with a very large record box which they bundled out of the lorry. This box was holding about 200 records. It was quickly taken into the club.

The inspector immediately restored the keys of the lorry to the group and they were allowed to go. The man from the club came up to him and said, 'Thank you very much, I'm very grateful for your help'. The inspector just said, 'All right, then'. The other officers helped the lorry to manoeuvre out of the tight space it was in. In discussion afterwards the inspector said that he thought the people in the lorry wanted to tempt the police 'into a situation which they would lose'. If the police had searched the lorry, he thought the people on the lorry would have provoked a fight in which those from the club might have joined in against the police as the situation became confused. This was exactly what DJS feared would happen at the time.

In our judgement, this was an excellent piece of police work. First, the relief inspector had gone out to deal with it himself; if he had not, there would have been the possibility of confusion. Second, there were enough police officers there to make the people on the lorry think twice before causing a disturbance, but they stood well back and offered no provocation. Third, the inspector kept control in the classic manner by remaining calm, speaking slowly and clearly and ignoring attempts to cause disruption. Fourth, he was very careful to avoid provoking a fight. One of the reasons for this was that he had his priorities right and preferred to resolve the matter peaceably if possible. However, a powerful reason was that he thought that all of the black people would stick together in a fight, so that the police would be heavily outnumbered. In this part of his thinking he was strongly influenced by the fact that the people were black: if they had been white, he would have considered that he had only 15 people (those on the lorry) to contend with. A further reason for caution was that he saw himself starting a new set of 'race riots' if he was not careful (indeed, a riot could be started by a far more trivial incident than this). Finally, it was interesting that the inspector squashed the expressions of racial hostility towards the Asian man.

A marked contrast *
The [. . .] case that we shall describe in this section involved misjudgements and bad behaviour by several officers. JG was working with a uniformed relief that came on duty at 2 p.m. for the late turn. However, as is usual, the area car crew belonging to JG's relief did not come on duty until 3 p.m., and the early turn area car crew towards the end of its shift answered a call to a council estate where a woman aged 27 had been pushed to the ground, punched and robbed of her handbag. The assailants were described as IC3 (that is, looking black, like West Indians or Africans) and between 15 and 17 years old. One was tall, had hollow cheeks and was wearing a blue duffle coat and a floppy hat; the other was wearing a yellow cap, a brown cord jacket and blue jeans. JG spent the first hour of the late turn (from 2 to 3 p.m.) out with the inspector. He heard about the robbery when two PCs from his relief reported over the personal radio that they had stopped three 'IC3s' as likely suspects for the crime. He and the inspector were not far from where the stop had been made, so quickly arrived at the spot.

The three boys who had been stopped were all aged about 14 (younger, therefore, than the 15–17 years quoted for the assailants). They were of slim build, and none of the three was tall (one of the assailants was described as tall). One of the three who had been stopped was wearing a yellow hat (like the description of one of the assailants) but was wearing a tweed jacket rather than a cord jacket. One of his friends had a floppy hat and a blue coat (like one of the assailants) but the coat was not a duffle coat and the boy was not tall.

It was clear that the PCs had done well to stop and question these boys: they had a number of points in common with the description of the assailants, and it was certainly justifiable to arrest them while the original descriptions were checked and further enquiries made. One of the two PCs who had made the stop checked the descriptions over the radio with the WPC radio operator on the early turn area car. It was evident that the fit was by no means exact.

As the inspector and JG transported Steven (the boy with the yellow hat) to the police station, each commented to the other that the boys looked too young for the description. In the car, the inspector asked Steven a few gentle questions about where he had been and what they had been doing. He protested that he had been at home with his mother until quite recently; the robbery had taken place at 2.30 p.m. and it was now 3.30 p.m. Steven then started to cry and said, 'I don't beat up old ladies, I don't do that sort of thing'. This comment could not have been calculated to deceive; Steven had lost control of himself at the time when he made it. It therefore very strongly suggested his innocence, since the victim was a 27-year-old woman. The inspector did not notice how significant Steven's remark was. No attempt was made to check his alibi with his mother.

At the police station the two PCs who had made the arrests (Barry and Bill) were taking the lead in handling the matter. The station officer performed purely administrative tasks in connection with the processing of the prisoners; he did not supervise or control the actions of the PCs. Although they (voluntarily) gave him a brief explanation of the circumstances of the arrest, he did not ask any further questions, or take any steps to satisfy himself that the matter was being apropriately dealt with. The inspector kept himself informed from time to time about what was going on, but did not intervene decisively at any point.

JG asked the two PCs whether the other two boys had said anything on the way back to the police station; apparently, they had not. As the boys were searched and asked routine questions (for example, the names and addresses of their parents) they were largely cooperative. Steven seemed genuinely frightened and was very compliant. Royston (who had a blue coat and floppy hat) was relaxed and friendly. Donald (the smallest of the three) was a bit cocky. When Barry (the PC who was taking the leading role) explained that he would arrange for the boys' parents to be contacted, Royston said, 'My mum said if I got into any more trouble she wouldn't come down'. He was therefore admitting that he already had a record. In fact, Barry knew him from having arrested him before.

When Steven was asked to sign for his property (as it was taken from him and sealed in a bag) he could only print his first name with the greatest difficulty.

The boys were then locked up separately, one in a detention room, the other two in cells. According to regulations, juveniles should only be put in detention rooms, but the PCs wanted to ensure that they could not talk to each other, and there was only one detention room at the police station. Donald said 'My sister says I can't go in a cell', referring to this regulation. One of the PCs was sure that he said 'My solicitor says I can't go in a cell', but JG is sure that he didn't.

The PCs found cards for all three boys in the collator's records. Steven had been in trouble twice before (criminal damage and carrying an offensive weapon). Royston had similar convictions and one for theft from the person. Donald had a considerable criminal record, including two convictions for robbery. Steven had so far told the truth about his previous record.

On searching the boys, the PCs had found plastic carrier bags on all of them (neatly folded in their back pockets). The PCs were convinced that the bags were for carrying stolen property, or for coats discarded to prevent being recognised.

Barry and Bill now interviewed the three boys one after the other in an unstructured way, hopping from one cell to another, often repeating questions and forgetting the answers that had previously been given. According to the rules of procedure with juvenile prisoners, no interviews should have been carried out except in the presence of the parents or other responsible adult. Acknowledging this, Barry said to JG, 'You realise what you've just seen is quite illegal'. (In fact, it offends against rules of procedure that do not have the force of law.) Also, according to police regulations, what was said during the interviews on both sides should have been taken down, but in fact nothing was recorded at the time.

Barry went in to see Steven first. He asked him what he had been doing during the day. Steven insisted that he didn't do 'that sort of thing' (while admitting that he did other sorts of things that were illegal). Barry raised his voice and said, 'You think about it. If you've done it, you tell me! Now think about it!' This little speech gives a fair impression of the level of subtlety that Barry used throughout the questioning. He and Bill carried out similar interviews with the other boys, though with Royston they were rather more friendly and used the opportunity to pick up information about local characters with criminal records, and to check their knowledge of their nicknames (such as 'Starboy', 'Ratman' or 'Gums') against the real names of the people concerned.

Barry and Bill had not obtained any useful information about the case from these interviews. However, when they discussed with each other what the boys had said they became convinced that two of them (Steven and one of the others) were responsible for the robbery. Although they did not try to justify their opinion in a rational way, their reasons were presumably that:

1   the boys had something in common with the descriptions;
2   they were picked up not far from the scene of the crime (but 45 minutes after it was committed);
3   they had criminal records.

At this point, the WPC who was operator on the early turn area car came into the police station. She said that while she was talking to the victim and walking through the estate, the victim thought she had spotted one of her two assailants five to ten yards away. The WPC approached the youth, who ran away, and the WPC lost him. She had now taken a look at the three boys arrested, and told Barry that Steven was the one she had chased. She did not seem to be entirely sure about this, and became aggressive when JG questioned her more closely about it. Arrangements were being made to bring the victim in, but the PCs did not wait until they had got a full statement from her before questioning the suspects further. The inspector checked up on what was happening, but did not prevent further questioning of the boys without their parents being present, and he did not advise the PCs to wait until the victim had made a statement.

Barry and Bill told JG that there had been two or three robberies or thefts from the person per week on this council estate for some months. They thought a team was at work. Barry said 'I *know* this lot are at it'. JG asked how, and he said, ''Cause I keep my ears and eyes open and I just know'. This illustrated a very important point about the approach of these two PCs. They had very little real evidence, so far, to implicate these youths in this particular crime, and they more or less realised that this was so. On the other hand, these boys had criminal records and were carrying plastic bags, and the PCs were quite convinced that they were engaged in criminal activities of some kind, probably theft from the person, possibly burglary. They were therefore willing to adopt a very low standard of evidence with regard to this particular crime on the argument that they 'knew that this lot were at it'. Whether or not they had committed this particular crime was, morally speaking, a matter of secondary importance – in fact, it was trivial. It was because they were locked into this mental set that the PCs did not attend to the details of the evidence about this particular incident and the possibility of the boys' involvement. It was not so much that they wanted to falsify the evidence as that they were not really interested in what that detailed evidence was.

The home beat officer for the estate (Matt) now came into the police station. He was an experienced and tough policeman who had acted as home beat officer for this estate for a number of years, but had lost none of his appetite for arresting people. He had with him a file on the spate of robberies and thefts from the person, which showed that nearly all the victims alleged that the offenders were black. Matt pointed out (triumphantly) that very few of the victims were black, although a high proportion of the population of the estate was black. Many of the victims were, however, Asians. Matt now visited each of the three boys two or three times, in rotation, to 'interview' them. The parents were not, of course, present. A fair example of his behaviour was his first interview with Steven. He put his face very close to Steven's and said,

> You're a fucking little cunt, aren't you? You've been at it, haven't you, you little bastard? You know what I'm gonna do, don't you? I'm going to nail your fucking hide to the wall! You'll stay here as long as I want you to. You'll stay here all weekend if necessary, until you tell me what you've done.

Matt's 'interviews' with the other suspects were similar.

By this time, Steven's parents had arrived and were left in a room to wait for 40 minutes. Meanwhile further interviews of their son took place. At no time were relatives of any of the boys present while they were interviewed.

The CID were contacted and a detective sergeant came down. JG was not in the charge room when he arrived, but saw him for the first time when he was concluding an 'interview' with Steven, who was crying. The detective sergeant said 'And you'd better stop crying or I'll give you something to cry about!' As he left the cell, he saw JG and asked 'Who's this?' After the explanations, the detective sergeant took Barry on one side to have a private word, making it clear he did not want JG to hear. Barry returned from this conversation full of resentment. He explained that the detective sergeant was not interested in interviewing the boys and going over crime book entries with them to see if they might admit to earlier offences. Not surprisingly, the PCs were annoyed that the CID officer did not want to do his job. Apparently his only contribution had been to bully one of the boys.

Matt and Barry tried again to hasten the arrival of the victim. JG left the charge room for 20 minutes at this time. When he returned, the inspector told him that Steven had 'put his hands up'. JG asked Barry how and why this had happened, and Barry said, 'Well, he's not so sure now'.

At last the victim arrived. She was quite sure she would recognise the two assailants again. She went over the descriptions, which were the same as before. JG asked her (while police were out of the room) whether she was quite sure that one was wearing a cord jacket. 'Positive', she replied. When Barry returned, JG pointed this out to him. He indicated that he began to see the case slipping away from him. The victim also emphasised that one of the assailants was very tall and had very hollow cheeks. None of the boys arrested fitted this description at all. Also, the victim was quite sure she had bitten one of the assailants on the hand – quite hard, because he had let out a yell. Matt went to check Steven's hands. He found one small dark mark, rather like a skin blemish. He suggested to JG that this was a bite mark, but JG disagreed. Five minutes later Barry went to check Steven's hands, not knowing that Matt had already done so (this was typical of the unco-ordinated nature of the investigation). He came back saying there were no bite marks. Various other details of the victim's description did not fit the suspects. Though Royston was wearing a blue coat, it was nothing like a duffle coat, while the victim insisted on the duffle coat description; also Royston's coat had red flashes on it, while the victim insisted that there was no red.

For the first time, the inspector made a positive decision about the investigation of the case. He decided they must let the victim and the suspects see one another and ask the victim whether she recognised them. First, they showed Steven's tweed jacket to the victim. She was sure it wasn't the one worn by her assailant. Apparently the parents or relatives were consulted about the 'confrontation' and agreed (JG did not witness the consultation). Steven's parents were led into the charge room and sat on the bench. Steven was produced and asked to stand against a wall; JG reminded the officers that he should be wearing his hat, which was an integral part of the description. The hat was accordingly produced and put on. The victim was brought in; she was rather nervous but firmly in control of herself. The inspector said, 'This is the young lady who was robbed today. Do you see one of the boys that attacked you in this room?' She answered 'No', and was quite sure about it. The procedure was repeated for Royston, whose mother muttered that this was all a 'disgrace' and that he shouldn't mix with those 'bad boys'. The victim was quite sure that Royston was not involved. When they presented Donald to her, she had to stifle a laugh, because he was so small compared with her attackers. As Royston was released and in the presence of his parents, Matt said to him, 'You don't shit on your own doorstep, all right?' The parents made no objection, and afterwards even thanked the inspector.

Throughout the handling of the case, the PCs involved made complaints to JG about the cumbersome nature of juvenile procedures, although they were not sticking to the procedures anyway. The inspector afterwards wrote up the 'persons at stations' sheet 'professionally' as he put it to JG. His account made it seem that events had turned on the victim's uncertain and changeable descriptions. In fact, the victim had given very clear descriptions, stuck to them consistently and always maintained that she would recognise the attackers. The official record finished with the words '... apologies tendered and no resentment noted', although Royston was sent on his way with the words 'Don't shit on your own doorstep, all right?', and no hint of an apology was offered to either of the other two boys or to their parents. The PCs consoled themselves by saying, 'Never mind, they'll come another day'; this illustrated again that they were concerned to get the boys for something and not to establish their guilt or innocence of some particular offence.

JG could not definitely establish whether the victim thought that Steven was the person she had pointed out to the WPC on the scene, but she gave no indication at all that she had seen him before. What probably happened was that the WPC thought Steven was a bit like the boy who had been pointed out and whom she had chased, and decided to say she was sure it was him because, like the PCs, she had no concern with being particular about the evidence. She was extremely uncomfortable when JG questioned her about the matter (before the victim had arrived at the police station). She would have stood by her identification of Steven if she had not (by implication) been contradicted.

The chief shortcomings in the handling of this particular case were as follows:

1 The decisions were taken in an uncoordinated way by the PCs; there was no effective direction by more senior officers, even though the inspector and, to a lesser extent, the station officer, kept themselves informed about the case.
2 All the officers involved failed to pay proper attention to the evidence as it emerged.
3 One of the officers involved (the WPC) came close to fabricating evidence, by her false identification.
4 Four of the officers involved (the two PCs, the home beat officer and the detective sergeant) used grossly oppressive bullying tactics in the effort to get confessions; at one stage, one of the suspects did confess, in response to these tactics, though it was later proved beyond doubt that he was not guilty.
5 The existence of rules is no guarantee of acceptable behaviour by police officers; the officers involved broke rules with impunity and quite without compunction, with the knowledge of their inspector.
6 The officers attached more importance to the pattern of crime on the estate and to their belief that the suspects 'were at it' than to any facts that might link the suspects with this particular crime.

It remains to consider how far the ethnic group of the suspects influenced the way the officers behaved. On the whole it seems likely that there was a considerable influence of this kind. Matt was particularly concerned to emphasise the racial dimension of crime on the estate and was triumphant in his assertion that virtually none of the victims were black. More generally, JG formed the strong impression that the hostility towards the three suspects, and their conviction that they were 'at it', were connected with a hostility towards black people.

10 Policy Evaluation:
The Use of Varied Data in a Study of a Psychogeriatric Service *
Gilbert Smith and Caroline Cantley

Introduction

Most people engaged in empirical research like to claim that the issues that they are investigating are rooted in scholarship. Nevertheless many of us for much of the time are hired hands without a great deal of academic freedom. We pick up other people's problems, claiming, for a living, some expertise in solving them. But we do not always have to solve them in the way that is expected of us and much of the skill of completing policy-relevant research lies in demonstrating convincingly that the problem is best formulated in a rather different way.

So it is with evaluation. Most often the term 'evaluation' evokes an image of rigorous experimental research design, rational assessment of output, the modification of inputs, and hard quantified data capable of supporting precise judgements of costs or benefits. Above all, objective grounds of judgement are required and this is taken largely to exclude both the 'subjective' views of the evaluator and the subjective assessments of those effecting and affected by the policy. Indeed the exclusion of judgements, views, perceptions and unquantified (as well as unquantifiable) material is frequently taken to be the very stuff of the evaluative exercise.

In this chapter we will discuss a rather different approach to the evaluation of health and welfare services; and it is one that is heavily, although by no means exclusively, dependent upon qualitative data. It also stresses the importance of understanding the perspectives of those

* This chapter draws upon the results of a research project titled 'A Study of Some Problems Associated with the Evaluation of a New Psychogeriatric Day Hospital', based initially in the Department of Social Administration and Social Work, University of Glasgow, and subsequently in the Department of Social Administration, University of Hull. Valerie Ritman was also a member of the research team in Glasgow. We wish to acknowledge grant support from the Scottish Home and Health Department (SHHD). We are also grateful to the members and officials of the (necessarily anonymous) Health Board, to the Consultant and staff of the day hospital, to the patients and their relatives and, for secretarial help, to Mrs Helen Dalrymple in Glasgow and Ms Sue Needham in Hull.

who participate in the programme. In discussing this approach we will, throughout, draw by way of illustration upon the results of a study of the problems of evaluating a new psychogeriatric day hospital. (For an overview of the project see Smith and Cantley 1983a.) Partly we do this because we find it more interesting to write (and read) about the results of specific research projects than to discuss research methods in abstract. Partly we do it because it is easier to argue some of the points that we wish to make through the medium of illustration. But mainly we write in this way because we believe that it is most important to site methodological debate in social context. Far too often textbook discussions of methodological issues bear only scant resemblance to the experiences of research workers who must seek sponsorship, collect data, write their reports and then try to ensure that their conclusions play some part in subsequent policy making and decision taking.

So the chapter will proceed in the following way. We start with the research problem and where it came from. We will then describe some research design difficulties. We will give an account of the data that we collected and will present a selection of these data from one part of the project. Finally we will indicate the kind of policy conclusions that we feel emerge from these data.

The policy problem

The project that is described here began like this. A central government agency with the job of promoting and funding health service research expressed an interest in 'naturally occurring experiments'. The idea was that the study and evaluation of novel, interesting and instructive policy initiatives in one geographical area or one sector of the health service might, if carefully documented, offer lessons of general relevance. At about the same time a local health authority was becoming increasingly concerned about the growing waiting lists for in-patient beds for seriously dependent psychogeriatric patients. The authority opened a 25-place day hospital for patients over the age of 65 with a history of psychiatric disorder. Health service administrators, the consultant in charge and the authority's medical advisers were then keen to have the initiative evaluated with a view generally to future policy on the care of the elderly mentally infirm and, specifically, with a view to deciding about the opening of a second and similar hospital in about two years' time.

It was at this point that one of the authors submitted a proposal for a study to evaluate the hospital from a university base. Although the investigation was planned as an exercise in the broad field of health services rather than within the narrower perspective of clinical medicine, the application was eventually succesful and the research has now been completed.

Smith (1982) has described the early phase of this research in some detail. In the present context a few points are particularly significant. First, our starting problem was essentially a problem for the practical policy maker: 'Was the hospital a success?' and 'Should the health authority build another institution of a similar kind in the near future?' but (and this is important), we did not automatically accept that the kind of study that the administrators and policy makers apparently had in mind was necessarily the best way of proceeding with the design and conduct of the research. Indeed, we concluded that many of the 'rationalistic' ways of thinking about health care evaluation that are often at the heart of the question, 'Is this policy successful?' were not valid in this context. This was because there was clearly a rather wide range of views about the aims and desirable modes of operation of the new hospital (and thus no agreed organisational goals to serve as criteria of success), because the controls of the clinical trial were not available in the setting (and thus nothing even resembling an experimental design was feasible), and because it was clear that in this rather novel institution much had yet to be decided about the service and much would change as the service evolved (and thus the nature of the programme that was to be evaluated could not be unambiguously described as the basis for the research). The design of the rest of the study had to take serious account of these points.

Research design and methods of data collection

On the basis of our analysis of some pilot data (including interviews, hospital records and field observations) certain aspects of the design task were clarified. The research design would have to cope with a plurality of perspectives on the organisation and its services. The design would have to entail ways of gaining an adequate qualitative understanding of several notions of the 'success' of the hospital and varying perceptions of its achievements. The study would therefore have to draw upon a wide range of data sources since it was unlikely that any one type of data alone would be adequate for these purposes.

In line with these requirements we adopted a broad approach to the investigation that we have described as 'pluralistic evaluation'. Elsewhere we have discussed the main features of this approach at some length (Smith and Cantley, forthcoming) but we should highlight some aspects of it here.

The stance draws draws quite heavily both upon theories of political pluralism and upon the 'subjectivist' school within sociology. Thus we are sensitised to the several sets of interests that interact within health service agencies, to the interpretations that are placed upon agency policy as a result of these interests and the tactics that the various groups adopt to pursue their interests as they see them, while nevertheless casting these strategies as being in the interests of the patients and the organisation as a whole. As a first stage, therefore, we identified the most significant constituent groups to the policy initiative and explored, through interviews, their ideological perspectives on the agency. In particular, we collected data on the several groups' interpretations and perceptions of 'success' in service provision. That is not to say that we took these perspectives to *represent* 'success' (on this point, see the discussion of 'pluralistic intuitionist' theory in House, 1980). But we did consider that any evaluative comment that we might wish to make about the agency should embody these criteria within the analysis. Thus, as part of such comment, we would be able to explain if need be why there was a difference between our own perspective and that of a particular group and why, too, perspectives within the agency differed between groups.

The study design also involved data collection on the practical strategies that each constituent group adopted to implement its perspective in its own interest. This entailed assembling material on how groups used their power bases, the negotiating strategies that they adopted, alliances entered into and, above all, how these were presented and justified within the context of a professional service. For we are arguing that an attempt to document the meaning, the pursuit and the public presentation of success in service provision is part and parcel of the evaluative exercise. Additionally, since success is a pluralistic notion, evaluative research must assess the extent to which success (or failure) is achieved on each of the several criteria employed within the agency and in terms of the several meanings assigned to these criteria.

These comments do complicate data collection. It is highly likely that any single data source will represent some perspectives and strategies better than others. For example hospital records are a semi-public presentation of nursing and medical staff views and are cast in terms of a medical perspective. Moreover their use in case conferences, staff meetings, and other group settings means that they have a tactical aspect that colours the way in which they are written. Observational methods are strong in some settings but are of little use, for example, in representing the views of patients' relatives since prolonged observation in the home is seldom possible. Interviews are powerful but are of little (or at least problematic) use with research on the elderly mentally confused themselves who probably most of the time assume that the research workers are medical staff. Thus we must collect as great a variety of data as possible, both qualitative and quantitative, and we must triangulate it upon our problem in order to represent as many perspectives as possible and have available as many checks as possible as to the interests of which constituent group are best being revealed at any one point in the research (see Denzin, 1970).

We decided that only by following these rather complex and difficult directives could we produce an ethnography of the service and some explanation of how it was developing and functioning to serve as the basis for an evaluation. For adequate evaluation in the context of health and welfare services must link the performance of an organisation to the problems, purposes and performance of the organisation as perceived by its members, broadly defined.

So we collected several data sets and by the end of the study our material consisted of transcripts of interviews with staff and with patients' relatives, extracts from patients' medical files and other records, notes on our observations in the field, fieldnotes on naturally occurring conversations, transcripts of the recordings of live meetings and some statistical data based upon our own sample of hospital records and upon some statistics which the hospital administration generated regularly. Sometimes we could use these materials to study different aspects of our problem. Sometimes we could triangulate our data by bringing different kinds of material to bear upon the same question or event. The most important point was that throughout the research our data should be sufficiently rich to reflect the plurality of perspectives that were such an important feature of both the hospital and our research.

In the next section we provide an illustration of the results of this research by discussing just one part of the hospital – a support group for patients' relatives. We draw upon interviews with staff, interviews with relatives, fieldnotes on observed meetings and extracts from the transcripts of recordings of complete meetings. We shall then discuss the implications of these kinds of material for future policy within the hospital and more generally.

Qualitative data on a group for the relatives of psychogeriatric patients

Interviews with staff

The interviews that we conducted with the consultant, health authority officials, nurses and other senior staff including a social worker attached to the hospital, indicated that one of the institution's main objectives (and thus one of the counts on which it should be evaluated) in the view of these respondents, is to provide a general service in support of the patients' relatives. The following quotations are typical of the view that was expressed repeatedly through these interviews:

> *So many of the relatives were just at the end of their tether, they just didn't think they could cope with the patient and they were really ... marriages were beginning to crumble and all sorts of things just because of the strain, and I really think the hospital has helped an awful lot of people that way.*

> *I think that when relatives get despondent and frustrated and there's no one to turn to, and they're on the waiting list that's all they'll get doing — I think it's a very desperate situation to be in and I think this is the biggest area of success that the day hospital has provided as well.*

> *We're offering support to the relatives, I think, even to the extent of, I think, saving somebody's marriage and somebody's family. I think support is a good thing that they [staff] are offering. You're offering comfort, help I suppose, sometimes I think it's more like throwing somebody a lifeline, a lifebelt, y'know, saying 'Well look, it might not be the best but it's the best we can do'.*

The day hospital's objectives in supporting relatives are held to be pursued, especially, through the medium of a relatives group. This group is held regularly and attended by some, but by no means all, of the patients' relatives. The group is described by staff as offering, in particular, emotional support to relatives and education in the care of the patient. For example, one nursing administrator said:

> *I think [the relatives group] possibly has helped some relatives to be able to share their problem with people who have the same problems or greater problems. I think it has helped them, and it has helped them to go back home to look after mother and father in a fresh light.*

And a social worker put the point in her way:

> *[The relatives group] gives this opportunity to laugh and to cry at times and to express anger and the second thing is to educate again, but in a very gentle educative way. It is not full scale education; 'You will come here and you will learn'. But it is a very gentle process.*

Additionally the relatives support group is seen as having therapeutic value for the relatives. The following extract is taken from our interviews with one of the psychiatrists in the area:

> *[The relatives group] provides a setting where people can abreact, they can talk about their feelings and embarrassment and aggression in a group of people who are all on the same footing and I think this is very valuable. .... I'm now sometimes going into a situation in somebody's home where the main problem really is, say, the daughter's feelings about her dementing mother or father where I almost feel that we don't really need to take the patient on but I'd like to take the relatives on. I don't think we have ever really divorced the two things completely. Now I think someone like this is being often helped through the relatives group. So that, I think, is a very valuable part of the day hospital.*

Now in these data and in others like them we have, apparently, a clear criterion for evaluating the day hospital – its success in providing a support service to the relatives of the elderly mentally infirm, in particular through the auspices of a relatives group. There is evidence, too, in these interviews, that the hospital is rather effective on this count. Such a straightforward conclusion, however, would be premature. For there is also evidence that at least some staff are aware that (for instance) 'helping relatives to cope' might be cast from a different perspective rather as 'persuading relatives to reduce their demands'. The following extract is taken from an interview with a social worker:

> *We know when they are asking for a bed without saying, 'Can you give me a bed?' Now they do of course say sometimes, 'We can't take it any longer.' Now because of [knowing relatives] we know how genuine this is. Because of the group, because of everything, we know how genuine this is for that person. ... I think from the hospital administration kind of point of view [the relatives group] is very, very strong – well, a lot of it, just it's a very strong thing in getting people not to ask for beds. ... Y'know we can live on this idea of always living in the community as long as we can keep the patient and the relatives going along. I think that's cruel. I don't believe in that. I believe that they should – there's a limit to these people. But what stops me, actually almost at times going along with this manipulation of relatives, because in a way that is what it is, is because I know there isn't anything to give. This is the biggest frustration of all. Because you know there isn't a bed.*

A psychiatrist presented the same point although in a somewhat different way. (Indeed in an exercise in quantification the two responses would probably be coded together but this would ride rough-shod over the way in which the same operational observations may be variously shaped.)

> *Now [the relatives group] seems to have been of great value – in all sorts of ways – like letting people know that there is a big problem in the shortage of accommodation because they hear other people and see other people with the same sort of problems.*

However, as a nursing officer explained, any tactic of bringing relatives together in order to convince them that they should not press for a bed in a ward because of the seriousness of other cases, may well backfire:

> *Some relatives can use the situation as well to their own advantage ... Because the relatives will possibly get to know other relatives and they will say 'Oh! I just phoned up and I got my father taken in. I just created, or I said I would go to the papers, and I just said I would get my M.P., and before you knew it there was a bed and I knew there was a bed.' You know, this is the kind of dialogue. Whereas they do not know at all what has gone before; the consultation that has been required and the fact that there just may have been a bed become available at short notice.*

So, to summarise, we have here one clear criterion for evaluating the success of the hospital. (Other criteria are discussed in Smith and Cantley, 1983b.) We also have evidence on the way in which staff see the hospital as relatively successful in these terms. However, we learn too that objectives may not always be interpreted in the same way. Also, achievements may not be perceived in the same way. Moreover, if we are to understand the workings of this institution, we shall have to study the tactics which the various groups employ as they seek to reconcile their differences. We must therefore now turn to the relatives' perception of the relatives group and set material from our interviews with relatives against the perspective of health and welfare staff.

Interviews with relatives
The reaction of relatives to the relatives group is by no means straightforward. The following extract from one interview gives some sense of the ambiguity of the data:

Interviewer: *You have been going to the relatives group quite regularly. What do you get out of that?*
Miss S: *Funnily enough after I came home I would say the majority of times I felt quite depressed for some reason and I found that night I couldn't really sleep. Maybe it was just all sinking in and I was thinking how long is this going to go on . . .*
Interviewer: *What made you keep going to the relatives group?*
Miss S: *I don't know, well, when I felt like that, when I came back I should just have said, 'Don't bother going' but while I was there I find it quite interesting.*
Interviewer: *In what way?*
Miss S: *Well, you were learning what they were doing and different things and talking to Sister. I was finding out things that I didn't know about, what Mum was doing, because when she came home she couldn't tell me and it was the one way I could find out how she was getting on.*

What *is* clear is that relatives relate the group to their problems as they see them and to the part that they see the hospital as playing in meeting their needs. Therefore, we, too, shall have to explore this relationship between 'the problem' and service provision if we are to understand how patients' relatives evaluate the relatives group as a part of the hospital service.

We have already noted that not all relatives attend the group and this was a point on which we questioned our respondents in interview. This questioning produced some material on how relatives see this particular service. There are, of course, many practical difficulties associated with attendance (not least of which is the fact that the patient has to be looked after) but attendance and non-attendance cannot be distinguished clearly on this count. Rather attendance depends upon how relatives see their 'problem' and how they expect contact with the hospital and its staff to contribute to solving their difficulties, as they see them. For relatives do not perceive their problem principally in terms of the clinical condition of the patient (as does the hospital, by and large) but rather more broadly in terms of their own overall social situation, of which the patient's infirmities are just one part. So when relatives construe the crux of their problem to be the effect that the patient has upon some wider aspect of their social life and networks which are not dealt with at the group, then they are disinclined to attend. Mr O'N, for example, was unemployed and felt that the task of caring for his mother, which involved visiting her twice each day, was restricting his job prospects:

> *To be quite honest with you I didn't think [that attending the group] would make any difference to me. I could be wrong. Maybe if I did go I'd find out differently. Primarily I'm concerned now – I'm getting a wee bit better now – because I am a skilled man and I haven't got a job and my prime concern is getting employment.*

This is not to say that relatives see no relevance of the group to the practical and emotional difficulties of caring for the elderly mentally infirm. One common expectation that relatives have of the group is that it will provide an opportunity for them to find out more about what is happening to the patient at the day hospital. (Most patients cannot themselves give a coherent account.) This need arises because there is no other routine arrangement made for relatives to visit the day hospital to see what is happening there, nor for them to discuss their relative with members of staff. In particular there are no routine arrangements for relatives to make an appointment with the hospital consultant. Relatives who expect the patient to improve and thus seek discussions with staff see point in attending the group in a way that is not shared by those who see little prospect of improvement and thus little point in going to this extra trouble. Similarly, relatives experiencing emotional stress as a result of caring for the patient may seek support at the group whereas others see little purpose in such activity. For example:

> *I don't think I'll get any benefit out of it. I don't see that I can be of any benefit to anyone else by talking about how I coped or why – it's a thing you've just got to do and that's it. I don't know. The only thing I could get out of it is to persuade somebody that she needs full time care, which is what she needs.*

An availability within the relatives' own social network of people with whom they can share their problem is also important in shaping relatives' views of the utility of the group.

Those relatives who do attend, describe the group as performing several functions. As we have just mentioned, a frequently cited benefit is the emotional support obtained through attendance. But although relatives do indeed appreciate the opportunity to talk to others with similar difficulties, even those who value it see this form of assistance as being somewhat limited. For although relatives undergo a good deal of general stress as a result of caring for the patients, they tend, as we have noted, to see their own problems in terms of the difficulties associated with their particular social situation (such as the problem of obtaining employment). They are all too aware that the benefits of emotional relief are limited and that the central problems for them are no nearer solution as a result. As one respondent explained:

Mrs M: *Well going to the relatives' night you realise that there are folk going through the same problems that you're going through. I mean it doesnae help you any but it makes you see that you are no on your own as far as the problems go. Because everybody seems – they all seem to react the same way and listening to the relatives, well they are having the same thing as you are having.*

Interviewer: *Does that make you feel a bit better about it?*

Mrs M: *Well it eases you that wee bit. I say it doesn't really help you any but it eases your mind that wee bit to realise you're no just having it on your own.*

Moreover, although relatives appreciate particularly having an opportunity to stress to staff what they see as their needs, they do not regard an open forum as always being the best setting for this. Mrs M. made the point:

At the relatives group, I thought it was good for the simple reason that it let me put my point of view to the staff, y'know, how I was coping. This is hard sometimes to do in front of strangers, tell them that your husband is an alcoholic and your sister drinks and things like that.

The point is that since for many relatives 'the problem' is not confined narrowly to the patient but arises from the disturbance which caring for the relative creates in their wider social network (we are stressing this point because it has so many ramifications), any discussion about the problem will entail not only talking about the patient but also talking about family, friends and even neighbours in a way that would not be usual. This discussion is then experienced both as embarrassing and as a betrayal of confidence. Staff are not always aware of this point because they define the problem in a different way.

A second expectation which the relatives have of the group is that it will serve as a source of information about the provision of resources, especially long-term beds. Some relatives think that the group provides them with an opportunity to press their particular case and hopefully influence allocation in their favour. The possibility exists in their mind that by attending the group and providing staff with a full picture of the difficulties at home they might enhance the prospects of a long-term admission. This perspective contrasts with the staff view, which we have reported, that one valuable spin-off from the group is that it *diffuses* some of the pressure which relatives may otherwise exert on the hospital in their efforts to obtain long-term beds.

Third, relatives see the group as an opportunity for the exchange of information about the hospital and the patient. As we have mentioned there is no occasion on which such exchanges *routinely* take place – sometimes with consequences that bordered on the comic. For example, at one stage several relatives were trying to persuade the patient to eat tea at home, not realising that patients had already been given their tea before leaving the hospital. One relative reported that the patient was becoming rather fat as a result, so it emerged, of eating an extra meal each day. More seriously information about drugs and their effects is a constant topic of concern to relatives. Staff tend to describe the exchange of information at the group as an occasion on which they can 'inform' and 'educate' the relatives.

Finally, relatives value the group as a substitute for personal consultation. It is clear that it is a *substitute* for undoubtedly most relatives would value an occasion to discuss the patient and their problems in private with the consultant psychiatrist. Frequently relatives do have a chance to meet the psychiatrist when he conducts a home visit as a basis for deciding whether or not to admit a patient to the hospital. However, relatives do not at that stage know if the patient will be admitted and they have not yet formulated the concerns that they subsequently wish to present to the staff and particularly to the doctor who in their eyes is making the major decisions. The following respondent expressed these feelings:

Interviewer: *Sometimes the relatives go along to the evening meeting because they feel it helps just to talk about the problems of the patient. You don't feel any need to do that?*

Mr B: *I would fine if I was talking to Dr [the consultant] personally. In fact the daughter and I were just saying that if it was possible if we could get an appointment with Dr just to have a wee quiet word with Dr and just talk to him as man to man, although he's a doctor – just to speak to him in a free way. 'Do you think doctor, do you think it's an advantage to my missis or is it more an advantage to me or to the missis?' Y'know that's how I'm wondering.*

And the same relative again made his position clear in a subsequent comment:

Well of course there was one evening we went down. There was a lad there showing a film of some description. Now as far as I was concerned it wasn't of any great interest to me, that is what I am seeking to say. I have no objection at any time to go down if Dr is there . . .

Now on the face of these materials it seems that relatives and staff have a certain amount in common in their approach to the relatives group. However, there are some very important differences in emphasis and presentation in the way in which relatives and staff perceive and construe the group. And these differences in presentation reflect some underlying conflicts between positions and interests. Relatives and staff emphasise different facets of the group in different ways. They present certain features of the group quite differently. And the group plays a different role in solving what staff on the one hand and relatives on the other see as their own and respective problems.

Some of these differences are subtle but significant nevertheless. Both groups mention emotional support. But whereas staff view the provision of such support to relatives as an end in itself, relatives view it as a palliative to the solution of their true difficulties. Both groups mention the importance of information about long-term beds. But whereas relatives see the meetings as occasions on which to press their demands, staff see them as occasions on which they can 'cool out' these demands. Both mention information about the hospital and the patient. But whereas staff speak of their attempts to 'educate' the relatives, relatives glean what they can from meetings in the absence of information conveyed to them in other ways. And both speak of personal consultation. But while staff see themselves as extending a psychiatric service to relatives, relatives are frustrated because they feel that they experience difficulties in gaining direct access to the consultant who (as they see it) is in primary charge of each case.

In order to see how these differences in perception and interpretation work out in social interaction within the relatives group we must now turn to conclusions that we reached about group meetings on the basis of meeting transcripts and field observations.

Observational material

A full analysis of our fieldnotes and transcripts of relatives group meetings is beyond the scope of this chapter. However, we can summarise our general view of the way in which the group works and give some examples of the qualitative materials that led us to these conclusions (see also Cantley and Smith, 1983). In this section, therefore, we shall outline the main categories of interaction which we observed and the main functions that the group performs as the perspectives and strategies of the relatives and the staff become operational. The main headings under which we group our data are similar to those that we have already used in reporting our interviews with staff and with relatives.

First, there is the exchange of practical information. Relatives frequently complain that they do not have a picture of what takes place at the hospital. Staff present relatives with information but they do so in a way that allows them to stress what they consider to be important about the hospital, especially if they sense that the relatives are not really prepared to share their point of view. The following is an exchange from one meeting:

Sister: [Responding to a relative's enquiry] *Each patient that comes to the department comes on an assessment basis; occupational therapy assessment, social work assessment, nursing assessment, medical assessment from Dr D. the Medical Officer, and psychiatric assessment from Dr R. the consultant. That period's usually a month – a month's assessment period where everybody's involved to get a full assessment of the patient and their capabilities the first month they come.*

Social worker: *When they're being assessed, each week we have a weekly meeting with Dr R. and all the staff involved with the patient, and each patient is discussed, how they are getting on, what's happening, something particular of concern . . .*

Mrs H: [She has been looking extremely tense throughout the meeting, not responding much to humour etc.] *How do you find out what they are capable of doing at home? Whether or not they can make themselves a cup of tea, whether or not they can wash themselves when they get up in the morning, how do you . . ?*

Social worker: [In response to this threat – this is not really her area.] *Well we would find out. [The occupational therapist] would find out here in the bedroom, that she's not capable of remembering that the cooker's on, or whatever. If there is such an alarm we would try to do something about that, or you may tell us before they ever get here, you may say to me, 'She can't do that, she can't be left' as all of you do, you all tell me that kind of thing. So I come armed with that kind of information at the start, but [the occupational therapist] and Sister do their own assessment as they're going along, which reinforces whether, not that you've been saying it wrong or it's a lie, but yes she's as bad here as she is there. Sometimes they're better here . . .* [The occupational therapist has tried unsuccessfully to put her point of view during the social worker's speech.]

Sister: *We work on what you call the Crichton Scaling Rate, so we can actually measure the patient's improvement . . . Although you may think your own relative is so demented they can't be rehabilitated at all, but [the occupational therapist] and the nursing team can maybe work on her, so they can dress themselves if they've just got out of the habit of dressing themselves, if their memory recall is not very good, reinforcing it all the time, that is a form of rehabilitation with them.*

Both staff and relatives derive benefit from this kind of exchange but while for staff it provides an opportunity to present to relatives an image of the hospital as an active therapeutically oriented institution, for relatives such occasions are more often used as a starting point for attempting to discuss their individual case.

So a second function of the group is that it serves as a substitute for individual consultation. The following fieldnote reports the attempt of one relative to gain advice:

> *Mrs H said that her mother was getting a good diet and she wondered if she was getting too much. Sister said that she could put her on a 1,000 calorie diet, but the conversation was not specifically conclusive. In some ways these meetings are a very unsatisfactory form of consultation about the patients. They certainly do provide a forum for relatives to talk to Sister especially, and the social worker, about the patients but on the other hand they are cast in fairly general terms so that if a relative wishes to seek some very specific piece of advice or make some very specific suggestion, they have to do this either by collaring a member of staff before or after the meeting (which they tend not to do because there really is not an occasion for this) or, as is more frequent, by interjecting a specific enquiry into the general discussion of the group. This is what happened on this occasion but it is somewhat of a confusion as to whether it really is a discussion about one particular patient or else a general question about, say, the diets of all the patients in the hospital which may be of interest to other relatives as well. Certainly Miss H did not get a very specific conclusion to her enquiry and was not really in a position to push home the point any further without seeming to introduce an inappropriately personal component into the general discussion.*

Quite often the consultations that relatives seek are (at least potentially) rather more disruptive than in this illustration because of the opportunity that they may provide for relatives to make demands on staff time and services. However, used as it is by staff, the relatives group functions to reduce this problem (for them) for genuinely individual consultations are limited to a minority of relatives. Consequently consultations with relatives have minimal impact on the life of the hospital.

A third function of the group which we have observed lies in its use by staff to convey to relatives a picture of the processes of admission, discharge and assessment. In this way the group serves as an instrument of resource allocation. The following is an extract from our fieldnotes on a discussion about discharge that took place at one group meeting:

> Social worker: (addressing relative) '*How do you feel . . . (hesitantly) . . . this is the nasty one now . . . about the possibility of the relatives coming home . . . (as if to anticipate the reaction) with the possibility of coming in again?*' The atmosphere was tense. One didn't have to be a very skilful observer to get that far. Sister filled the vacuum: '*To give everyone a fair share – and not just twenty-five*'. The social worker and Sister both explained that, '*There is a six-weekly assessment – everyone is assessed each six weeks*'. There was a period of quiet and it was clear what all of the relatives were thinking but Miss N was the first to express it: '*It would be no good for me . . .*'

The social worker: *'Would it be important to know?'* (i.e. that discharge was coming in order to be able to make some arrangements). Mrs E: *'For us? ... I think he has improved a bit ... but I was at the end of my tether before he came here ... I could not take any more. I thought he would have to be committed.'* Miss N: *'Well that is how it was for me ... that was the alternative for me.'* Sister said that she well understood that but: *'That is O.K. for twenty-five but there are perhaps three thousand with the same problem – the situation is so chronic – so we just give you a break, that is what the day hospital is for.'* The social worker: *'But I think we shall make it clear – or else you will get a shock ...'* (she is explaining that they will not simply be faced with a very sudden announcement of the imminent return of their relative). Miss N: *'Well I did get a shock – I didn't realise that it was on a six-week basis.'* The social worker explained that perhaps the patient would be discharged for a period but might then be taken back after that. Miss N: *'Well you tell us how we can cope in that period – that is it and you tell us ... I was at the end of my tether.'* Miss D: (entering the discussion without being prompted) *'Yes ... in that period.'*

Staff members who run the group express some pride in the fact that because of such discussions and the work of the group, relatives who attend are most unlikely to exert pressure on the hospital in other ways. Thus again potentially disruptive behaviour is confined in its scope and its troublesome consequences minimised.

In its fourth function the group acts as a forum for negotiation between relatives and staff as to the nature of the patients' conditions. We have already noted that much of the hospital is organised around the view that the patients have potential to recover whereas many relatives do not share this perspective. The following is one record of the way in which discussion between staff and relatives at the group is used, especially by staff, in an attempt to reconcile these differences:

Sister was explaining that what the hospital hoped to do was to get a particular patient 'to a peak'. Mrs T (the patient's wife): *'Then do they come only for a short period?'* Sister said that they were hoping to discharge and then perhaps pick the patients up again and *'then we can give more people benefit ...'* Mrs T: *'But to me – he is making no progress'*. Mrs T Junior: *'He's getting worse'*. Sister: *'But we get him to shave'*. Mrs T: *'Aye, but he won't do it with me'*. Sister: *'I'll have to give you a uniform'* (joking).

Finally, the group serves to provide what, as we have noted, staff describe as a therapy for relatives. However, it is a major ambiguity of the meetings of the group that relatives perceive the *patient* as requiring attention (in the context of the difficulties of their own social situation) whereas staff (and the social worker in particular) view *relatives* also as 'clients' (if not perhaps quite 'patients') and the group as an occasion for providing them with 'support'.

Relatives do indeed experience very intense emotional reactions because of the stress of coping for long periods with their severely disturbed patients. The group is a setting in which they are encouraged and to some extent do feel able to express pent-up anger, guilt and distress. However, the important point in the context of the present analysis is that this kind of emotional release is not encouraged at other times nor in other areas of the hospital where coping with irate or distressed relatives is viewed by staff as an encroachment on their time and a disruption to hospital routines. So this is yet another way in which the relatives group confines organisationally the activities of one constituent party to the institution (the relatives) which might otherwise pose a threat to another constituent party (the medical and social work staff).

Conclusions

Let us now draw some conclusions, or at least indicate the kind of conclusions that can be drawn from qualitative data collected in pursuit of policy evaluation. We began the chapter by suggesting that one of the tasks of the research worker in the field of policy analysis may be that of revising the terms of the original policy question. (It is, after all, a well known principle of the advancement of science that the most difficult part of the investigation is not in finding the answers but in asking novel questions.) We turn back to that point as we give an affirmative response to the query, 'Can qualitative data, of which we have presented examples, assist in the evaluation of social and health policies?'

First, if nothing else, these data show that the simple question, 'Is the hospital a success?' is indeed simplistic. 'Success' is not a unitary concept. We have shown that the important question is not about whether 'the hospital' is successful but rather about whose notions of success we use, what these notions are, in what contexts and what occasions they are employed, how they are pursued, with recourse to what resources, with what objectives, in whose interests, with what consequences, to whose benefit and so on. Answering these questions – an activity that we might describe as the deconstruction of success* – is hardly a task upon which we could embark without heavy reliance upon qualitative data.

Even the limited examples that we have presented in this chapter, however, allow us to take the argument somewhat further than this. It is clear that there *are* important differences in perspective, especially in the context of the present study, as between staff and relatives. Of

* We are grateful to the anonymous reader of another manuscript for suggesting this term. Some might regard it as a piece of jargon but it does capture the essence of the task and it is economical. An alternative phrase might be 'unpacking success'.

course, there are also differences of perspective within as well as between groups and these differences may be equally significant for studying some aspects of the institution. We have discussed in particular the way in which staff adopt a primarily 'clinical' perspective on the patient whereas for relatives the problem is generally a rather broader one entailing various aspects of their social setting. Although some staff (especially social workers) may espouse a perspective which is at variance with the 'medical model' our observations have shown how this poses a threat to the smooth running of the hospital, the routines of which, as a medical institution, are geared to 'curing' patients and are organised around the traditional hierarchies of professional medicine. The question which Howard Becker (1970) posed for students of institutions over a quarter of a century ago has not lost its point. Data on significant differences in perspective on the organisation throw into sharp relief his question, 'Whose side are we on?'

Having addressed this question, data of the kind that we have described may take us a little further still. One of the major weaknesses of institutional evaluations which rest very heavily upon the *quantification* of output measures is that they do not in themselves give much information about the social processes at work within the institution that produced the outputs. But because the research approach that we have followed does entail documenting the various groups' alliances, power bases, negotiating strategies and so on – all in pursuit of success – it offers an explanation of *why* success in particular terms has been achieved. In turn this allows policy makers to understand why success in some other terms may *not* have been achieved and they are offered some clues about what action to take in order to rectify that state of affairs if they so wish. As an illustration, we have shown in the relatives group of this hospital how relatives' criticisms of the service are disarmed, how their demands are contained and how their reactions which may be disruptive are stifled. We have also shown how relatives, for their ends, use the group to press their demands (albeit not very successfully) and to obtain some services that cannot be obtained in other parts of the hospital. And, if they feel that they are clearly at odds with the staff perspective, they simply do not attend. We can draw from these observations indications of several ways in which, in practice, relatives could be placed in a more powerful position with respect to hospital services. For example, staff membership of the group could be changed. Consultation arrangements could be altered. Relatives, as a matter of routine, could be involved in several other aspects of the hospital in order to ensure that their perspective was taken more seriously.

Indeed one possible implication of our data is that relatives might actually be in a stronger position to influence hospital services without the relatives group. At least some of our material suggests that the group functions to confine relatives to a relatively isolated part of the institution and thus limit the organisational impact of their influence. The group therefore has what might be described as the 'ghetto' effect. If this conclusion has merit it is certainly an ironical one. For it means that the relatives group, established on the face of it, to provide a service to relatives, may actually be functioning with an almost opposite effect. Noting what have been termed the 'unanticipated consequences' of policies in organisations is, of course, by no means novel but it is nevertheless a clear strength of qualitative data of the kind that we have presented that they are inclined to highlight (rather than obscure) such features of health and welfare services.

There is at least one further important advantage in the use of qualitative research in policy evaluation and it is this. It is all too easy in a highly quantified account of organisational inputs and outputs to concentrate on the service but give very little attention to the problems that the service is purportedly designed to solve. As we have pointed out it has been an important part of the methods of data collection described in this chapter that we have paid very close attention to the 'problem' as perceived, presented and incorporated into the action strategies of those providing and in receipt of the service. Indeed our approach to describing the service and evaluating it has meant that analysis of the 'problem' has been a central part of the evaluation of policy. Thus the way is open for an understanding of the interaction between 'policy' and 'problem'. As we have stressed throughout, this interaction is such that it is not sensible to try to change or understand the one without the other.

Finally, we wish to conclude the chapter on a note of caution. Qualitative material is by no means a complete substitute for quantified analysis in policy evaluation. But in a field such as the evaluation of innovative health or social care programmes, the potential of observational materials, in particular, has not been explored as fully as it might have been. This is particularly true where the problems of researching 'success' that we have described at the start of this chapter are concerned. We are aware too that some of the problems of power, authority and control that we have touched upon are beyond the scope of a study in which little data have been collected beyond the organisational boundaries. Tactics are only a part of the story. We would argue, however, that in any study of the place of the institution and its constituent groups in the wider social system, qualitative data should play as significant a part as they should play in a study of the evaluation of 'success' from within.

References

Becker, H. 1970, 'Whose side are we on?', ch. 8 in *Sociological work: method and substance*, Chicago, Aldine Publishing Co.

Cantley, C., Smith, G. 1983, 'Social work and a relatives support group in a psychogeriatric day hospital: a research note', *The British journal of social work*, vol. 13, no. 6.

Denzin, N. K. 1970, *The research act in sociology: a theoretical introduction to sociological methods*, London, Butterworths.

House, E. R. 1980, *Evaluating with validity*, London Sage.

Smith, G. 1982, 'Some problems in the evaluation of a new psychogeriatric day hospital', in Taylor, Rex, Gilmore (eds.), *Current trends in British gerontology*, Gower, Aldershot, England.

Smith, G., Cantley, C., Ritman, V. 1983a, *Pluralistic evaluation: a study in day care for the elderly mentally infirm*, end of grant report submitted to the SHHD, University of Hull, Department of Social Administration (mimeo.).

Smith, G., Cantley, C., Ritman, V. 1983b, 'Patient turnover in a new psychogeriatric day hospital: a pluralistic evaluation, *Ageing and society*, vol. 3, no. 3 (in press).

Smith, G., Cantley, C. (forthcoming), Pluralistic evaluation in Lishman, J. (ed.), *Research Highlights*, University of Aberdeen.

PART IV
The Product

11 Evaluating Applied Qualitative Research
Robert Walker

My intention in this chapter is to draw together much of the material presented in earlier chapters in order to assist the reader to answer the following questions:

1   How good is a proposal for a qualitative research project?
2   How can I ensure high quality qualitative research?
3   How good is a piece of qualitative research? How reliable are its conclusions?

Questions 1 and 3 raise important issues for both the producers and consumers of qualitative research. Question 2 is of most concern to the person commissioning and managing qualitative projects.

How good is a proposal?

A research proposal or tender should provide sufficient information for the reader to make a reasoned judgement as to the value of the research proposal. It must as a minimum:

1   establish the rationale for the project, whether based in theory or policy reality;
2   clearly specify the objectives;
3   discuss the choice of design and describe the methods proposed;
4   describe the procedures of analysis;
5   describe the research outputs and method of presentation;
6   discuss staffing;
7   define timing;
8   present costs.

This minimum specification applies equally to proposals for qualitative or quantitative work; moreover, it is worth noting that each item is dependent on earlier ones in the list and a well constructed proposal will make these relations explicit. This is not to say that cost is the last thing to be considered; policy makers are prone to ask, for example, 'What can be learnt for £20,000?' and most research is subject to an externally/extraneously determined budget. However, for presentational purposes the iterative process of tailoring methods and objectives to cost is frequently omitted except where costed alternatives are considered to be appropriate.

Rationale

By definition applied research is likely to be conducted within a policy context, an understanding of which may be a prerequisite to the production of valued and implementable findings. Where research is commissioned by policy makers, an understanding of their interests, motives and those of their political and bureaucratic masters should be (though rarely is) apparent from the research brief which they prepare for researchers. It is encumbent upon the researcher to try to establish a firm grasp of his client's needs by initiating further discussions or by other means before submitting a proposal. The perspective of other actors in the policy arena will probably be less well understood at the beginning of a project and indeed a research objective may be to describe them more fully. Nevertheless, whatever is known should serve to inform the rationale of a project.

The nature of qualitative research is such that the theoretical rationale is likely to be less well developed than with a quantitative study. Typically quantitative research is concerned to investigate specific theoretical propositions deduced from a more general theoretical system. Even where this process is not made explicit, quantitative research requires *a priori* statements or assumptions about the relevance of particular concepts and about the means of operationalising them (see Chapter 1). Qualitative research is more frequently concerned to identify concepts in the data and to develop a theory which incorporates them. Only rarely, however, does this exclude the qualitative researcher from the need to acquire a knowledge of the empirical and theoretical research likely to impinge upon the research issue. This should be applied to identify pertinent issues that might be illuminated by research but care should be taken not prematurely to foreclose potentially fruitful lines of enquiry. Such scholarship also provides the research commissioner with an indication of the researcher's ability to handle conceptually the study findings.

Objectives

Without a clear statement of objectives it is impossible to assess how useful the results of a research project are likely to be or whether an appropriate methodology is proposed. Certain generic sets of objectives attainable by qualitative methods are listed in Table 1.2 but a full list would be very long. One important consideration, however, is whether the qualitative research is to complement quantitative research at any stage in a project. In such circumstances, the objectives of the qualitative research may differ markedly from those of the quantitative component and from the project as a whole. These differences should be made explicit. It is rare that a single research design can optimally meet all the objectives and so it is therefore useful to give them priorities.

Choice of design

Table 1.1 compares the characteristics of four methods discussed in this volume. These should be borne in mind together with the objectives of the project, the nature of the research topic or topics and the characteristics of the research subjects when choosing a particular strategy. The reasons for the final choice and the strength and limitations of the resultant design should be made explicit in the proposal. Of course, it is frequently not a matter of a single method but of a number used on different occasions for different purposes. The real art of design is to select from the many techniques and to marry the chosen ones in mutually supportive ways. Moreover the flexibility inherent in qualitative methods means that it is often inappropriate to specify all stages in advance. To avoid an open-ended financial commitment it is wise to arrange the budget so that it contains contingency reserves.

The research proposal should include a discussion of the sampling method although it may be impossible to characterise fully the sample in advance. The sampling unit or units should be specified; hierarchical designs will not infrequently be appropriate where, for example, the focus may be upon individuals within different institutions. The sampling method will probably be purposive – or theoretical – rather than representative. That is, the sample will comprise small numbers of people with specific characteristics, behaviour or experience which may be postulated to offer different perspectives on the research problem. These groups may not be known in advance; rather the sample may be specified incrementally as analysis of completed interviews suggests other groups which might usefully be included for analysis. A sample would be deemed complete when no new groups were suggested by the analysis or when the marginal insight from additional interviews levelled off. (In practice a more immediate criterion might be the marginal cost of obtaining additional insights.)

The proposed method of recruiting respondents should also be outlined. For group and individual interviews, this may be undertaken by specially trained recruiters charged to fill quotas systematically from partial or complete sampling frames. (A complete frame might, for example, be the register of a professional association; a partial frame would be every ninth dwelling in a roughly defined neighbourhood.) With fieldwork, recruitment and the final sample may be less formal and depend on accidental contact or snowball sampling (i.e. contacting persons suggested by persons already contacted).

A proposal should briefly discuss the implications of sampling and recruitment for analysis and the extent to which they undermine the general applicability of the results. Where appropriate, the methods proposed to minimise sample bias should also be described.

One would expect a section on method also to state where the interviews or group discussions are to be held and why; to discuss transport provisions if appropriate; to outline the kind of briefing which interviewers and field staff will receive and the procedures for facilitating information exchange during fieldwork; and, finally, to detail the method of recording interviews and, if they are not to be taped and fully transcribed, to justify why.

Analysis

Without competent analysis, the yield from a rich crop of data may be negligible. Unfortunately what a proposal can reveal about analysis is strictly limited. It should state who will undertake the analysis and their track record is perhaps the best guide to the final product. It should specify the time set aside for the analysis which will suggest the extent and detail of analysis envisaged. (For some purposes, exhaustive analysis may be inappropriate although in such circumstances thought needs to be given as to whether less comprehensive methods of data gathering might not suffice.) One would also look for some statement of how transcriptions are to be handled, how the data are to be organised, what software is to be used and, ideally, an outline of the analytic model proposed (see below). It should be remembered that with qualitative research, data gathering and analysis are very often neither in time nor logic distinct and a good research proposal will discuss ways in which the potential interaction between these twin processes will be exploited and managed.

Research outputs and presentation

A written report is unlikely to prove sufficient as a means of reporting qualitative findings. Qualitative material cannot be adequately summarised – there is no qualitative equivalent of descriptive statistics. Instead a report must be selective and, while a skilled researcher should be able to report adequately to his brief, the client will undoubtedly welcome the opportunity to explore certain issues in greater detail. Also, the understanding acquired through the very personal, frequently interactive process of qualitative research is often best conveyed through verbal presentation and discussion. Therefore, depending on the nature of the project, a good proposal will be characterised by provisions for supplementary verbal presentations and, most probably, by extensive debriefing ahead of the final reporting to decide the foci to be adopted.

Finally, some mention of the degree of confidentiality which is to be accorded the research subjects should be included. (There may be a case for a more general statement as to how their interests should be protected, see below.)

Staffing

The depth interviewer, group moderator or fieldworker needs to be able to receive and comprehend a broad brief and to use it as a 'springboard rather than as something to be slavishly followed' (Hedges, 1981). In the light of their understanding of the brief, they have to take decisions about which lines of enquiry to pursue and which to forego. Such 'executive-level' skills of interpretation and decision are seldom possessed by junior researchers.

Similar executive-level skills are required for analysis and the symbiotic nature of data collection and analysis is sufficient reason for the same people to be involved in both stages. Indeed, where this is not to be the case, a proposal should be specific about how insights gained during fieldwork are to be passed on to the analysts. As noted above it is often appropriate for the proposal to name the principal researchers involved and the precise contribution they are to make.

Timing

Qualitative projects are highly variable in length depending on the objective and techniques employed. Sometimes lead times are very short giving qualitative projects an edge over quantitative ones. However, certain aspects of qualitative research are very time-consuming and cannot readily be skimped. If a proposal allows less time than the minimum figures given in Chapter 2, the research is likely to be less than thorough.

Cost

The combination of expensive research time and time-consuming processes means that a competent research proposal is likely to work out expensive when expressed on a per-respondent basis. In research, as in many things, you tend to get what you pay for. What a proposal should do is to indicate precisely how the money is to be spent.

Ensuring quality research

The leverage which a research client has over the quality of research is of two main kinds: facilitating and coercive. The first is about communication and, as far as is practicable, consumer involvement in the research. The second is about the steps that may be taken to ensure that best practice procedures are adopted. Both strategies entail additional costs to the consumer and contractor although if successful these should be well justified. As on so many occasions, a mixed approach is perhaps the most productive although adoption of the first strategy lessens the requirement to apply the second.

Good communication begins with the research brief. This should state as clearly as possible what the client needs to know and why. Initially, at least, the research brief provides the researcher's only window on the policy context and yet for research to have maximum value it must be sensitive to this context. The closer the researcher is permitted to get, the more directly relevant will be the research questions asked and the less the interpretation that is required before the findings can be used for policy purposes. A good research brief will elicit a better research proposal. Moreover, the dialogue should continue in such a way that revisions to the research brief can reflect advice as to how policy questions may be formulated in research terms.

Often, in lengthy projects, communication channels ossify at significant cost to the research. Changes in the policy environment need to inform the development of the research. But more specifically, there is a strong case for continued involvement of the research client, the policy maker or decision taker in the process of research (Walker, 1981). Participation of the client in the briefing of fieldworkers can markedly increase the latter's sensitivity to key policy issues. Moreover, visiting the research location, observing group discussions and meeting observers is likely to add greatly to the policy maker's understanding of the policy world and of his contribution to it, provide a grounding in reality for his interpretation of the research findings, and may increase his appreciation of the research task and its related difficulties. Similarly, involvement in analysis, as Sue Jones proposes, can ensure that policy relevances are given appropriate attention in the interpretation of the data and increase confidence in the reliability and validity of the findings.

Perhaps many researchers would interpret extensive involvement by policy makers as an unwelcome interference. Maybe, also, the final product would differ little from that produced by a good researcher working to a good research brief. But, if 'first hand involvement' is seen as crucial to a researcher's understanding of the social world, it would seem to be equally the case for the policy maker (Filstead, 1970).

The second approach to quality control is to initiate checks that what should be done is done. Malpractice may be more frequent in qualitative research than in quantitative because the opportunities and incentives are greater and because consumers are unaware, or too little concerned, with matters of quality control.

However, it is equally true that, because of the heavy reliance on tape recorders in data collection, malpractice is simpler to check. Many of the procedures suggested below are already standard practice in reputable research agencies. Conscientious recruitment of respondents is essential for the reliability of qualitative research. Recruitment is frequently a soulless task and the temptation to cut corners is strong. Recruiters should be asked to complete returns on all contacts, i.e. including those excluded from the quota, and random checks should be undertaken. Tapes of interviews and transcriptions should be obtained to confirm that the interviews have actually taken place and that the interviewer was the person named on the proposal. Lists of times and venues for group discussions should be obtained in advance to facilitate spot checks for similar reasons. Annotated transcripts should be inspected to check the quality of analysis. Material quoted in reports is best indexed to individual transcripts so as to establish that it is drawn from a greater rather than a lesser range of respondents. Fieldstaff and analysts should be 'debriefed' to confirm that they have indeed 'immersed themselves in the data'.

How good is a project?

Evaluating a final 'report' is in many ways easier than evaluating a proposal. Instead of peering into the future and backing hunches as to whether, for example, the sampling will prove sufficiently robust or the researchers be capable of handling the analysis, the results are at hand. While many of the same considerations remain relevant, the substance of the data and the way in which they are marshalled to enrich understanding of the policy issues bear most heavily on one's final judgement. It should be stressed that for much of this section it is assumed that the final report will be a written document. As has already been noted, this may not be the most appropriate way of presenting the output of qualitative research (see also below).

Gerry Rose (1982) has provided a framework for deciphering reports based on qualitative methods which may be expressed, slightly modified, in question form:

Summary
1 What is the natural history of the research?
2 What data were collected and by what methods?
3 How was the sampling done?
4 How was the analysis done?
5 What were the results presented?
Evaluation
6 How valid are the concept-indicator links?
7 How valid are the theories or hypotheses?

8　When theorising, has the author kept to the limits imposed by his sample selection?

9　What is the external theoretical validity of the research?

Answers to questions 1 through 5 serve to summarise the report and to classify the raw material of evaluation. Questions 6 through 8 provide a mechanism for addressing the fundamental question of whether the author's conclusions are consistent with his data. Question 9 focuses on the contribution made by the research to understanding of the phenomena considered.

It should be emphasised, as Rose (1982, p. 140) does, that the above list constitutes 'a framework for the presentation of the reader's analysis, rather than an inflexible step-by-step procedure'. Moreover, 'the most common problem in applying the procedure will be lack of information in the research report' (Rose, ibid). Reporting a qualitative study in a fully detailed form is difficult but a failure to do so inevitably lessens the reader's ability to evaluate the research adequately and must consequently undermine his faith in the validity of the findings.

Many of the issues in the above list have already been covered and the focus here is therefore selective.

Natural history

Qualitative research is rarely tightly structured in advance. Progress, in terms of evolving hypotheses and design, is usually contingent upon what has been learnt before, so that in evaluating the final output it is valuable to know which avenues were followed and which were rejected and why. The importance of a project's natural history is sometimes recognised formally in the procedures of data collection and analysis. Becker and Geer (1982) see the fact that a participant observer constantly redesigns his study in the field in the light of new data as evidence of a continuous analytic activity. They therefore propose that it is possible to conduct a sequential analysis in a formal and self-conscious fashion leading to a 'set of tentative conclusions based on a running analysis of the field data instead of a mass of undigested fieldnotes' (p. 240). Similarly Schatzman and Strauss (1973) suggest that fieldnotes should be organised into observational notes, theoretical notes and methodological notes resulting in three developmental strands.

Regardless of whether analysis is handled in this fashion, a report should be expected to discuss the policy context in which the research was conceived, the original purpose of the study and the initial design, how these developed and, particularly, what factors or findings led to major shifts in direction and, most notably, how the report relates to the present policy context. Whether it is appropriate to cover all these points in a specific section of the report will naturally depend on context. Moreover, certain projects, particularly those with short lead times, may have undergone relatively little development since conception: this is nevertheless worth recording.

The significance of the natural history is that it provides a context within which to evaluate all subsequent aspects of the study according to the Rose framework. It can help explain why the study may in some respects be deficient and provide a basis for assessing how far those deficiencies undermine the value of the findings.

Data and analysis
Throughout this volume it has been stressed that data yielded by different techniques differ in kind: interviews provide information on reported behaviour, attitudes and beliefs; discussions yield respondent reports offered in the knowledge that they may be subject to group criticism; observation offers descriptions of behaviour in a specific context. It is therefore necessary to ask whether the kind of data collected is that demanded by the problem at hand.

Another aspect of the same question, 'how good are the data?', focuses on the implementation of the data gathering techniques. Were the procedures, outlined above and discussed in earlier chapters, followed? We need to ask, for example, what or who is the source of the data? What faith we have in this source? How far are the data contaminated by prestructured questioning or biased sampling or distorted by poor microphones or by over-selective listening? What is the effect of context? Who else was present at data collection? What was the impact of the interviewer or significant others? Do the respondents say what they mean and mean what they say? What might have been the ulterior motives of the respondents? In what ways might prior contact with the researcher or knowledge of the project and/or its sponsor have affected responses? Would their considered response have differed from the spontaneous one (or *vice versa*)?

One must also ask whether the analysis suits the data and, moreover, whether it can illuminate the policy problem. Previous chapters have illustrated the personal nature of qualitative analysis but also the fact that it must be rigorous, systematic, comprehensive and sensitive to the data at hand. Analysis involves 'fracturing' data into 'lumps of meaning' (e.g. events, actions, acts, statements, concepts) and a subsequent restructuring, first by categorisation and then by developing relationships between categories. At one level this raises practical issues about the technology used to facilitate this laborious process. Schatzman and Strauss's system of recording fieldnotes has already been cited (see also Burgess, 1982, and Lofland, 1971). Moreover the advent of sophisticated text management systems (INFOTEXT, BASIS etc.) expands the boundaries of qualitative research both with respect to the complexity of relations that can be explored within the data and perhaps also to the scale of qualitative studies that can be envisaged.

A more fundamental issue concerns the nature and origin of the categories used in coding; the extent, in particular, to which they emerge from the data or are imposed upon them. This links both with the objectives of the research (i.e. whether the intention is to generate theories or policy ideas or to test them) and with the methodological tradition within which the research is being pursued.

The latter is, at first sight, the simpler point. A researcher of the humanistic tradition will want the respondent's view of his world to stand uncontaminated. The positivist is more likely to structure the data through the questions he asks; even in a preliminary project he will primarily be interested in concepts that would be amenable to later measurement (Halfpenny, 1979; Faraday and Plummer, 1979). In applied research things are never quite so simple since the researcher will approach the data with the research relevancies of the client foremost in his mind. Sue Jones, in effect, proposes a triangulation when she notes the value of repeating the process of categorisation basing it first on the 'concrete concepts' of respondents and, then, on the client's policy agenda.

Turning to the role of theory, Glaser and Strauss (1967) have compared several approaches to the analysis of qualitative data according to whether they are most frequently used, and/or most suited, to theory generation or testing. Their typology is presented in Table 11.1. Many would argue (e.g. Rose, 1982; Ford, 1975) that, in practice, each approach involves elements of theory creation and testing. Thus, for example, ethnographic description (strategy 1), which typically aims to present a description expressed entirely in the terms of the participants' concepts and categories, is presented by Glaser and Strauss as neither generating nor testing hypotheses; in reality much of an ethnographer's time is spent checking 'hunches' (hypotheses) against experience as they search for patterns in their data.

Strategy 2 seeks to test *a priori* propositions by coding and analysing all *relevant* 'data'. A paper cited by Glaser and Strauss describes a three-stage process of sequential analysis:

(1)   the selection and definition of problems, concepts and indices;
(2)   the check on the frequency and distribution of phenomena; and
(3)   the incorporation of individual findings into a model of the organisation under study (Becker and Geer, 1982, p. 241).

'Sequential analysis' fits Glaser and Strauss's typology most closely

Table 11.1
Analysis and theory

Theory generation	Theory testing	
	No	Yes
No	(1) Ethnographic description	(2) Test prior hypotheses against data (e.g. sequential analysis)
Yes	(3) Inspection for hypotheses	(5) Inspection for hypotheses followed by preliminary testing
	(4) Constant comparative method	(6) Analytic induction

Adapted from Glaser and Strauss (1967) and Rose (1982).

when the researcher has a 'larger problem in mind and [searches] for specific indicators to use in studying it' and when his conclusions are 'implicitly numerical' even though they are not precisely quantified. Such an approach is a close analogue to the normal quantitative/ positivist model of research and may be most common when existing technologies prevent precise measurement of the phenomena under consideration.

Sequential analysis need not be as rigid as portrayed by Glaser and Strauss and when concepts are allowed to emerge from the data it has much in common with strategies 3 and 5. The latter two both involve an iterative process of theory development whereby concepts and relationships are formulated from the data through inspection, the data are then reviewed leading, where necessary, to a redefinition of the initial concepts. However, strategy 5 involves the preliminary testing of the results and hypotheses usually in quasi-quantified fashion before concluding the research (see Becker, 1958; Lofland, 1971). Strategy 3 may typically be associated with pilot or preliminary projects where subsequent numerical analysis is anticipated.

Strategy 4, the constant comparative method, is presented by Glaser and Strauss as a means of systematising strategy 3. Three stages are involved before write-up:

1 Each incident in the data is coded into as many categories as possible, comparing each incident with the previous incidents in

the same and different categories and with incidents occurring in different comparison groups.

2 Continued coding is accompanied by a shift in the unit of comparison. Instead of comparing incident with incident, the characteristics of each new incident are compared with the properties of the category that resulted from the initial comparison of incidents. This leads naturally to an integration of categories and then of their properties.

3 Underlying uniformities in the original set of categories or their properties are identified such that the theory can be formulated with a reduced set of higher-level concepts. The categories themselves become 'theoretically saturated' so that new incidents cease to contribute to an understanding of the categories' properties (and cease to be coded unless they do). The theory 'solidifies', at which point it is possible to write it up.

During the first two stages the data base will typically expand rapidly as new comparison groups are sampled according to 'their theoretical relevance for furthering the development of emerging categories, properties and integration of the theory' (Glaser, 1982, p. 228).

Glaser and Strauss (1967, p. 103) argue that the constant comparative method does not facilitate theory testing because:

> In theoretical sampling, the data collected are not extensive enough and, because of theoretical saturation, are not coded extensively enough to provide provisional tests as they are in the... [second and fifth approaches]... They are coded only enough to generate, hence to suggest, theory.

In this approach, therefore, the concepts and theory would seem to be grounded to such an extent that generalisation is impossible. In practice, of course, the responsibility of generalisation passes to the reader who evaluates the theory's applicability to his areas of interest. Also, further comparisons of one substantive theory with others can lead to the generation of formal theory (i.e. that relating to a formal or conceptual area of sociological enquiry) which should be applicable to further diverse substantive areas with minimal qualifications (see Glaser, 1982).

The final approach discussed by Glaser and Strauss is analytic induction which is described by Cressey (1950, p. 31; quoted in Robinson, 1951) as follows:

1. A rough definition of the phenomenon to be explained is formulated.
2. A hypothetical explanation of that phenomenon is formulated.
3. One case is studied in the light of the hypothesis with the object of determining whether the hypothesis fits the facts of that case.
4. If the hypothesis does not fit the facts, either the hypothesis is

reformulated or the phenomenon to be explained is redefined, so that the case is excluded.

5. Practical certainty may be attained after a small number of cases has been examined, but the discovery by the investigator or any other investigator of a single case disproves the explanation and requires a re-formulation.

6. This procedure of examining cases, redefining the phenomena and re-formulating the hypothesis is continued until a universal relationship is established, each negative case calling for a re-definition or a re-formulation.

At its most ambitious, therefore, analytic induction aims to generate and prove an integrated, limited, precise, universally applicable theory of causes accounting for phenomena identified during field-work. Despite its many limitations (see McCall and Simmons, 1969), the analytic induction model remains very influential and indeed appears in Peter Abell's recent exposition of comparative narratives (see Chapter 1 above and Abell, 1983).

It is important that the reader of a research report should understand the analytic model that is adopted and be provided with sufficient information to judge both the credibility of the categories, relationships and concepts which are used (or emerge) in the analysis and to gauge the stringency of any tests performed.

> A cardinal rule for the researcher is that whenever he himself feels most dubious about an important interpretation – or foresees that readers may well be dubious – then he should specify quite explicitly upon what kinds of data his interpretation rests. The parallel rule for readers is that they should demand explicitness about important interpretations, but if the researcher has not supplied information then they should assess his interpretations from whatever indirect evidence may be available (Glaser and Strauss, 1970 pp. 232–3).

The information provided may take the form of quotations, incidents or anecdotes. For these to be convincing, they must be accompanied by adequate detail concerning the source, the context and the rationale for selecting them as examples (i.e. they are typical, counter-intuitive, etc.).

Evaluation

Questions 6 to 8 in Rose's schema force consideration of the validity or accuracy of the findings and of their reliability; that is whether the same findings would have been discovered by another researcher. It is helpful to identify four aspects of validity: descriptive, conceptual, theoretical and external.

At one level *descriptive validity* involves asking whether each incident, event, act or indicator is really what it is thought to be (by the researcher). Evidence needs to be sought as to the quality of the data (see previous section) and particular attention paid to whose perspective most conditions the description of an incident and with what consequences. Descriptive validity is in this case analogous to measurement validity in quantitative research (Smith, 1975).

But judgements appertaining to the 'authenticity' of the description are also important. Runciman (1983) has proposed a number of forms of 'misdescription': incompleteness, oversimplification, suppression, exaggeration and ethnocentricity. Incompleteness may arise from the neglect of institutions and practices which are only peripheral to the researcher's own theoretical interests but which are of much closer significance to the people he is studying. Similarly, oversimplification may result from a failure to ask informants for a description in *their* terms which would have resulted in further elaboration. Suppression and exaggeration may be deliberate, the former when details are excluded which would make the description less favourable to the researcher's chosen cause, the latter when description is overstated to make a case for purposes of his own. Ethnocentricity arises when assumptions of the researcher's own milieu are inappropriately mapped onto the experiences of members of another.

In judging authenticity the reader is again forced to rely in part on indirect evidence and, most notably, on his own experience and intuition.

Conceptual validity concerns the extent to which the concepts used fit the data. Does the content of the category correspond with the description of it? Are the instances included sufficiently similar to be included together? Are the categories comprehensively defined (i.e. 'saturated') or still emerging? Are different categories in fact different? Are the concepts those used by respondents, and if so, by which respondents, or are they conceptual tools of the researcher, in which case, were they established *a priori* or *a posteriori*?

Consideration of both conceptual and descriptive validity are necessary to establish the validity of the concept-indicator links (Rose's question 7). In most, but not all, qualitative research the concepts will be derived from inspection of the data. If the concepts themselves are of suspect validity, so must be the resultant theory.

Theoretical validity relates to the way in which concepts are handled and the 'coherence' of the resulting theory. Consideration needs to be given to the following questions: what is the intended relationship between data and theory, and the balance between the building and testing of theory? How are concepts and categories merged? What are the relationships between concepts and how are they defined and determined? Do the relationships stand in a logical relationship to one another or are they empirically determined? How well are empirical relationships established? Which concepts and relationships are least supported in logic or evidence and how significant are these for the theory as a whole?

External validity is here used in a more restrictive sense than in the Rose's framework and equates with his question 8, not question 9. The concern is with the scope and generalisability of the theory and is largely dependent upon the nature of the samples used.

Samples are unlikely to be statistically representative and may be so married to the emergent theory as to prevent generalisation (see 'theoretical sampling' above). More often the issue is one of deciding whether the limitations of the sample, e.g. in terms of its coverage or selection bias, could materially affect the conclusions and whether the analyst is justified in generalising beyond the data in the way that he does. The key questions to ask are: 'Are the subjects typical of the group as a whole?' and 'Is the group typical of other groups?' (Orenstein and Philips, 1978). Whenever the analytic induction model is employed, it is also pertinent to ask whether the sampling provided a sufficiently stringent test of the hypothesis under examination.

Reliability concerns the extent to which results are reproducible. It has been argued that quantitative research is high on reliability and low on validity while the reverse is true of qualitative research (Filstead, 1970). It is to be hoped that the rigorous, systematic and transparent approaches to qualitative research advocated by this volume should in themselves lead to a substantial improvement in reliability. Frequently it is possible to build in internal checks prior to, during and after fieldwork (Smith, 1981). Another means of enhancing reliability may be to involve more than one person in the research process. This could be another researcher, or, in applied research, the research client or other persons in the policy domain (Heron, 1981).

Once again the reader of a report has a role to play, this time through the process of discounting:

> This discounting takes several forms: the theory is *corrected* because of one sided research designs, *adjusted* to fit the diverse conditions of different social structures, *invalidated* for other structures through the reader's experience and knowledge, and deemed *inapplicable* to yet other kinds of structure (Glaser and Strauss, 1967, pp. 231–2).

The 'worth' of research and the importance of presentation

Rose acknowledges the ninth question in his schema to be the most important but chooses not to elaborate it because 'external theoretical validity is not a matter of methodology as such' (Rose, 1982, p. 105). By 'external theoretical validity' Rose means 'the relationship of the study to the wider body of sociological literature' (Rose, 1982, p. 105).

As such, external theoretical validity is one aspect of what is here termed the 'worth' of a project. 'Worth' refers first to the value placed on a project by those who commissioned it (this may satisfactorily be established only in the long term – say by a continued willingness to commission research – since even the continued involvement of policy makers in research cannot guarantee that it will yield the substantive results they desire).

A second related aspect concerns the *use*, or non-use, made of the results and theory by the policy makers who commissioned the project, by others in the client organisation and by people elsewhere in the policy domain including, for example, pressure groups and opposition parties in government-sponsored research.

The project's impact on the development of policy and on the understanding and definition of the policy domain constitutes a third component of worth, while the fourth is its impact on other policy domains. Clearly, the importance of these components will be mediated by the adeptness of policy formulation based on the research and by other contextual factors. Finally, the assessment of worth would take account of the contribution made to the general body of social science theory appertaining to the phenomena studied.

The worth of research is crucially affected by its presentation. No matter how valid or reliable the research may be, it is worthless if it proves inaccessible to those who need it. The above discussion of evaluation has pointed already to the desirable features of a qualitative report, not least the necessity to present as much data as possible and to take the reader close to the process of analysis.

However, such cardinal rules need to be balanced against the audiences' willingness, and ability, to digest information. The potential audiences for the research must be identified, their information requirements carefully defined and the presentation appropriately tailored and packaged.

The commissioners of the research will usually require a written report. With large studies, it may often be appropriate for this to be modular in form with separate sections addressing distinct policy issues (which may reflect different interests within the commissioning organisation). Typically each module will open with a summary, perhaps as short as a single side, establishing the context, distilling the policy implications of key findings and indexing the subsequent sections where matters are discussed more fully. The ideal is to try to convey the excitement of the real world even in this short summary and this is made easier if concepts are grounded in the language of the respondents. It is also useful to include a section that explicitly relates analyses included in the module to the project as a whole.

The main sections of each module present the arguments, data and results. No blueprint is possible although it is frequently appropriate to structure the discussion according to the policy questions raised in the research brief. Sometimes, of course, the inadequacies of this initial conceptualisation will have been highlighted by the research and in such cases it would be necessary to construct a new policy framework. According to context, individual modules might be organised by concept, group, level of aggregation or, indeed, by way of a narrative of discovery.

The overriding concern, however, is to put the description and analysis across in a way that is vivid, credible and meaningful to the client (or reader). In part, this is a matter of demonstrating a rigour in method but it also entails thinking about what data are to be presented and in what form. A number of devices are available. The researcher may, for example:

> ... quote directly from interviews or conversations that he has over-heard. He can include dramatic segments of his on-the-spot field notes. He can quote telling phrases dropped by informants. He can summarise events or persons by constructing readable case studies. He can try his hand at describing events and acts and often he will give at least background descriptions of places and spaces. Sometimes he will even offer accounts of personal experience to show how events impinged upon himself. Sometimes he will unroll a narrative (Glaser and Strauss, 1967, p. 229).

The data reported will be chosen primarily because they have value in defining, supporting or elaborating the researcher's interpretation of events but the choice may legitimately be conditioned by knowledge of the sensibilities of the client or of the wider audience. It is only through the careful choice of examples, adjectives, metaphors and similes that the experiences of the research subjects, as experienced by them, can be made understandable and significant to the reader.

As Runciman (1983) has noted, the issues raised by presentation are already familiar to students of literature and biography if not to social scientists. However, the qualitative researcher differs from, say, a novelist, in that he has a greater obligation to be explicit about the basis for his interpretation of events and, as far as possible, to provide evidence that would facilitate re-examination. Such evidence may need to be included in the main body of the report when an important interpretation is difficult. Otherwise there is usually a case for annexing fuller accounts of the data which, when in the form of cognitive maps, facilitate the simultaneous presentation of data and analysis.

In the same way that the involvement of a client in analysis can improve reliability, so the interactive interpretation of project findings can add substantially to the potential worth of a project. (Analysis and

interpretation are a continuing process which is arbitrarily dichoto-
mised here at the point where a final report is written.) This is perhaps
best achieved through verbal presentation, possibly supported by
audio or video tapes. Such presentations need meticulous planning.
Material cannot be so densely packed as in text – particularly when
real interaction is sought – and so the content must be carefully matched
to the objectives of the presentation. There is also a danger that the vivid
example may become the anecdote which is remembered out of context
and which diverts attention from the central issues. Equipment failure
can also be disastrous. Nevertheless, the risks are outweighed by the
possibility of direct and immediate influence.

In applied qualitative research there are two significant audiences
for whom a research report is seldom appropriate: the research subjects themselves and others who may be affected by policies arising
from the research findings. Chapter 1 discussed how qualitative techniques can facilitate the involvement of the research subjects in policy
interpretation resulting perhaps in the researcher acting as an adviser
or advocate. Where the numbers likely to be affected by policy
decisions are large, the researcher may only be able to reach them
through the mass media, in which case careful thought needs once
again to be given to the way in which the material is presented.

Inclusion of the above two groups among the audiences for applied
qualitative research is perhaps contentious, not least when it may
adversely affect the interests of the research client. It also raises
the issue of a researcher's responsibility to his research subjects
(Sjoberg, 1967; Becker, 1969; Heron, 1981). Some would subordinate
the interests of research subjects to the need to discuss 'facts' (Vidich
and Bensman, 1958, discussed in Becker, 1969). Others believe that
the researcher has a duty at least to 'warn those studied of the effects
of publication and to help them prepare for it' (Becker, 1969). Yet
others propose 'co-operative enquiry' as a means of preventing research
becoming 'another agent of authoritarian social control' (Heron,
1981, p. 34).

The applied researcher, on behalf of his client, can all too easily
exploit the researched. Wide dissemination of research findings might
go some way to redress this imbalance but, in practice, the bulk of
applied social research is never published. It is instead 'protected' by
proprietorial rights and by the Official Secrets Act. The rights of the
researched receive some protection through the codes of practice
supported by the Market Research Society and the Social Research
Association but these codes say virtually nothing about any right of
access to research findings. As a consequence it is for the individual
researcher to negotiate the best deal possible for those who potentially
have most to lose.

Postscript

Neither this chapter, nor the volume as a whole, is intended as a blueprint. What we have attempted is to provide the simple guidance that has generally been lacking. In this way we hope both to encourage researchers to be more confident in their use of qualitative methods and research sponsors to be more prepared to provide the necessary funding. But nothing succeeds like success and much qualitative research is already of the highest quality.

References

Abell, P. 1983, *Comparative narratives: some rules of a sociological method*, Mimeo, University of Surrey.

Becker, H.S., 1958, 'Problems of inference and proof in participant observation', *American Sociological Review*, vol. 23, pp. 652–60.

Becker, H.S. 1969, 'Problems in the publication of field studies'. In G.J. McCall and J.L. Simmins (eds.), *Issues in participant observation*, London, Addison-Wesley, pp. 260–75.

Becker, H.S., Geer, B. 1982, 'Participant observation: an analysis of qualitative field data'. In R.E. Burgess (ed.) *Field Research*, London, George Allen and Unwin.

Burgess, R.C. (ed.) 1982, *Field Research*, London, George Allen and Unwin.

Cressey, D.R. 1950, *Criminal violation of financial trust*, Dissertation, Indiana University.

Faraday, A., Plummer, K. 1979, 'Doing life histories', *Sociological Review*, vol. 27, no. 4, pp. 773–798.

Filstead, W.J. 1970, *Qualitative methodology, firsthand involvement with the social world*, Chicago, Markham.

Ford, J. 1975. *Paradigms and fairy tales: an introduction to the science of meanings*, London, Routledge and Kegan Paul.

Glaser, B.G., Strauss, A.L. 1967, *The discovery of grounded theory*, Chicago, Aldine.

Glaser, B.G., Strauss, A.L. 1970, 'Discovery of substantive theory: a basic strategy underlying qualitative research'. In W.J. Filstead (ed.), *Qualitative methodology*, Chicago, Markham.

Halfpenny, P. 1979, 'The analysis of qualitative data', *Sociological Review*, vol. 27, no. 4, pp. 799–825.

Hedges, A. 1981. *An introduction to qualitative research*, a paper presented to the Market Research Society, Winter School.

Heron, J. 1981, 'Philosophical basis for a new paradigm'. In P. Reason, J. Rowan (eds.), *Human inquiry*, Chichester, John Wiley, pp. 19–36.

Lofland, J. 1971, *Analyzing Social Settings*, Belmont, Wandsworth.

McCall, G.J. 1969, 'Data quality control in participant observation'. In G.J. McCall, J.L. Simmons (eds.), *Issues in participant observation*, London, Addison-Wesley, pp. 128–141.

McCall, G.J., Simmons, J.L. (eds.) 1969, *Issues in participant observation*, London, Addison-Wesley, pp. 260–275.

Orenstein, A., Philips, W.R.F. 1978, *Understanding social research*, Boston, Allyn and Bacon.

Robinson, W.S. 1951, 'The Logical Structure of analytic induction', *American Sociological Review*, vol. 16, pp. 812–818.

Rose, G. 1982, *Deciphering sociological research*, London, Macmillan.

Runciman, W.G., 1983, *A treatise on social theory: the methodology of social theory*, Cambridge, Cambridge University Press.

Schatzman, L., Strauss, A.L. 1973, *Field research: strategies for a natural sociology*, Englewood Cliffs, N.J., Prentice Hall.

Sjoberg, G. 1967 (ed.), *Ethics, politics and social research*, Cambridge, Schenkman.

Smith, H.W. 1981, *Strategics of social research*, Englewood Cliffs, Prentice Hall.

Smith, H.W. 1975, *Strategics of social research*, 2nd edition, Englewood Cliffs, Prentice Hall.

Vidich, A., Bensman, J. 1958, *Small Town in Mass Society*, Princeton, Princeton University Press.

Walker, R.L. 1981, *Improving the quality of Government Research*, paper presented to the Annual Conference of Government Social Science Research Officers, London, December.

Further Reading

Methods

Burgess, R. E. 1984, *In the field: an introduction to field research*, London, George Allen and Unwin.

Cook, T. D., Reichardt, C. S. (eds) 1979, *Qualitative and quantitative methods in evaluation research*, Beverley Hills, Sage.

Filstead, W. H. (ed) 1970, *Qualitative methodology: firsthand involvement with the social world*, Chicago, Markham.

Glaser, B. G. 1978, *Theoretical sensitivity*, Chicago, The Sociology Press.

Glaser, B. G., Strauss, A. S. 1967, *The discovery of grounded theory*, Chicago, Aldine.

Hammersley, M., Atkinson, P. 1984, *Ethnography: principles in practice*, London, Tavistock.

Maanen, van, J. 1983, *Qualitative methodology*, Beverley Hills, Sage.

McCall, G. J., Simmons, J. L. (eds) 1969, *Issues in participant observation: a text and reader*, Reading, Addison-Wesley.

Miles, M. B., Huberman, A. M. 1984, *Qualitative data analysis: a sourcebook of new methods*, Beverley Hills, Sage.

Patton, M. Q. 1980 *Qualitative evaluation methods*, Beverley Hills, Sage.

Spradley, J. P. 1980, *Participant Observation*, New York, Holt, Rinehart and Winston.

Young, K., Mills, L. 1980, *Public policy research: a review of qualitative methods*, London, Social Science Research Council.

Examples

Andrews, L. A. 1979, *Tenants and town hall*, London, HMSO.

Bryon, R., MacFarlane, G. 1980, *Social change in Dunrossness: a Shetland study*, London, Social Science Research Council.

Burgess, R. G. 1983, *Experiencing comprehensive education: a study of Bishop McGregor School*, London, Methuen.

Corden, A. 1983, *Taking up a means-tested benefit: the process of claiming Family Income Supplement*, London, HMSO: DHSS Social Security Research.

Cragg, A., Dawson, T. 1981, *Qualitative research among homeworkers*, Research Paper 21, London, Department of Employment.

Flynn, R., 1979, 'Urban managers in local government planning', *Sociological Review*, 24, 4, pp 743–753.

Gill, D. 1977, *Luke Street: housing policy, conflict and the creation of the delinquent area*, London, Macmillan.

Miles, R., Phizacklea, A. 1981, 'Racism and capitalist decline' in M. Harloe (ed), *New perspectives in urban change and conflict*, London, Heinemann, pp 80–100.

Glendinning, C. 1983, *Unshared care: parents and their disabled children*, London, Routledge and Kegan Paul.

Hedges, A. 1978, *Employment and the small firm: a survey of Covent Garden*, London, Social and Community Planning Research.

Hedges, A., Stowell, R. 1978, *Community panels in Southwark*, London, Social and Community Planning Research.

Smithin, T., Sims, D. 1982, 'Ubi caritas? – modelling beliefs about charities', *European Journal of Operational Research*, 10, pp 237–243.

Walker, R. 1985, *Housing benefit: the experience of implementation*, London, Housing Centre Trust.

Name Index

Subject Index